LE ᠎᠎ ᠎᠎ ᠎᠎ ᠎᠎ SERIES

How to Think, Write and Cite: Key Skills for Irish Law Students

SECOND EDITION

Round Hall's Nutshell, Nutcase, Exam Focus, and Legal Skills Series

NUTSHELL TITLES

Specially written for students of Irish law, each title in the **Nutshell Series** from Round Hall is an accessible review of key principles, concepts and cases. Nutshells are both the ideal introductory text, and the perfect revision aid.

- **Administrative Law** by Matthew Holmes
- **Company Law** – 3rd edition by Catherine McConville
- **Contract Law** by Fergus Ryan
- **Constitutional Law** – 2nd edition by Fergus Ryan
- **Criminal Law** – 3rd edition by Cecilia Ní Choileáin
- **Equity and Trusts** – 2nd edition by Miriam Dowling
- **Employment Law** – 2nd edition by Dorothy Donovan
- **Evidence** by Ross Gorman
- **Family Law** by Louise Crowley
- **The Irish Legal System** by Dorothy Donovan
- **Land Law** – 2nd edition by Ruth Cannon
- **Succession Law** by Karl Dowling and Robert Grimes
- **Tort** – 2nd edition by Ursula Connolly

NUTCASE TITLES

Round Hall Nutcases are written to give you the key facts and principles of **important cases** in core legal subject areas. Straightforward, no-nonsense language makes Nutcases an easy way to understand and learn key cases.

- **Criminal Law** by Majella Walsh
- **Evidence** by Neil Van Dokkum
- **Tort** – 2nd edition by Val Corbett

EXAM FOCUS TITLES

The **Exam Focus Series** is especially designed to support students in the weeks coming up to exams by providing a unique tutorial approach to answering questions.

- **Criminal Law** by Sarah Carew

LEGAL SKILLS TITLES

The **Legal Skills Series** helps students master the essential legal and research skills needed to succeed in their studies and in their future careers.

- **How to Think, Write and Cite: Key Skills for Irish Law Students**, 2nd edition by Jennifer Schweppe, Rónán Kennedy and Lawrence Donnelly

LEGAL SKILLS SERIES

How to Think, Write and Cite: Key Skills for Irish Law Students

SECOND EDITION

by

JENNIFER SCHWEPPE
BCL, LLM, PG Dip
School of Law, University of Limerick

RÓNÁN KENNEDY
BComm, HDipSysAnal, LLB, LLM, PG Cert, PhD, Barrister-at-Law
School of Law, National University of Ireland Galway

LAWRENCE DONNELLY
BA, JD, Attorney-at-Law
School of Law, National University of Ireland Galway

ROUND HALL

THOMSON REUTERS

Published in 2016 by
Thomson Reuters Ireland Limited
(Registered in Ireland, Company No. 416940. Registered Office
and address for service 43 Fitzwilliam Place, Dublin 2)
trading as Round Hall.

Typeset by Carrigboy Typesetting Services

Printed and bound in the UK by
CPI Group (UK) Ltd, Croydon, CR0 4YY

ISBN 978–0–41405–655–8

A catalogue record for this book is available from the British Library.

Contents

Foreword to First Edition   vii
Preface to First Edition   viii
Preface to Second Edition   x

1. **Introduction**   1
   Structure of the Book   1
   What is Distinctive about Irish Law?   2
   What is Different about being a Law Student in Ireland?   5
   A New Opportunity: Clinical Legal Education   7
   What is Distinctive about this Book?   9
   Other Key Reading Materials   10

2. **Legal Thinking**   11
   Introduction   11
   'Thinking like a Lawyer'   12
   Conclusion   18
   Further Reading   18

3. **Reading Judgments**   19
   Introduction   19
   Why you Read Case Law   20
   Why is Reading Case Law Different?   20
   Where can I Find Irish Case Law?   21
   The Structure of a Reported Case   22
   How to Read Case Law   23
   Reading the Same Case in Different Ways   26
   More Complex Issues   27
   Ratio Decidendi and the Use of Precedent   29
   Writing a Case Note   31
   Further Reading   37
   Sample Case Notes   37

4. **Reading Legislation**   44
   Introduction   44
   What is Particularly Unique about Legislation?   44
   What Does the Word 'Legislation' Mean?   45
   How Does an Act of the Oireachtas Come into Being?   46
   What are the Parts of an Act of the Oireachtas?   50
   Where do you Find Legislation?   52
   Has the Act been Amended?   53
   Is the Act in Force?   55
   How should you Read Legislation to Discover its Meaning?   55

Other Aspects of Legislation 59
Further Reading 61

5. **Legal Writing** **62**
Introduction 62
Clarity 62
Formality and Legal Writing 65
Technicality 67
Audibility 77
Further Reading 78

6. **Writing Law Essays** **80**
Introduction 80
Legal Research Methods and Methodologies 81
General Advice on Assignments 85
Getting Started 87
Structuring your Essay 90
Writing your Essay 93
Using Technology 96
Citations 100
Further Reading 109
Sample Essay: Should the Supreme Court of Ireland Follow
a Strict Rule of Stare Decisis? 110
Sample Essay: The Preamble of the Constitution has no Place
in a Modern Secular Demoracy. Discuss. 114
Sample Essay: Extra-judicial Comment by Judges 120

7. **Writing Law Exams** **130**
Introduction 130
General Examination Tips 131
Essay Questions 134
Problem Questions 135
Examples 138

8. **Legal Research** **146**
Introduction 146
Library-Based Research 147
Selected Databases 149
Using Databases—Searching Tools 156
Conclusion 159

Appendix 1. OSCOLA Ireland—Second Edition 161
Appendix 2. OSCOLA Ireland Quick Reference Guide 195

Index 199

Foreword to First Edition

This book is an excellent reminder that lawyers need to think and write about law; that's because a good lawyer is a problem-solver, and usually arrives at a solution through writing. Before thinking about lawyers, it's important to remember that we all get into situations that need to be resolved, and that we can often arrive at a solution ourselves by sensible discussion. Large organisations, as well as individuals, do this every day, without the need for a lawyer. Lawyers often become involved because the problem can only be dealt with through 'the law'. Where an individual or organisation has been charged with a crime, the lawyer is needed to assist in navigating the procedurals as well as advising on whether 'to plead'. Similarly, in a civil dispute, the lawyer will advise on procedural issues and, often, be used to arrive at an out-of-court settlement.

Increasingly, with civil disputes, the resolution does not involve an adversarial setting, because mediation and conciliation have become much more significant processes. Mediation and conciliation place the parties in dispute at centre stage, and also require lawyers to think differently, not just in the context of a single dispute that has to be resolved in a win-lose adversarial way. Strategic thinking is, therefore, an extremely important part of being a lawyer, and this is why you should take seriously the advice in this book that you read more than just law books.

As to writing about the law, this book also provides exactly the right advice: write clearly. Maybe the Plain Language campaign could be rebranded the Clear Language campaign, because often writing clearly about the law requires a lot of thought (thinking, again), which the word 'Plain' does not necessarily capture. In particular, the authors remind us that good legal writing is, first and foremost, good writing. This also follows from the advice to think clearly. No client wants to hear a lawyer ramble on about how difficult their problem is: they want as clear an answer as possible. Bear in mind, though, that an examiner may want to hear an analysis of the complexity of the legal problem they set in any essay or exam script you write.

By following the advice in this book, you should be able to retain the good habits you learned up to now about writing well. In this digital age, writing clearly about the law is a necessity and more common than might have been the case in the past; and don't forget to enjoy learning the law while you're at it.

RAYMOND BYRNE
Bunclody, Co. Wexford,
July 2011

Preface to First Edition

This book was written largely because we wished it was already available. As experienced legal researchers, who have taught legal research and writing to many students, we found ourselves looking for a good textbook on the topic from an Irish perspective. As it became obvious that no one else was going to come forward, we decided to fill the gap ourselves.

We were also interested in applying modern technology to enhance student learning. We have set up a website at <www.legalwriting.ie> to support this book and see this as an integral element of this text and of teaching and learning this topic.*

In addition, we became increasingly frustrated with the inconsistency in citation styles between Irish researchers. We hope that the conversion of OSCOLA, a legal citation standard developed by the Faculty of Law at Oxford University, to Ireland will be a first small step toward rectifying this difficulty. OSCOLA Ireland is one of the appendices to this book and is also available on <www.legalcitation.ie>.

This book has been a work-in-progress for a long time and many people helped along the way. Most important, the School of Law and the Faculty of Arts, Humanities and Social Sciences' Faculty Teaching Board at the University of Limerick, the Teaching and Learning Strategy Committee at Dublin Institute of Technology and the School of Law at the National University of Ireland Galway provided generous funding at various points in the process. Michael Coyne and Rob Smyth provided technical help. Frieda Donohue and Catherine Bermingham-Thomas oversaw the conversion of our text into this book with skill, care and patience. Dr Eimear Spain of UL Law School was kind enough to allow us to road-test an early version of the material on her students, and they were enthusiastic and constructive participants in this first experiment. A number of individuals gave us vital feedback on the text, including Dr Eimear Spain, Patrick McInerney, Dr Cliona Kelly and Ursula Connolly, and we are most grateful for their comments and suggestions. The audience at the 4th Legal Education Symposium at the University of Limerick in 2010 gave us helpful feedback on an initial presentation of our work. We would also like to thank Raymond Byrne. No Irish law student in the past

---

* The authors of this book have also created a companion website. Please note that this website, while complementary to the book, is an independent endeavour by the authors and Thomson Reuters Ireland Limited bears no responsibility for the content or maintenance of that website. This book is sold as a stand-alone text. Views expressed on the companion website are those of the authors and not the publishers.

two decades, including ourselves, has graduated without reading his book, *The Irish Legal System* (co-authored with Paul McCutcheon), and we are privileged to have him write the foreword to this text. We would like to thank all of them for their assistance, though all errors remain our own.

JENNIFER SCHWEPPE, RÓNÁN KENNEDY,
ELAINE FAHEY, LAWRENCE DONNELLY
June 2011

Preface to Second Edition

One of the challenges of writing a textbook such as this, which deals with the practical uses of real-world skills, is that it is out of date almost as soon as it is published. With the passage of some five years since the first edition, we felt that it was time to update its contents and we have therefore revised the information on how to use online databases, expanded the section on the use of software to automate and simplify referencing, and added material on completing assignments, clinical legal education and different research methods, including doctrinal, historical and socio-legal research. Our thanks to Nora Burns for her help with the online questions, Aisling O'Connor for proofreading, and Michael Coyne for ongoing technical assistance. At Thomson Reuters, Pamela Moran was always helpful, even when we sought additional time to put the finishing touches on the text, while Donough Cassidy read and re-read the text with great care and attention to detail. All responsibility for any remaining errors is, of course, solely ours. Last, but certainly not least, we would like to record our thanks to Elaine Fahey for her many contributions to the project over the years and for her work on the first edition of this textbook, for which we are very grateful. We wish her the best in her new role at City University London and hope she can re-join the team for future editions.

JENNIFER SCHWEPPE, RÓNÁN KENNEDY,
LAWRENCE DONNELLY
May 2016

Introduction

When entering law school, most students are surprised when they are told that they need to learn how to read and write legal materials. Surely, reading legal materials is not that different to other forms of reading? The reality is that legal writing uses different language and structures. This book is intended to assist you in learning how to read and write about the law in Ireland. After reading this book and completing the exercises which it contains, you will be able to:

- identify the key elements in a court judgment;
- analyse judicial reasoning;
- apply a knowledge of statutory interpretation;
- decide when you need to cite in support of your writing, and how to do so;
- explain the difference between legal and non-legal reasoning;
- identify good and bad legal writing styles; and
- find primary and secondary legal materials useful for your research.

STRUCTURE OF THE BOOK

What follows this introductory chapter are seven chapters which will guide you through some of the key areas we regard as important in learning legal writing and research in Ireland. These chapters are as follows:

Legal Thinking: This chapter explains the basics of legal reasoning, including how to identify the core legal issue in a question.

Reading Judgments: This chapter gives you a set of questions that can serve as a guide for writing case notes that solidify your understanding of case law.

Reading Legislation: This chapter explains how to find, verify and dissect a piece of legislation, and the process of 'statutory interpretation'.

Legal Writing: This chapter will help you to understand what good legal writing is, what pitfalls to avoid and how to deal with the Irish language in legal writing.

Writing Law Essays: This chapter builds on the preceding chapter and helps you to get started on writing essays, to use technology appropriately, to structure your work clearly and to avoid common problems and pitfalls.

Writing Law Exams: Following on from the previous chapter, this chapter discusses general examination techniques, essay questions in law and 'problem questions', which you may not have encountered before.

Legal Research: Finally, the last chapter will give you practical guidance on how to access the wealth of material that is available through various online services, and your law library.

WHAT IS DISTINCTIVE ABOUT IRISH LAW?

While Ireland is a common law country, sharing a legal heritage with many other countries, it has a number of distinctive features which mean that materials prepared for students in other jurisdictions may not be immediately useful to you. As you will encounter case law, textbooks and articles written in these other countries during your studies, it is very useful to have a good understanding of what is different about Irish law and the Irish legal system.

IRELAND AND THE UNITED KINGDOM OF GREAT BRITAIN AND NORTHERN IRELAND

The United Kingdom of Great Britain and Northern Ireland (more commonly referred to as the United Kingdom, or the UK) is our nearest geographical neighbour and a jurisdiction which has been (and continues to be) a dominant influence on the development of our legal system. As you will probably hear in your lectures, Ireland shares a common legal heritage with the UK, as Ireland was the first country to which the 'common law' system which developed in England and Wales after the Norman conquest was exported. The UK Parliament could pass legislation for Ireland for long periods of time. This means that the common law approach is the fundamental basis for our legal system and many older statutes are still common to Ireland and England and Wales. Even after independence in 1922, the Oireachtas tended to look to English legislation as a model for changes, and Irish judges continued to refer to decisions of the higher British courts. It is only in recent decades that Irish law has begun to significantly diverge from that of England and Wales, and you will still be referred to law from there from time to time in your lectures and readings. (It is important to remember that Scotland is its own jurisdiction, with a particular legal tradition, as is Northern Ireland, although the latter is not as distinct from England and Wales.)

Other jurisdictions, particularly 'civil law' countries such as France and Germany, with their roots in Roman law, are not as significant in the development of Irish law. However, with greater European integration, you will see more and more references to legislation and case law from these types of legal systems. They are all useful, but you need to be aware of the need to put them in their proper context before you apply them when writing about the law in Ireland.

Europe has become a significant influence on Irish law, with some specific subjects (such as environmental law) almost entirely based on European legislation and case law. When discussing European law, it is important to be clear on the difference between the laws of the European Union and the Council of Europe. On the one hand, European Union law (formerly known as European Community law) can and often does have a direct effect in Ireland. On the other hand, the Council of Europe is an important international organisation, but cannot directly change Irish law. Ireland has long been a signatory to the European Convention on Human Rights and incorporated that instrument into Irish law in 2003. The Convention is an international treaty agreed within the framework of the Council of Europe. As such, it is not as directly effective here as European Union law. The two are often confused by students, particularly in the context of human rights.

It is also important to be clear about the two major European courts: the Court of Justice of the European Union (which includes other courts) and the European Court of Human Rights. These courts are not identical and do not have the same powers. They exist within different international organisations. They are located in different places—the Court of Justice in Luxembourg and the European Court of Human Rights in Strasbourg. The Court of Justice will eventually be subject to the jurisdiction of the European Court of Human Rights if the EU treaty for accession to the European Convention on Human Rights is ratified. This makes precise referencing all the more important. Do not confuse the two. Do not refer in a haphazard fashion to 'the European courts' or 'going to Europe'. Specify which court you mean and be clear as to other laws that apply.

THE CONSTITUTION AND CONSTITUTIONAL LAW

Unlike the UK, the Irish Constitution is contained in a single document. As any UK lawyer will be quick to point out, this does not mean that there is no constitutional law in the United Kingdom, but it does mean that there is no single reference point for constitutional questions there, and that constitutional law can develop and change in a somewhat more organic fashion than in Ireland.

This has a number of consequences. In some ways, our constitutional law is more rigid: there are written rules that govern procedural issues, such as the enactment of legislation. In other ways, our constitutional law is more flexible: the provisions of the Irish Constitution that govern fundamental rights were not examined closely by lawyers for several decades but were then given life in the 1960s by a Supreme Court that pointed out some unanticipated features of the guarantees which they contained. (You will not learn more about this aspect of constitutional law in this book but you will in your other courses.) The rights provisions of the Constitution continue to be relevant to modern issues and provide us with a framework that can be adapted to apply to new questions. This does not mean that the Constitution is perfect, but only that it is not frozen in time.

IRELAND AND THE UNITED STATES OF AMERICA

The United States of America, another important influence, does have a written Constitution, including features such as a Bill of Rights. These were a clear inspiration for aspects of the Irish Constitution. However, the American Constitution is a much sparser document than ours, even slower to change and in many ways a product of a particular historical period. For example, it still mentions the institution of slavery, although this has long since been abolished in the US.

Nevertheless, while we will sometimes look to the US in the context of the development and understanding of constitutional law, the US legal system has other important differences to ours: it is a large federal system with a population that is very diverse geographically and culturally. As a result, the federal government, based in Washington DC, has 'limited powers' and much is reserved to the governments of the individual states (and to local governments below them) to decide. 'Limited powers' does not mean 'small'—the powers of the federal government are wide-ranging and extensive. However, there are limits to those powers, and states and individuals will often challenge the right of the federal government to intervene in matters which they think should be decided at a more local level.

Ireland is a much smaller country, with a small population. While local government has a role to play, it is not a federal system, and the Oireachtas has wide freedom to introduce laws. (Although this freedom is not absolute, as we shall see.) This means that US legal precedent is not easily 'importable' into the Irish context, and there are sometimes important differences in legal culture between the two systems, such as the much stronger protections for freedom of speech in the United States.

None of this is to say that material from the UK, Europe or the US is not useful in Ireland. It is, and it is often read, cited and relied upon. However, be aware that these are different countries with different basic assumptions about the law. Over time, you will learn to adapt what you learn from these countries to Irish law. As Ireland is a small country, with a small market for legal materials, the choice of textbooks and journals is not as wide as it is in the UK or US. Indeed, for many years after independence, Irish lawyers would study using English textbooks. This was partly because the two systems were quite similar—even now, for example, Irish and English contract law are not that different—and partly because there was no choice: there were no authors or publishers preparing books specifically on Irish law. The range of Irish materials has begun to grow as Irish law begins to diverge from its roots and as Irish lawyers take the time to write about those differences. Indeed, as you progress through your studies and beyond, you may contribute to this literature yourself.

Due to the relatively limited range of literature available about Irish law, you will find that some of it is very foundational. There may be only one textbook on a specific area of law, and there is not the wide range of legal journals, some on very specialist topics, that exist in the UK, and nothing like the vast numbers of legal publications in the US. Many of the journals in Ireland are oriented towards legal practitioners, and therefore Irish journal articles tend to be more descriptive than analytical, and certainly not as 'inter-disciplinary' (meaning that they contain a mix of discussion from the perspective of law and some other discipline, such as economics or psychology) as they can be in the US. When referring to materials from jurisdictions other than Ireland, be aware of the purpose and value of those materials: while informative and persuasive, they do not represent the law in Ireland.

WHAT IS DIFFERENT ABOUT BEING A LAW STUDENT IN IRELAND?

As law students, you are probably already used to strong reactions—one way or another—from friends and family when you tell them that you are studying the law. Promises to seek a loan in a few years after you are well-established in practice as a solicitor or barrister, and derogatory comments made only half in jest about lawyers, come with the territory and are very familiar to all of us who are currently studying or once studied law. In truth, however, it is a privilege in many ways to study law and, as both an academic and vocational discipline, it is distinguishable from many degrees. With that privilege come some additional duties and responsibilities that you as law students must take on, at least in part, to be successful.

Note-taking from the Spoken Word

First year law students often voice a concern that they are not given enough in terms of notes—whether in traditional handout form, in detailed slides or via online teaching and learning resources, such as Blackboard. To some extent, this may conflict with the experience of their fellow students in other disciplines. But there is a method to what may at times seem to you as students like madness.

Active listening is something seldom practised or discussed in today's technology-driven world. Yet it remains vital for lawyers or for anyone working in a law-related career. Many law lecturers are cognisant of this reality and, from day one, take a firm stand against 'spoon-feeding' students the material. Students must rapidly grow accustomed to listening carefully, pinpointing what the key information is, and making note of it accordingly. As most lecturers are keenly aware, this is a skill that takes time and practice.

By way of concrete example as to why this is so important, a farmer who walks into a solicitor's office in the west of Ireland and is aggrieved by a boundary dispute with a troublesome neighbour is not going to present the facts either in a set of slides or a neatly compiled set of notes. The difficulties will be communicated verbally, and may not be entirely objectively accurate. It is down to the solicitor to listen patiently, distill the essence and discern fact from fiction. You, as law students, must acquire a similar capacity. That strongly militates against a consumerist view of legal education in which lecturers simply provide the information that you must learn and then be examined on. Law study requires active listening and learning at all stages, and you are responsible for taking the initiative, independently. Your lecturers are there to guide you in this process.

Being Civically and Politically Engaged

Law does not exist in a vacuum. One of the weaker attributes of their own studies recounted by lawyers and judges is what can be a fixation on the decisions—both majority opinions and dissents—of appellate courts as the essence of legal education. Of course, the most significant cases in all areas that you will focus on are vital and absolutely central to your educational and professional formation. However, decisions of appellate courts are only one way in which the law is formed and evolves in common law jurisdictions like Ireland. More often than not, the law—legislation, regulations, treaty provisions, etc.—that govern the people and that solicitors and barristers have to work with in seeking to resolve ordinary disputes, are the by-product of politics, whether in Dublin or in Brussels. Furthermore, although the Irish judiciary is nowhere near as politicised as the American judiciary, it is a fact that political leanings also play a role in the appointment of judges to the superior courts and, eventually, in the opinions those judges write. Having due regard for the aforementioned difference in the relative import of appellate court decisions in law study and law practice, Irish law schools now increasingly devote time to statutory interpretation and legislative drafting in lecture theatres and in other settings (eg moot court exercises and clinical placements/externships). However, to get a fuller sense of the political, social, economic and cultural context from which both case and statute law emerge, it is necessary that you, as law students, monitor the news and stay abreast of current affairs and the manner in which the political system responds.

LAW STUDENTS AND THE PUBLIC INTEREST

Today, many law students have a real belief that law can make a significant difference in the lives of vulnerable individuals and groups in society and have a passion for one or more specific issues. This is a most welcome development and serves as an effective rebuttal to cynics who charge that those pursuing the study of and a career in law are in it 'just for the money'. Of course, careers in the law are often lucrative and there is nothing at all wrong with the desire to do well financially. Yet it is gratifying to see large numbers of law students for whom achieving professional success and helping to promote the public interest are not mutually exclusive goals.

The Free Legal Advice Centres Ltd (FLAC), together with its project, the Public Interest Law Alliance (PILA), supports law students who wish to obtain valuable exposure to public interest law while in law school. 'The main purpose of student FLAC societies is to operate information clinics where the student population can come and receive once-off legal information from qualified practitioners who supervise law students. For students who want to get involved in using their growing legal skills to help others, it's a great way to become more socially active and aware.'[1] As well as those directly affiliated with FLAC and PILA, other law schools operate legal information clinics with similar aims and objectives.

Law students are encouraged to explore the potential for working to advance the public interest at their law schools and to utlilise the resources offered by FLAC and PILA through their websites (<www.flac.ie>; <www.pila.ie>).

A NEW OPPORTUNITY: CLINICAL LEGAL EDUCATION

Clinical legal education has been described as the 'greatest single innovation in law school pedagogy—and certainly in student learning—since the

---

[1] For more detail, see <www.flac.ie/getinvolved/student/>.

'science' of the Socratic case method was brought to Harvard by Christopher Columbus Langdell.'[2] Clinical legal education programmes were established in Ireland in the 1970s, and have been formalised and expanded significantly in the past decade. Now, you, as students at Irish law schools, can supplement the instruction you receive in classrooms and lecture theatres with exposure to the law in practice in a variety of 'real world' settings. Crucially, most of these clinical legal education programmes offer academic credit for participation in them.

Internationally—and in the US, particularly, where clinical legal education is most advanced—law students assist in the representation of real clients in real cases under the supervision of practising lawyers who are also full- or part-time members of academic staff. The explosive growth in clinical legal education programmes around the world over the past 50 years stems from the reality that law is both an academic and a vocational discipline. Law graduates must certainly know and be able to apply the law. However, it is an added advantage—from both a purely educational point of view and in light of the very competitive job market law graduates will confront—to have a good understanding of how the law operates in practice.

At Irish law schools, building on the skills inculcated in legal research and writing modules, as well as in moot court and related activities, clinical legal education programmes now offer many students the opportunities to undertake placements/externships (the terms are interchangeable) as part of the academic curriculum. These placements are typically with firms of solicitors, barristers, non-governmental organisations, governmental and quasi-governmental bodies and with academics working on public policy-oriented research and activism.

In order to expand and enhance existing and planned clinical initiatives, academics at Irish law schools have formed the Irish Clinical Legal Education Association (ICLEA). This will promote the interests of students, academics and external supervisors as Irish law schools strive to replicate the extraordinary successes of clinical legal education programmes around the world, especially with respect to the role students can play in advancing the public interest and the interests of those on the margins of society. ICLEA will also encourage moves toward the involvement of law students in Ireland in the representation of clients in actual cases and their assisting in the public policy and law reform campaigns of non-governmental organisations. There are already some promising developments on this front, in particular at postgraduate level.

If you wish to add a further practical dimension to your legal training, you are strongly encouraged to avail of the broad range of clinical legal education offerings at Irish law schools.

---

[2] Richard Wilson, 'Western Europe: Last Holdout in the Global Acceptance of Clinical Legal Education' (2009) 10 German Law Journal 823, 823.

What is Distinctive about this Book?

This book is distinctive in two ways. First, it provides an Irish perspective on legal writing. Secondly, it is supported by a website, <www.legalwriting.ie>.[3]

Legal Writing from an Irish Perspective

While there are many books on the market about legal research and writing, there are very few from an Irish perspective and none that cover the full range of basic legal skills that you need as a law student: research, reading legal materials and legal writing, both for essays and for examinations.

This book also contains a comprehensive and modern citation guide specifically tailored for Irish material, but based on an internationally-recognised standard. The lack of such a guide has been a difficulty for Irish researchers for some time. We hope that it will be widely used with time, avoiding the need for students to adjust their citation style as they move from lecturer to lecturer and institution to institution.

How to Use this Book

This book is supported by a website, <www.legalwriting.ie>, to which you will have access as you work through the book. As you read the chapters, you will see that there are a number of assignments built into the materials. These assignments are to aid your learning and to ensure that you understand the key issues being raised. You should complete these assignments as you go. All of these assignments can be completed online so that you can get immediate feedback. The website also contains additional material and updates to the book.

In order to begin using the site, use your web browser to navigate to <legalwriting.ie>. On the home page, you will see a column on the right hand side headed 'STUDENT LOGIN'. Click on the login link there to access the site.

On your first visit, you will need to create an account. On the right hand side of this second screen, you will see a column headed 'Is this your first time here?' Click the 'Create new account' button at the bottom of this section and fill in the form to register for the site. Accounts are free of charge. Please keep a record of your username and password, and take care when providing your email address, as it is easy to mis-type this.

---

[3] The authors of this book have also created a companion website. Please note that this website, while complementary to the book, is an independent endeavour by the authors and Thomson Reuters Ireland Ltd bears no responsibility for the content or maintenance of that website. This book is sold as a stand-alone text. Views expressed on the companion website are those of the authors and not the publishers.

Once you have an account, you can enter your username and password on the login screen. When you are successfully logged in, you will see 'How to Think, Write and Cite: Key Skills for Irish Law Students' on the list of available courses. Click on this and then on the 'Enrol me' button in order to gain access to the assignments.

You will then see the list of online exercises, grouped by chapter. You can take these at your own pace, as directed by the textbook, or following the instructions of your instructor.

OTHER KEY READING MATERIALS

There are a number of texts that we would recommend you refer to in order to build on the knowledge imparted through this book. What is important to note, however, is that most of these are not written for an Irish context, and so there may be differences of approach between this jurisdiction and others.

- Butt P and Castle R, *Modern Legal Drafting: A Guide to Using Clearer Language* (2nd edn, Cambridge 2006)
- Byrne R, McCutcheon P with Bruton C and Coffey G, *Byrne and McCutcheon on the Irish Legal System* (6th edn, Bloomsbury Professional 2014)
- Donnelly L, *Clinical Legal Education in Ireland: Progress and Potential* (Free Legal Advice Centres Ltd 2015)
- Garner B, *Legal Writing in Plain English: A Text with Exercises* (Chicago 2001)
- —— *The Elements of Legal Style* (2nd edn, Oxford 2002)
- Gowers E, *The Complete Plain Words* (3rd edn, Penguin 2004)
- O'Malley T, *Sources of Law* (2nd edn, Round Hall Sweet & Maxwell 2001)
- Strunk W and White EB, *The Elements of Style* (4th edn, Longman 1999)

Legal Thinking

2

Reason is the life of the law; nay, the common law itself is nothing else but reason ...[1]

INTRODUCTION

One of the basic skills which a lawyer must have is the ability to think like a lawyer. This might seem a little self-evident, but it is something that takes some time and effort to master.

If you are studying the law for the first time, you may have the impression that it is a very cut-and-dried subject, with black or white answers and no grey areas. Many students beginning their legal careers are surprised to find that it is not like that. It is true that legal questions can often have clear answers, but sometimes they do not, and sometimes they have no answer at all. After all, if law was simple, the world would not need lawyers. One thing is certain: much of what you will study will not have a straightforward answer. The purpose of a formal education in law is not to learn the rules that everyone agrees on (although you will need to do that) but to understand how to deal with situations where the rules are not agreed.

The law is not straightforward for a number of reasons. The first is that it is there to govern people, and people are not straightforward. The situations in which people find themselves are often complex, and a legal system that was strict and inflexible would often lead to unjust decisions.

Secondly, the tools of the law are words, and words can have many different meanings. Putting words with other words changes the meanings of those words. Applying those words to a particular situation can have different meanings to different people, particularly if they are on different sides of the argument. For example, what does 'reasonably practicable' mean as a standard for employers to meet in ensuring the health and safety of their employees? Is the burden that this places on a particular company dependent on its financial resources? Are there minimum thresholds which must be met? If financial cost can be taken into account, can a company which is struggling to pay its bills take unreasonable risks with the welfare of its workers?

---

[1] Co Inst 97.

Thirdly, law does not operate in a vacuum, separate from people and the ebb and flow of change in a society. It is a human tool, to be applied to human situations. As social, economic and environmental conditions change, so will the law, although not always at the same pace or as responsively as some might like.

Finally, law can be a tool of social change itself. This is most obvious if you consider civil rights as an issue. In many countries, Ireland included, legal tools such as employment law have been used to promote the protection and advancement of women, disadvantaged communities and minority groups. However, law can be used for social change in less obvious areas, such as encouraging small business, creating incentives for research and development and environmental protection. There is a continuing dynamic of interaction between law and society.

'Thinking like a Lawyer'

There is no substitute for experience. You cannot learn to become a lawyer in an afternoon: it requires sustained effort and repetition of the types of exercises contained in this book over a long period of time. Through study of this material, your lectures and other coursework, you will gradually absorb what makes legal thinking distinctive.

'Thinking like a lawyer' is easier to do than to describe. In other words, you will need to learn through practice rather than through a simple mechanical application of a set of rules and procedures. The mental processes involved may seem and feel difficult at first, but over time, as you study the law you will become comfortable with what you are doing and eventually find yourself thinking like a lawyer without even realising that you are doing it.

What follows are simply some tips to help you along the way. These are only guidelines, not strict requirements. They should be used as a support, not as a limit to your thinking. Everyone approaches the law in a different way. Over time, you will develop your own individual perspective.

Clear Thinking

Legal thinking is, first and foremost, clear thinking. A good lawyer works with definite categories and deductive processes to arrive at a clear conclusion (even if it does not completely answer the question).

In contract law, damages are only payable if there is a breach of contract. The late delivery of the second shipment is not a breach of contract because there was advance notice and the change of plan was accepted by the purchaser. Therefore, no compensation is due.

In order for there to be liability in tort, there must be an injury or loss which arises as a consequence of the actions of the defendant. While the plaintiff suffered an injury in this car accident, it is not as a result of the actions of the defendant but is due to the carelessness of the bus driver. Therefore, there is no liability in tort.

International human rights law emphasises the importance of protecting the survivor of rape both from the crime itself and from mistreatment at the hands of those investigating and prosecuting the offence afterwards. The laws on rape in Ireland do not take sufficient account of this. Therefore, reform is required.

A lawyer thinks, to a certain extent, like a mechanic or an engineer. You need to check whether or not all of the required elements are present and 'functioning' correctly. This does not mean that you think in a mechanistic or mechanical fashion. Lawyers deal with people and with words, which are much more flexible and malleable than machinery and physical objects. It is this requirement of fluid thinking which makes the law both interesting and challenging.

You should also remember that clear thinking does not mean rigid or simplistic thinking. Law involves the application of principles from other disciplines, taking abstract discussions from politics, economics and philosophy and turning them into practical rules. This process is considerably more complex and challenging than it might seem, particularly when changes to the system have to fit with what is already there, and work around what can and cannot be changed. It is at these limits that a lawyer must be creative and that the rigid, technical approach must give way to a more fluid, pragmatic and nuanced process.

IDENTIFY THE CORE QUESTION

In order to arrive at a clear conclusion, what thought process must you go through? You must clearly identify the core legal question to be answered. If you are working in the context of an examination, that will often be made clear to you. If you are working on an essay, it may be less definite and you may need to state your understanding of the issue in your introduction. As you progress through your career as a law student, you may tackle larger and more challenging research projects which raise more subtle questions, or sometimes an interrelationship of questions. Nonetheless, you should always be able to summarise your enquiry as a single sentence question.

Is the late delivery of the second shipment a breach of contract?

In what circumstances can a driver who has driven into another car escape liability for careless driving?

Should the laws concerning rape be reformed?

If you cannot sum up your core question into one key issue, you probably have not thought enough about the problem and you will almost certainly have a very difficult job in answering it. This is true for the most basic and the most advanced types of legal analysis.

Identify the Ancillary Questions

Identifying a central question should help you to identify a number of ancillary questions which must be answered before you can answer the central question. You will need to decide the most logical order in which to answer these questions and then proceed with the type of legal research outlined in the chapters on 'Reading Judgments' and 'Reading Legislation'. You will need to carefully consider the facts (including any written documents) and then deal with these issues one by one.

Identifying the ancillary questions is a skill in itself, and different topics will require different approaches. Start by brainstorming the obvious questions that occur to you.

A good second step is to clarify the law that governs the topic. Does it come from statute law, common law or some mix of the two? Put together a comprehensive overview of the relevant law and, from that, you should be able to identify the fundamental definitions, requirements and consequences.

You should also begin to grasp the underlying principles that inform and motivate the development of this area of law. You can move from that to ask: what are the social issues here? Does the law make sense in this broader context? A good way to explore this aspect of the topic is to see what academic authors have to say on the topic.

What is non-performance of a contractual obligation?

What types of non-performance constitute a breach of contract?

What are the consequences of non-performance of a contract?

What is meant by reasonable care in tort?

What are the general defences to a negligence claim?

What are the specific defences to a claim of careless driving?

What are the laws concerning rape in Ireland?

What defects have been identified in these laws?

What are the arguments for and against changing these laws?

Avoid Assumptions

As you deal with these ancillary questions, take nothing for granted. Always ask 'why?' or 'why not?' Verify that the law is the way that you think it is. Read the case law. Look at the legislation. Read the interpretation section. Check that the legislation is actually in force. (You will learn how to do all of these things in the relevant chapters of this book.) Do not assume that because you think that something is illegal (whatever that means), that this is in fact so. A good lawyer knows what the state of the law is, even if that state is somewhat confused or entirely non-existent.

A good way to build the capacity to ask these types of questions, and to understand the practical implications of the law, is to expose yourself to a wide variety of sources and arguments. Read as much as you can. A good grasp of history, economics and politics and an understanding of different social contexts are a great help to a lawyer. As a minimum, you should be reading a quality newspaper every day.

Binary Answers and Fuzzy Logic

The examples of legal thinking given above might lead you to think that legal logic always gives rise to clear, binary (yes or no, right or wrong) answers. This is not always true. In certain circumstances, the legal answer to a question is quite clear. In many others, it is not. There are many reasons for this: the complexity of human dealings with each other, the difficulty in ascribing precise meanings to words, the challenge of predicting all of the possible situations which could arise in the future, and so on. Legislators and judges will sometimes deliberately leave the law open-ended and vague, so that it can easily be adapted to changing circumstances. Bear in mind also that almost every rule has an exception.

All of this means that the 'correct' answer to a legal question is rarely in black and white. You need to remain aware of this, and open to giving subtle answers to what might seem to be very straightforward questions. Never assume that two particular situations are legally identical. There may be small differences which make a great difference in practice. Lawyers will often agree to disagree on the legal answer to a particular question, and may settle a case without resolving it. If they cannot agree, they must go to court for a definitive ruling from a judge. What is important is that an answer can be found which everyone agrees upon as a 'good' answer: certain, legally valid and a reliable guide for future conduct.

While the case of *Mosshart v Hince* seems similar to the circumstances outlined, there is one significant difference: the purchaser did not consent to the non-delivery of one shipment of goods.

Determining what constitutes a careful standard of driving would seem straightforward but there is, in fact, very little case law on the issue and it is a question that must be answered in the circumstances of each case.

It is not easy to find out how survivors of rape feel about their experiences of the criminal justice system. They are understandably reluctant to speak out or be interviewed about it.

ARGUE FOR BOTH SIDES

A good lawyer knows the arguments from both sides. Sometimes students think that they should only discuss the legal arguments which support their point of view. This could not be further from the truth. If you are advising a particular client (in an exam context, for example) or arguing for a particular change in the law, you need to be clear about the strong and weak arguments on your side and any counterarguments that might be made, as well as how strong they are. You should be like a chess master who can deal with the board being reversed, and be able to argue the other side's position just as well as your own.

It is only by having a good understanding of the weaknesses on your side that you can make sure that you are putting forward a strong case. You should explicitly mention those weaknesses in your writing and deal with them. This applies even if you are constructing an argument as an advocate, for example, when you are writing an answer to a 'problem question' (which will be discussed further in the chapter on examination techniques) or if you are working on a moot court exercise.

In the case of *Black v Gass*, the court held that the fact that the purchaser orally accepted a change to the delivery arrangements did not alter the obligations under the original contract. However, the situation here is different as the change was conditional on a discount to the final price, effectively creating a new contract.

While it is true that the usual rule is that a driver is liable for their actions, this does not apply when some third-party action intervenes, such as a bus driver braking suddenly without warning.

While there is no comprehensive survey of the experiences of survivors of rape, what evidence there is points clearly to a need for reform.

Authorities and Proofs

Another aspect to ensuring that your argument is solid is making sure that you have good legal authority so that you can prove that the facts are on your side. As mentioned above, always verify that the state of the law is what you think it is. It is far better to be able to point to a particular phrase in legislation or a quotation from an eminent judge than to appeal generally to some vague concept such as the 'common good' or 'prudence, justice and charity'. You also need to be able to point to facts which support your arguments. In the context of a 'problem question', these will be facts stated in a hypothetical situation. In the context of an essay, this might be official reports, academic commentary or media reports. You need to be able to both argue *and* prove your case.

In order to do this well, you need to know the hierarchy of authorities. With legal authority, you should understand the difference between the Constitution, case law, and primary and secondary legislation. These are all types of *primary* legal materials, which are sources of law in and of themselves, at least for the jurisdiction from which they come.

Of lesser importance, but still very useful in your research, are *secondary* legal materials, such as legal textbooks, journal articles and government reports. These can help to explain and explore the law, but are not a direct *source* of law. They are not equally reliable or correct.

■ To learn more about this distinction, go to <www.legalwriting.ie> and complete Assignment 2.1.

With academic commentary, you need to find out what the main journals in your field are, and which authors are more respected. This can be difficult, but look to see who your lecturers are citing and using on your reading lists for initial clues.

This judgment is from the UK Supreme Court. I need to pay more attention to it than to the Court of Appeal case.

There is an article on standards and duties of care in negligence in the 'Modern Law Review'. I must read it carefully as this is a well-respected journal.

There are some articles on reform of the criminal law in Ireland, including rape, on the Judicial Studies Institute Journal website. I must download these as they will be very relevant to my essay.

LEGAL THINKING

Conclusion

This chapter is an overview of the basics of legal reasoning. The following two chapters will deepen your knowledge of this topic by bringing you through how to read, analyse and apply case law and legislation. You will come back to these basic principles again and again, but they are only useful if you understand how to read a legal text, extract its meaning and use that to support your argument.

Further Reading

- Hanson S, *Learning Legal Skills and Reasoning* (Routledge 2016), Chapters 13–15

Reading Judgments

3

As for attempts to dispense with first-hand reading and digesting by printed summaries and other like devices, they are absolutely to be rejected. No man ever became a lawyer by putting his trust in such things ...[1]

INTRODUCTION

Learning the law would be easy if all that lawyers needed to do was to memorise and strictly apply the rules contained in legislation. Unfortunately, human language is much too flexible and open to different meanings to make this possible. Consider, for example, the different ways that one could read a roadside sign saying 'Fine for Parking'. Even long-standing and well-developed systems of rules can contain gaps and confusion—Irish law does not clearly define who is a 'motorist' or a 'pedestrian'.[2] Is a person in a motorised wheelchair a 'driver'? Is a person on a skateboard a 'pedestrian'? The 'Plain English' movement argues that laws should be drafted in simpler language, and while this is a good guiding principle, simplicity is not the same as precision.[3] Too much precision can create inflexibility: road traffic law needs to be able to accommodate new types of transport, such as Segways or so-called 'hoverboards', without requiring extensive re-writing. Strict rules can also be blunt instruments and often need to be applied with some flexibility in order to achieve results that are 'just' or 'fair'.

When the meaning of legislation is unclear, it is for the courts to determine how it should be understood. They do this only in the context of real-life cases, where there is a difference of opinion over words that matter to people in an important way. In this way, the law develops. This chapter deals with the legal reasoning adopted by the courts in this context.

To establish the legal rules to be applied to a particular set of facts, you need to be able to read case law—the judgments given by courts in past

---

[1] Frederick Pollock, *Oxford Lectures* (1890) as quoted in ATH Smith, *Glanville Williams: Learning the Law* (13th edn, Sweet & Maxwell 2006) 27.

[2] Neil Van Dokkum, '"Is it a Car? Is it a Man? No, it's a Cyclist": Plain Language in our Legislation' (2012) 30 Irish Law Times 99.

[3] Brian Hunt, 'Plain Language: The End of the Road for Recondite Legislation?' (2001) 7 Bar Review 47.

cases. This is an important source of law in the Irish legal system. Court judgments are not case studies or examples of legislation in action. They are real law as developed by judges in real cases involving real people. Principles developed in case law are just as authoritative as legislation.

WHY YOU READ CASE LAW

If case law developed in a neat progression, it would be easy to study. Unfortunately for law students, it does not. In general, courts will not deal with hypothetical cases or give advisory opinions, though as with nearly all legal rules, there is of course an exception in the Irish context—by way of references to the Supreme Court under Article 26 of the Constitution.

Case law is formed from the cauldron of real-world litigation, which arises in the same unpredictable and haphazard way as everyday life unfolds. It often leaves more questions unanswered, particularly for students and academics who are trying to understand a body of law as a coherent whole. This happens because interesting arguments were not advanced by the lawyers in the case or the particular circumstances did not allow a particular proposition to be explored. Similarly, the court may hypothesise on what the outcome may have been were those arguments advanced, or what the outcome would be given a different set of facts—while these comments are useful (or, as lawyers would say, 'persuasive'), they do not form part of the law. One of the skills which a lawyer must develop is the ability to read a judgment and extrapolate how a court dealing with a similar, but not identical, set of situations might decide a case.

WHY IS READING CASE LAW DIFFERENT?

Reading case law is different from reading a book, a journal article or a piece of legislation. The reason for this is that, in case law, the answers you look for will often be buried in information that is irrelevant to the purpose for which you are reading the case. If you simply read journal articles, case books or core texts which analyse the judgment, the richness and depth of analysis in the case will be lost on you. In the same way, a different judge may regard issues in a different way and will bring different perspectives.

Further, in reading a case, you will, almost by osmosis, learn how to think like a lawyer. The complexity of the language used, the way in which arguments are formulated, posed, rejected or accepted, and the structure of thought will, after a spell, become second nature to you.

Having said that, it will take some time for you to become accustomed to this distinct method of analysis, and it cannot be emphasised enough that you should read as many cases as possible in your early years as a student.

WHERE CAN I FIND IRISH CASE LAW?

There are a number of places to find case law. First, in the library, the reported cases are collected into volumes of reports. There are also a number of databases where reported judgments are available. LexisLibrary, Justis, Westlaw IE and <irlii.org> are probably most useful. Sometimes, the judgment will be unreported or not yet reported. We will return to this question later in the chapter on legal research.

The first thing to note about case law is that there are very few cases where the judge will deliver a written judgment, and even less of those will actually be reported in one of the series of law reports. Usually, written judgments are given only when the case concerns a new point of law, or the application of established law to a novel fact pattern.

Reported cases are usually reported in Ireland in one of the two main law reports: the *Irish Reports* (IR) and the *Irish Law Reports Monthly* (ILRM). While cases may be reported elsewhere (in any of a number of specialised law reports, such as the *Employment Law Reports*), the IRs should be cited if at all possible, with the ILRMs the second preferred choice.

There is a considerable time delay in reporting cases, and sometimes it will be months or years before a reported version is available. Therefore, if you are writing about a topic that is particularly current, involving recently delivered judgments, you may find that you cannot find a proper report of the judgment. Indeed, sometimes, important judgments are never properly 'reported' and you will have to rely on an 'unreported' version of the text. Bear in mind that the reports are for convenience and the definitive version of a judgment is the one which is approved by the judge. If a judgment is reported, this confirms but does not confer status on it, and there is nothing wrong with using an unreported version.

It used to be the case that unreported judgments were issued in paper copy and were available in law libraries. Most unreported decisions from before around 1997 will have to be accessed in this manner. Today, however, websites such as <irlii.org>, <courts.ie> and <bailii.org> offer faster access to recent Irish decisions than was ever envisaged, perhaps months before the cases will be 'officially' reported. These cases appear in an online format and contain a neutral citation.

Every judgment given by a court will have a 'code' or citation which helps readers find the case, and for the writer to specify the exact judgment they are referring to. (Think, for example, how many decisions there will be called *DPP v Murphy*.) For reported decisions, the 'code' or citation is as follows:

[Year] or (Year) 'Volume of Report' 'Name of Report' 'Page number'
Thus, at [2005] 4 IR 504 you will find the case *People (DPP) v Murphy*.

For unreported decisions not available online, the code is:

(Court, Date)
Thus, the citation for *S v Eastern Health Board* is (HC, 22 July 1988)

There is also a code for neutral citations—this is the year in square brackets; followed by IESC (Supreme Court), IEHC (High Court), IECA (Court of Appeal), or IECCA (Court of Criminal Appeal); and then a number, which seems to represent where the decision falls in the chronological order of decisions issued by that court or posted online in the relevant year. Thus, the case above is also found at [2005] IECCA 52.

For neutral citations, the code is:

[Year] Court Number
Thus, the neutral citation for *People (DPP) v Murphy* as cited above is: [2005] IECCA 52.

■ To learn more about how to find cases, go to <www.legalwriting.ie> and complete Assignment 3.1.

THE STRUCTURE OF A REPORTED CASE

There are thousands of cases heard in the courts every year. Most legal disputes will never result in a final decision, because they are settled (agreed in private, between the parties) or withdrawn. For many others, the court will simply apply accepted law to the facts as established and give judgment. For these, the court will not deliver a written judgment. However, in certain circumstances, the court will decide to issue a written judgment. The court will do so for a number of reasons:

- cases which introduce, or appear to introduce, a new principle or a new rule;
- cases which materially modify an existing principle or rule;
- cases which settle, or materially tend to settle, a question upon which the law is doubtful; and
- cases which for any reason are peculiarly instructive.

These reasons were first set out by Lindley, and are known as the 'Lindley Principles'.[4]

While the number of reported cases is increasing annually (compare, for example, the 1980 *Irish Reports* with the 2010 *Irish Reports*), the number of reported cases is still only a fraction of those cases heard and decided in the courts.

Each case is reported in a similar manner. A number of things will always be set out at the top of the report: the name of the case, the court in which the case was heard, and the date on which the case was decided.

Underneath all of this information will be a series of words and phrases, called 'catchwords' or 'keywords', which represent the key issues of the case. From reading these keywords, you can quickly establish the general gist of what the case is about. Underneath this section is the headnote. It is vitally important to understand that this does *not* form part of the written judgment of the court and therefore should never be cited as authority. The headnote will normally summarise the facts of the case, briefly refer to arguments by counsel, and finally set out the ratio decidendi, or reason for the decision, of the case. If there is a minority or dissenting judgment, this will also be set out, as well as any important obiter dicta, or statements made in passing by the judges. Headnotes are useful for establishing the key points to the case, but the nuances of the decision are lost. Remember also that the headnote is written by a barrister, and will necessarily be a subjective account of the case. Following the headnote, a brief summary of the procedural history of the case will be set out.

The names of the barristers in the case will be set out directly above the judgment, and the names of the solicitors are set out directly after the judgment.

Most cases will involve two parties—A and B. The name of the case will be *A v B*. In Ireland, this is pronounced 'A and B', not 'A versus B', or 'A V B'. If a case involves more than two parties, it is generally known by the names of the first party on either side, so *A, B and C v D, E and F* will be referred to as 'A and D'.

■ To learn more about how reported judgments are structured, go to <www.legalwriting.ie> and complete Assignment 3.2.

How to Read Case Law

Reading case law is a particular skill and one which requires training and practice. Once learnt, however, it is an ability that will be of great assistance

---

[4] See ATH Smith, *Glanville Williams: Learning the Law* (13th edn, Sweet & Maxwell 2006) 30.

to you in your study of law. After learning how to read a case, and practising this repeatedly, you will then learn some more sophisticated skills in reading case law. You cannot learn these overnight. What follows are the five stages required when reading and evaluating a case on a basic level.

WHERE DID THE CASE ARISE?

When reading a judgment, the first thing to consider is its source. Where did it come from and why was it written? Ask yourself:

- Which court decided the case? Where is this court in the hierarchy of courts?
- Was it decided in a first instance court or on appeal, or by some other procedure (such as a case stated)? Is this the final domestic appeal or final determination of the issue?
- Which judge(s) wrote the judgment(s)? (With experience, you will begin to understand the background and perspectives of individual judges, and why that matters. While all judges are in theory interchangeable, in practice, everyone brings their own unique approach to a legal question. On a panel of different judges, they may all arrive at the same result, but by different means. This can be interesting and useful to observe. What can be even more educational is noticing when and why judges disagree.)

WHAT ARE THE FACTS?

You then need to look at how the case arose. Litigation always emerges from a dispute between two or more parties—individuals, corporations, State bodies—who disagree about some issue of fact or law. What was the problem which was serious enough to demand all of the effort and expense involved in taking a case to court? Generally speaking, law students are concerned with learning the black letter legal rules and principles that they will invariably be examined upon. Too often, an extensive study of these rules and principles that emanate from seminal cases is undertaken at the expense of any serious consideration of the specific facts of these cases. This is, to some extent, understandable in a traditional academic context, but in a practical sense, as one United States Supreme Court Justice once famously remarked, '[I]t may sound paradoxical, but most contentions of law are won or lost on the facts.'[5] Ask yourself:

- What were the facts of the case? This will usually (but not always) be summarised at the beginning of the judgment by the judge. Often the

---

[5] Robert H Jackson, 'Advocacy Before the United States Supreme Court' (1951) 37 Cornell LQ 1.

facts can be complex—try to boil them down to the essentials without over-simplifying. Is *Carlill v Carbolic Smoke Ball Co*[6] a case about truth in advertising, or about whether an advertisement can be an offer to the world? Sometimes, the summary of the facts can be intertwined with the procedural history of the case. Do not get lost in the procedure—your starting point should be the dispute before the lawyers got involved.

- Arising from those facts, what was the legal complaint on the part of the plaintiff or prosecutor? In order to get into court, the aggrieved party had to argue that the law was being broken or ignored. This will generally involve a breach of some legal duty, arising out of the Constitution, common law or statute, which is allegedly being committed by the defendant.
- What legal relief was sought? If a legal duty has been breached, the plaintiff will want a remedy for that breach. Sometimes that will be immediate and short-term, such as an injunction, or more long-lasting, such as a declaration of unconstitutionality. In a criminal case, it might involve the defendant being convicted of an offence, and perhaps being sent to prison.

WHAT IS THE LEGAL ISSUE?

The particular facts of the case, and the legal complaint made, will leave the court with a decision to make. Sometimes this will turn on a question of fact—was the surgeon paying proper attention when performing the operation? Did the defendant start the fight, or was he acting in self-defence? These questions will often be decided by a trier of fact, which may be a jury, with no written judgment. In situations where they are decided by the judge, this will rarely merit detailed written consideration and you will therefore not consider these types of cases further.

However, other cases will require the resolution of a legal question. Correctly identifying this issue is at the heart of reading a judgment. By the time you have answered the questions above (on the origins of the case and the demands of the parties), you should be able to state the legal issue at stake in one or two sentences. If you cannot state the issue briefly, you probably have not identified it clearly enough. There may be sub-questions, but there should be one principal question. However, bear in mind that different judges may identify different principal questions. Before you go any further, therefore, be sure that you can state:

- What is the legal issue in the case? The judgment will often state what this is, just before it begins to discuss the law in detail. However, sometimes it will not be made clear and you will need to re-read the introduction carefully.

---

6 [1893] 1 QB 256.

What did the Court Decide?

The next step in making sense of a case is to see what the answer to the question is. Sometimes, the judgment will summarise its reasoning before giving a detailed exposition of the relevant law. This is particularly helpful in understanding what the judgment means.

However, the court will not always make it this easy. You will therefore need to skip to the end of the judgment and read the concluding paragraphs to see what the judge's final decision was. This is not absolutely necessary, and you may prefer to wait until you have read through all of the judgment before discovering what the ruling of the court was. However, knowing what conclusion the judge came to can make it easier to understand the discussion of the law which follows.

Why did the Court Decide that?

The difficult part of reading a judgment is figuring out why the court decided in one way and not in another. This ability is a core legal skill: having a proper understanding of how a court arrives at a conclusion is what allows lawyers to advise their clients on new, unanticipated situations. You should be able to answer the following questions:

- What arguments were made by the parties? The lawyers on both sides will have taken different points of view on the issue(s) in the case. It is important to clearly identify these. You may find it useful to sketch a diagram of these, possibly as two columns, 'for' and 'against'. In the chapter on legal thinking, you learned about ancillary questions. This is a good way of identifying these.
- In reaching its conclusion, how did the court weigh these arguments? The court should go through an exercise of considering the relative weight of the reasoning for and against the legal arguments put forward by the parties. Which arguments did it think were strongest and why? What were the policy rationales, if any, that it identified?

Reading the Same Case in Different Ways

You may find that you read the same case again and again in different contexts. In these situations, the issue you are interested in will be different, depending on why you are reading it. For example, you may read the case of *Norris v Attorney General*[7] a great many number of times throughout your time in law

---

[7] [1983] IESC 3, [1984] IR 36.

school, in criminal law, in constitutional law and in international human rights law. You'll need to filter the case through the prism of your particular interest, and focus on different aspects of it as appropriate. You may not have to read all of it every time but can simply read the relevant portions.

More Complex Issues

Once you have carefully read a judgment and fully understand the majority opinion and the reasoning in support of it, and the nature and reasoning behind dissenting opinion(s) (if any), it is crucial to 'take a step back' from it. Knowing what a judgment holds and why it does so are obviously important, but being able to contextualise the judgment and use it to support your own legal reasoning and argument in an essay, exam or moot court exercise are perhaps even more important skills. You need to be able to place the judgment, and its usefulness to you, in a broader context.

Questions to Ask

In common law jurisdictions like Ireland, every judgment establishes a precedent. However, it is in establishing the applicability or non-applicability or, stated another way, relevance or irrelevance of that precedent to subsequent factual situations or to other precedent, that sharp legal reasoning is crucial. Does an existing precedent require a certain result in another instance? Is a judgment that might seem to depart from a long line of precedent actually a legal departure or does it only reflect the particular facts and circumstances presented by that case? These are questions that law students will be forced to confront and answer throughout their studies. To resolve these questions, you must employ legal reasoning skills and, more specifically, know how to use judgments to support your own reasoning.

In order to be able to do this, a lawyer must understand the operation of *precedent*. This is how the courts work from case to case, by trying to boil a case down to its essential elements, extract the legal rule from the text of the judgment, and reason by analogy to future situations. The part of the judgment which is binding for future cases is the ratio decidendi of the case—this is the reason for the decision, and consists of the principle of law as it applies to the facts of the case. Any other principles of law set out in the judgment are obiter dicta. This occurs where, perhaps, the court speculates on how the case would have been decided were the facts any different, or if the court decides the matter on a particular issue, and then asks whether it could be decided in any other way. These statements of law are not determinative of how the case was decided, and so are not binding for later courts.

Using judgments requires that you use your legal analytical skills. Again, understanding a judgment and the reasoning that underpins it is only the first step towards being able to use it. You must think analytically and critically about a judgment. In so doing, you must ask and consider a number of new questions. When was the case decided? What was the political, economic, cultural and social context? Finally, and most importantly, what were the facts of the case? This last question is the most important to consider in evaluating how a judgment can be used, and it is a question that law students spend too little time thinking about.

Revisiting the Role of Facts

It is important to consider the role played by the facts in any judgment. First, when reading any judgment, you must be aware that no two cases are exactly alike, although the differences may be very small. Secondly, when reading a judgment, you must pay special attention to the particular facts that are deemed legally salient and play an explicit role in the opinions of the judges. Thirdly, you must evaluate the facts of all cases carefully in light of the eventual outcome. This evaluation must be both critical and cynical in that, because judges are human beings, they are inevitably moved to decide cases based on the facts before them. Put simply, this third step requires that you always 'read between the lines'.

Analogising and Distinguishing

When you understand and can contextualise judgments, you can then use them to advance or support your own legal reasoning. This is accomplished by two primary vehicles: analogising and distinguishing. Analogising means showing the similarities between the two cases; distinguishing means showing the differences between the two. Why must you do this? When you are asked to construct a legal argument as a law student, it is likely to be a tricky endeavour. Whether it is in the context of an exam, essay or moot court exercise, there will be precedent on both sides—some judgments would seem to favour one side of the argument, other cases would seem to favour the other. There will not be straightforward right or wrong answers. You should be far more concerned with how you arrive at an answer than with the actual answer itself. Your legal argument needs to be based on the relevant legal authorities—again, the authorities will invariably conflict—and you need to show why one line of authority is more relevant to the scenario you are confronted with and why the other is less relevant. You do so by analogising and distinguishing precedent.

To analogise cases, you need to:

1) identify the potentially relevant cases to which you want to draw analogies;

2) point to the similarities and explain why they are legally significant; and

3) explain why the differences are not legally significant.

To distinguish cases, you need to:

1) identify the potentially relevant cases you want to distinguish;

2) point to the distinctions between the cases; and

3) explain why these distinctions are legally significant.

Ratio Decidendi and the Use of Precedent

As you study law, you will spend a lot of time reading, or at least reading about, cases. You do this because they contain legal rules which are applied in future cases. How to identify those rules is a skill that requires some practice to acquire, but is vital to the learning of the law.

To begin with, you must identify the distinctive facts of the case, the ones which distinguish it from others in ways which make it a new rule of law. There will be something about the circumstances of the case which is new and raises a novel question for the court to answer. Of course, many of the facts of a case will be unique, but the key is to find the ones which matter. Imagine a case involving a car accident. Is it important that the car was blue? Probably not. Is it important that the driver was drunk? Probably. Is it important that the car was moving? Most likely. Does the injured party's clothing matter? If it includes a reflective jacket, it may be very important; otherwise it may be irrelevant.

Once you have identified the salient facts, you must identify the legal rule: a statement of the law as applied by the judge in this case which can be taken as applying to similar cases in future. It is this rule which is the ratio decidendi in the case. Sometimes the judge will helpfully state what this rule is; more often, the judge will not, or the rule that you are looking for is a peripheral issue in the case and is not dealt with directly. In the abstract, the rule will take the form 'In circumstances where X, Y and Z are true, the legal outcome is A.'

Defining X, Y and Z clearly can take some effort. In the car accident example, you might find the judge saying 'Where a car driver has an accident while drunk, the driver is liable for any injury or damage caused.' That seems straightforward by itself, but you may find that other statements by the judge in the case will add additional dimensions to the rule. These will most likely be obiter dicta. For example, does it matter if the accident was caused by the driver or by some other person, or by circumstances out of anyone's control, such as bad weather? Does it matter whether the drunkenness was a direct contributor to the accident, or that the accident would have happened to a sober driver? To deal with these ambiguities, you will need to read the judgment carefully.

You will then need to state the rule in a way that can be applied to future cases. This will involve abstracting the circumstances in such a way that the rule can be used in analogous cases in the future. For example, a case that involves a drunken car driver will become a rule that applies to any operator of any moving mechanically propelled vehicle. This is the application and development of precedent, which is a distinctive feature of the common law.

■ To learn more about how to identify the ratio decidendi in a case, go to <www.legalwriting.ie> and complete Assignment 3.3.

THE USE OF PRECEDENT FROM OVERSEAS

Often, there will not be clear precedent on a particular issue from the Irish courts. The courts will then look to cases decided in other jurisdictions (countries). This is very useful when the Irish courts have not already dealt with the particular issue involved, and can offer insight into different policy perspectives on questions without easy answers.

However, precedent from other jurisdictions is only *persuasive*, which means that the Irish courts do not have to follow it. An Irish judge will take it into account but is free to decide a case in a way that contradicts the decisions of the UK House of Lords or Supreme Court, or the Supreme Court of the United States. In assessing the usefulness of a precedent from another jurisdiction, you should start by looking at the position of the court in that legal system. Is it a court of first instance? A court of appeal? Is it the highest court? The higher the place of the court in the overall hierarchy, the more weight will be given to its judgments.

What is also important to identify is how similar the laws in that country are to the laws of Ireland. In many areas, the laws of England and Wales are quite close to Irish law, such as in contract law. However, the United States of America tends to be a better source in the area of constitutional law, as the Irish Constitution is more similar to the American than to the (unwritten) UK system. However, this depends on the context and the particular legal topic, particularly since the European Convention on Human Rights Act 2003, which made that international treaty part of Irish law. We can now draw on the experience of the UK with this instrument under their Human Rights Act 1998.

Think about what case law your lecturer regularly refers to in your module, as this may indicate which jurisdiction is the more helpful in the particular subject area.

The Importance of Dissenting Judgments

Judgments in appeal courts are decided by majority vote, which means that minority decisions are, strictly speaking, not a source of law. However, dissents are always worth reading. As a point of contrast, they can be useful in understanding the majority judgments.

They can also, over time, be seen as containing more compelling reasoning than the majority decision, and it does occur that a judge in a later case will adopt the minority judgment, giving it the force of precedent. Thus, dissents can develop into the mainstream view in time. For example, in the case of *People (AG) v O'Callaghan*,[8] the High Court suggested that one reason to refuse bail is the likelihood of the individual re-offending while on bail. This was forcefully rejected by the Supreme Court in the case, but the issue was ultimately put to the people in a referendum, and now courts can take it into account when determining if an individual should be granted bail or not.

How to Establish the Majority Opinion

In an ideal situation, identifying the majority decision is a simple matter of counting the votes. However, in complex cases, it may not be this easy. The judges may have identified different issues, or answered them in different ways, which means that clearly defining what the case is actually authority for is not straightforward. A careful reading, and probably re-reading, will be required.

Writing a Case Note

In learning about the law, and preparing for examinations, one tool that is very useful is to prepare a *case note*: a brief summary of a judgment that can be quickly read later. The process of writing it will help you to understand the case, and it can be a significant help when revising.

Format of a Case Note

Although a case note can take various shapes, in its most basic form, it should deal with the following:

---

[8]   [1966] IR 501 (HC).

- name of the case;
- court that decided the case;
- date on which judgment was given (year is usually sufficient);
- facts of the case, in summary form;
- legal issue, in one or two sentences;
- ruling, including any dissents; and
- reasoning, summarised for each judge, including dissents.

ASSIGNMENT 1: PRACTICE—WRITING A CASE NOTE

Introduction

Using the case of *Shannon Regional Fisheries Board v Cavan County Council* SC, 30 July 1996, reported at [1996] 3 IR 267, you will learn how to read a case. You will find the judgment in *Shannon Regional Fisheries* online at <www.bailii.org/ie/cases/IESC/1996/7.html>. You should find the document and read it either on screen or on paper, whichever is most convenient for you.

As with most things, the best way to learn is to practise. What you will do now, therefore, is draft a case note for the case of *Shannon Regional Fisheries v Cavan County Council*. You will be guided through it, so that you understand how to identify the important information in the case. This will build your skills so that you can tackle more complex cases soon.

If you like, before continuing to read the remainder of this section, which will help you to draft a note on this case, try to answer the questions given above, even if only in a rough, outline form.

Where did the case arise?

The first question to ask yourself is: In what court was the judgment given? The answer to this question is fortunately very clear. The name of the court which decided the case is given at the top of the judgment: the Supreme Court. Now ask what is the procedural history of the case?

The first judgment is written by Mr Justice Blayney, abbreviated as 'Blayney J'. (Note that this is pronounced 'Mr Justice Blayney'—*never* 'Blayney J'.) You will see that in the first paragraph, he helpfully gives the circumstances of the case: it is a case stated from the District Court to the High Court, which has been appealed to the Supreme Court.

What are the facts?

You will find that most court judgments begin with a recital of the facts of the case. You will also find that in cases where there are multiple judgments, one judge will write a summary which the other judges will adopt. Blayney J provides such a summary (which is in fact taken from the District Court judge) and if you skip to Keane J's judgment, you will see that his first sentence agrees with it.

However, this summary is somewhat long for our purposes. If you are writing a case note, you are doing so for the purposes of understanding and study. You will probably be looking at the note when you are revising for examinations, and therefore you will want to be as brief as possible.

You should therefore write your own short summary of the facts. The important things to look for are:

- What action of the defendant led to it being charged with an offence?
- Why was it doing this? (Was the County Council polluting the river out of malice, or was there another reason?)
- Why did it not take action to prevent the pollution?

Make an attempt at this now, and then move on to look at the legal issue in the case.

What is the legal issue?

Identifying the legal issue in a case is probably one of the trickier tasks you will need to do. Obviously, in a legal judgment, there will be many legal issues raised and it can be difficult to make out which is the important one. You need to read carefully to see what it is. It will generally be stated immediately after the summary of facts.

In this case, it is easy to identify, as the District Court judge had to identify the issue when forwarding the case stated for determination by the High Court. You will find it under the numbered paragraphs, where the District Court judge looked to the High Court for guidance. You will see that there are a number of questions which he asked, but the essential one is the first one. If you read the remaining questions, you will see that none of them matter if the first question is answered in the negative.

What did the court decide?

(Before going on to consider what the court decided, you need to be clear about what is meant by mens rea. This is the 'guilty mind' or intention to commit an act which is criminal. Mens rea, along with the actus reus, or 'guilty act', is required in order to prove criminal liability.)

If you can identify the question, it is usually easy to identify the answer. It is usually right at the end of the judgment, as in this case: look at the last sentence of Blayney J's judgment to see what he decided. (You do need to go back up to see what the High Court judge said, but the answer to the question asked by the District Court judge is 'yes'.)

Keane J's answer is also in the last sentence of his judgment, but you will need to dig a little deeper to determine what exactly he is saying. When he says he would allow the appeal, he is saying that he disagrees with the answer given by the High Court judge, so you need to go back to the start to see what that answer was.

The matter does not end there. There are two written judgments, each of which gives a different answer to the issue. However, the final decision of the court must be one answer. This is determined by majority vote. You will see from the top of the judgment that there were three judges hearing this case. The third judge was O'Flaherty J. He agreed with one of the other judges. Which one? What does this mean the overall decision was?

Why did the court decide that?

Once you have determined what it was that the court decided, you need to determine why. This is so that you can learn what policy reasons directed the judges in the directions they went, and use this to predict how they might decide future cases.

This can be the most time-consuming part of reading a judgment, but it is the most valuable learning exercise. It is easy to memorise the rule in a case; it is quite another to understand the reasoning process behind that rule, and perhaps the counter-arguments to it.

In some cases, the reasoning is quite straightforward. So it is with Blayney J's judgment. He disposes of the mens rea issue quickly—how? He finds that there are no effective defences—why? He cites a House of Lords decision—why? Does he need to do this to make his argument?

Keane J's decision is more complex. He outlines the traditional understanding of criminal liability, and the impact of absolute liability on this. What difficulties does he see with this latter doctrine? How does he deal with the *Alphacell* case cited by Blayney J? What other approaches does he find in the persuasive precedent from overseas? Which approach does he prefer? Why?

Which answer, Keane J's or Blayney J's, do you find most convincing? Why?

ASSIGNMENT 2: PRACTICE—WRITING A CASE NOTE

Introduction

For your second exercise, you will prepare a case note for a somewhat more complex case. The case is *Norris v Attorney General*, which is very important in the development of constitutional jurisprudence in this country. You will find the case at <www.bailii.org/ie/cases/IESC/1983/3.html>. Download or print the case now, and read it carefully before proceeding.

Where did the case arise?

The first point in our analysis is the procedural history of the case. That is easy to identify: it is given in the first paragraph of the Chief Justice's judgment.

What are the facts?

The essential facts of the case are also brief and easy to find, as the Chief Justice's judgment conveniently provides them. However, you will also need to read carefully through Henchy J's judgment, where he summarises what he calls the 'general tenor' of the evidence which the court heard. The information given here is also important in understanding the final decision of the court. Can you say why?

What is the legal issue?

You may be thinking that the legal issue in the case is straightforward, and on the surface, it is: the Chief Justice states it in the first paragraph of his judgment. However, if you read through the judgments, you will see that this seemingly simple question contains a number of other, more complex, issues.

For example, the Chief Justice's judgment contains a section headed 'Locus standi'. What is this about? He also discussed the European Convention on Human Rights. What is the issue to be decided by the court here?

Perhaps a more subtle example is the issue of the impact of Christian and Catholic moral teaching on constitutional law. Read carefully the paragraph in the Chief Justice's judgment that begins 'The preamble to the Constitution …'. What is the legal issue here?

From these examples, you should begin to see that although a case can be reduced to a single legal issue where necessary, it will often include a number of sub-issues, as mentioned above. Depending on how and why you are reading the case, those issues will be more or less important. Read the judgments carefully again to see if you can identify any other legal issues.

What did the court decide?

Determining what the court decided is relatively straightforward. Skip to the bottom of each judgment and see how each judge ruled on the issue of constitutionality. Count the number of votes in each direction.

Why did the court decide that?

What is a little more difficult is to understand why they each voted in this direction. From the work which you did above to identify the legal issue, you should have a list of questions that the judges set out to answer.

Read through each judgment in turn and examine the logic of the judge's thinking. What reasons does he put forward for his final decision? Does he rely on previous court decisions? Does he rely on the evidence heard by the High Court? Does he look to the decisions of courts in other countries? Try to reduce the flow of argument of each judge to a few sentences. This can be difficult, particularly with a long and complex case like this, but it is a skill which is well worth learning.

ASSIGNMENT 3: PRACTICE—WRITING A CASE NOTE

Introduction

For the final exercise, you will write a case note on an interesting and controversial case, *North Western Health Board v W* [2001] IESC 90, [2001] 3 IR 622. You will find this case at <www.bailii.org/ie/cases/IESC/2001/90.html>. Download and read it carefully. As the Chief Justice says at the outset, the issue is easy to state, but the answer is not easy.

Where did the case arise?

To determine the procedural history of the case, you will need to read the Chief Justice's judgment carefully. From paragraph 11 on, he gives the history of the case, both before it came to court and afterwards. Be sure that you are clear as to what the plaintiff (the Health Board) was seeking when it went to court, and why, before reading on.

What are the facts?

The facts are also found in the Chief Justice's judgment, from paragraph two on. There are a number of essentials that you need to understand: the science behind the PKU test, the objection of the parents and the concerns of the Health Board. Try to distil these to a few sentences before proceeding.

What is the legal issue?

As the Chief Justice says, this is not a simple case. The legal issue can be simply stated, but what are the sub-issues that can be identified? Whose rights need to be considered? What are the issues regarding the family? Freedom of conscience? Education?

What did the court decide?

This part, at least, is straightforward. Skip to the bottom of each judgment and see what answer the judges gave to the main question in the case.

Why did the court decide that?

What is more complex is figuring out what motivated the judges to decide in one way or another. Each judge gives thorough consideration to the issues. However, they do not analyse the case in the same fashion, and you will need to structure your summary in different ways to take account of this.

Thus, the Chief Justice summarises the arguments made by lawyers for both sides, the relevant law and cases from other jurisdictions before arriving at his conclusion. Denham J starts from the High Court judgment and the grounds of appeal put forward against it, then analyses the relevant constitutional law. Murphy J prefers to use Catholic moral teaching as the main plank of his reasoning. How the other judges structure their judgments is something you should consider carefully yourself.

What you need to do at this point is summarise the main thread of their argument into a few sentences. This is not always easy, but if you can reduce a complex judgment to a few pithy phrases, you will have gone a long way to understanding it. It will also be much easier to review and revise it once you have done this.

Take your time and work through each of the judgments in turn. When you are done, review your previous summaries. Does your understanding of a later judgment give you a better perspective on one you have already summarised? Go back through them and see if they can be polished in any way.

Further Reading

- Smith ATH, *Glanville Williams: Learning the Law* (15th edn, Sweet & Maxwell 2013)
- Samuelson D, 'Introducing Legal Reasoning' (1997) 47 Journal of Legal Education 571
- Byrne R and McCutcheon P with Bruton C and Coffey G, *Byrne and McCutcheon on the Irish Legal System* (6th edn, Bloomsbury Professional 2014)

Sample Case Notes

What follows are some examples of different approaches to case notes, prepared for different purposes. They are intended as guidelines rather than strict templates. Try out various methods and discover what works best for you and your audience (which may be yourself, if you are using these as a revision tool).

Example for Private Research Purposes

Case name and citation

McGee v Attorney General [1974] IR 284

Facts

The plaintiff was a married woman with four children, of child-bearing age. She was told that a further pregnancy could be fatal. After consultation with her husband, she decided to use contraception. The pill was legally available but she could not safely use it. She was prescribed a contraceptive jelly, but this could not be imported or sold in Ireland. When she tried to import the jelly, it was seized as it was prohibited under s 17(3) of the Criminal Law Amendment Act 1935.

Question

Was s 17(3) of the Criminal Law Amendment Act 1935 compatible with the 1937 Constitution?

Holding

No (4–1). Walsh, Budd, Henchy, Griffin JJ: No. Fitzgerald CJ (dissenting): Yes.

Reasoning

Fitzgerald CJ (dissenting): She is treated equally with all other citizens and there does not need to be an exception for her. The Act does not prohibit the use of contraceptives. The spouses have no right to prevent expansion of the family. The use of 'conscience' in Article 42.3.1° does not extend to the decision not to have children. The US cases are not relevant. Spouses must face these natural hazards together.

Walsh J: It is for the husband and wife to decide how many children to have. Their sexual life is private; the State cannot intrude. Section 17 of the 1935 Act is an unjustified invasion of this.

Budd J: The citizen's right to privacy is universally recognised and is most important in marriage. The 1935 Act does not defend or vindicate that right.

Henchy J: By denying access to a suitable contraceptive, and therefore risking her health and life, the 1935 Act endangers the plaintiff's marriage. Following *Griswold v Connecticut*, it violates her right to privacy and to make her own decisions regarding her marriage.

Griffin J: The plaintiff is entitled to marital privacy. In the US, *Poe v Ullman* holds that the family can be regulated, but *Griswold v Connecticut* holds that the marital bedroom is private. The aim of the 1935 Act (the protection of morals through the deterrence of fornication and promiscuity) is a legitimate one, but s 17(3) sweeps unnecessarily broadly and thereby invades the area of protected freedoms.

EXAMPLE IN HEADNOTE STYLE

McB v L

[2010] IESC 48

Facts: The appellant was the natural father of three children born to parents who co-habited in a non-marital relationship. Ireland was the place of habitual residence of the children until the respondent removed the children from Ireland to England. The issue for resolution related to whether the appellant had rights of custody in respect of the children on the date of their removal. The appellant sought a declaration in earlier High Court proceedings that the removal was wrongful and in 2010 the High Court had determined that the appellant had not enjoyed rights of custody as to the children and that the removal then had not been wrongful. The appellant submitted that Council Regulation 2201/2003/EC had substantially replaced the Hague Convention and that provisions of the Treaty on the European Union after the Treaty of Lisbon and the binding legal effect given to the Charter of Fundamental Rights warranted the recognition of 'inchoate rights' of a natural father who had not obtained recognition of his position in the form of a court order. The issue arose as to the position of the unmarried father under Irish statutory and constitutional law.

Held, by the Supreme Court (Fennelly J; Denham, Macken, Finnegan and O'Donnell JJ concurring) that the appellant did not have rights of custody as to his children for the purposes of art 5 of the Hague Convention. The Supreme Court sought an order for a preliminary reference on the interpretation of 'rights of custody' within the meaning of Council Regulation 2201/2003/EC on the recognition and enforcement of judgments in matrimonial matters and parental responsibility. The court urged the Court of Justice to deal with the case pursuant to the urgent procedure pursuant to art 104b of the Rules of Procedure of the Court of Justice. The Supreme Court recognised that the definition of 'custody rights' for the purposes of the application for the return of children on the basis of the Hague Convention was contained now in art 2.9 of Regulation 2201/2003/EC. The wording of the provisions introduced additional words subsequent to 'custody rights', namely, 'and duties ...'. The court took note of the submission of the appellant that the provisions of Council Regulation 2201/2003/EC should, in light of art 6 TEU, be interpreted to conform with the right to privacy and family life as protected in art 8 of the Charter of Fundamental Rights of the European Union. The Supreme Court referred a question to the Court of Justice pursuant to art 267 TFEU as to whether Council Regulation 2201/2003/EC, interpreted pursuant to the Charter of Fundamental Rights, precluded a Member State from requiring an unmarried father to obtain an order of custody to have 'custody rights' so as to render the removal of the child wrongful. The Supreme Court suggested a negative answer to this question.

FORMAL NOTE FOR EXAM/JOURNAL ARTICLE

This case note takes a thematic view of the case, examining the case issue by issue rather than judgment by judgment.

North Western Health Board v HW and CW [2001] IESC 90, [2001] 3 IR 622

Facts

The case of *North Western Health Board v HW and CW*[1] dealt with the complex issue of parental autonomy and State interference with reference to a medical procedure. Here, the parents had refused to allow their newborn son to undergo a screening test. The test is routinely carried out on all children in the State between 72 and 120 hours after their birth, and was highly recommended by the medical profession.[2]

High Court judgment

In the High Court, McCracken J considered the rights of the family under Articles 41 and 42 of the Constitution, and came to the conclusion that the orders sought could not be granted. His reasoning was that the State could only interfere with parental rights in 'exceptional cases', which this case was not.

---

[1] [2001] IESC 90, [2001] 3 IR 622.
[2] Indeed, the court stated that on average, only six children per year did not have the test.

Supreme Court judgment

Medical consent

Denham J began by discussing the doctrine of consent in medical law. Referring to her judgment in *Re A Ward of Court*[3] in which she discussed the notion of medical consent in considerable detail, she emphasised the fact that where a child is unable to consent for reasons of immaturity, the parents of that child are endowed with the responsibility of giving consent to medical treatment. Hardiman J went so far as to say that the position adopted by the Health Board in the case was that the consent requirement for the PKU test was a 'mere empty formula since the parents have no right to refuse to consent'.[4]

Family and the Constitution

All four of the majority opinions referred to Articles 40.3, 41.1, 42.1 and 42.5 of the Constitution. They agreed that the family has a unique position in Irish law, as the fundamental unit of society. They also all referred to the rights of children as members of that family, and the rights children possess autonomously from that family. The judges referred to *G v An Bord Uchtála*,[5] and noted that under Article 40.3 of the Constitution, the State has a duty to protect the personal rights of all of its citizens.

The 'best interests' test

All of the five judges seem to have been of the opinion that, had the best interests test or a test of 'medical benefit' been used, the test would be ordered. Murphy J explicitly declared what is implicit in the rest of the majority judgments when he stated, 'It is beyond doubt that the performance of a PKU test is unquestionably in the best interests of the infant tested'.[6]

The 'best interests' test and State intervention

Denham J noted that what was at issue in the case was the balancing of three interests: those of the parents, those of the Health Board (the State), and the interests of the child as a member of the family and as a person. Despite the apparent primacy of the welfare principle, she then went on to maintain that State intervention into affairs of the family could only be justified under Article 42.5 where the parents have failed, for physical or moral reasons, to care for their child. Murphy J agreed. He noted that, while under Article 40.3, the State

---

[3] *Re A Ward of Court (withholding medical treatment) (No 2)* [1996] 2 IR 79.

[4] [2001] IESC 90 [234], [2001] 3 IR 622 (SC), 741.

[5] [1980] IR 32.

[6] [2001] IESC 90 [200], [2001] 3 IR 622 (SC), 729.

has a clear duty to intervene in certain cases, 'it would be incorrect to suggest that the State could or should intervene merely because by doing so it would advance significantly the material interests of the child'.[7]

Murray J agreed with Murphy J that if the test were authorised in the case, it would lead to a situation where the State could intervene when a parental decision was unwise. He was of the opinion that the State could only intervene in exceptional circumstances in the interests of the common good, where the parents had failed for physical or moral reasons in their duty to the child.

Test for State intervention

The four judges then went on to establish a constitutional test for State intervention. Denham J was of the opinion that the State could only intervene in affairs of the family in exceptional cases, for example, where the child was in immediate danger and needed a life-saving operation. Murphy J stated that a particularly ill-advised decision, such as that made by the parents in this case, did not amount to a default of the parents' moral and constitutional duty. Murray J was only willing to go so far as stating that there should be some 'immediate and fundamental threat to the capacity of the child to continue to function as a human person, physically, morally, or socially, deriving from an exceptional dereliction of duty on the part of the parents'[8] before State intervention would be justified. Hardiman J was of the opinion that where the parents have not failed in their duty towards their child for physical or moral reasons, their decision should not be interfered with by the State or the courts in the absence of a jurisdiction conferred by statute. The presumption that the welfare of the child is best addressed within the confines of the constitutional family could be displaced, he thought, where there were countervailing constitutional considerations, or perhaps in the case of an immediate threat to the life of the child.

Dissenting judgment from Keane CJ

Chief Justice Keane gave the only dissenting judgment of the court. He discussed the constitutional protection of the family in great detail, and referred to a number of cases which discussed the rights of children and their families.[9] He then discussed a number of cases from Australia, Canada and the United Kingdom.

---

[7] ibid.

[8] ibid 740–741.

[9] The Chief Justice referred to *PW v AW* (HC, 21 April 1980); *Re JH (an infant)* [1985] IR 375; *Re Article 26 of the Constitution and the Adoption (No 2) Bill 1987* [1989] IR 656; *G v An Bord Uchtála* [1980] IR 32; *FN v Minister for Education* [1997] 1 IR 409; *DG v Eastern Health Board* [1998] 1 ILRM 241; and *Ryan v Attorney General* [1965] IR 294.

Keane CJ noted at the outset that if the case were to be determined by what was in the best interests of the child, the order should have been granted by the High Court. He concluded by stating that in refusing to give consent for the procedure, the parents had refused to protect and vindicate the rights of the infant to be guarded against unnecessary and unavoidable dangers to his health and welfare. These constitutional rights, the Chief Justice concluded, could and should be protected by the court.

Comments and conclusion

The judgment of the Chief Justice in the case correctly placed more emphasis on the right of the child to fulfil his potential as a human being, and his right to medical care, than the judgments of the rest of the court. While the other judgments referred to the personal rights of the child, it would appear that if these rights are not being afforded due consideration by the parents of the child, there is almost no way in which the State can intervene and protect his interests. A child's personal rights under Article 40.3, the Convention on the Rights of the Child and other international conventions and agreements will, seemingly, always be compromised by Articles 41 and 42 of the Constitution. Whether the long-awaited referendum on the rights of the child will change this constitutional preference remains to be seen.

4 Reading Legislation

> In theory, there is nothing to prevent the whole of the law being set out clearly and logically in statutory form ... In practice, human sloth, indifference and perversity have combined to keep the statute book in a state far short of perfection.[1]

INTRODUCTION

In addition to the Constitution, there are two other primary sources of law in Ireland: case law and legislation. A good deal of your time as a lawyer will be spent looking at this second type of law. Legislation is law made by politicians in the Houses of the Oireachtas, and there are rules regarding what they can and cannot achieve by this means. Reading legislation requires a particular approach. Extracting meaning from the words is a complex, layered activity.

The starting point in our discussion of legislation must be the Constitution, which sets out certain rules about how legislation is written. The first and most important rule is that legislation must be consistent with the Constitution. The second important point is Article 15.2.1° of the Constitution, which provides that the sole and exclusive law making power in the State is the Oireachtas. This means that no other body in the State can make law: while the legislators make law, the courts interpret it and apply it.

WHAT IS PARTICULARLY UNIQUE ABOUT LEGISLATION?

Legislation is written, or to use the technical term, drafted, with particular terms and phrases. It is very precise in its wording, and sometimes the way it is written can make it seem excessively formal, strained and very particular to the first-time reader. The main reason for this is that legislation is prescriptive, that is, it is written to provide for or *prescribe* a specific state of affairs or rule or principle. It is very tightly drafted using special terms so that it can have a certain and definite meaning attached to it.

---

[1] ATH Smith, *Glanville Williams: Learning the Law* (13th edn, Sweet & Maxwell 2006).

Legislation then differs from other types of law in its form and its purpose. For example, if we compare a piece of legislation with the text of the Constitution, we note that the latter contains general statements of principle as distinct from detailed rules; lofty aims and ideals rather than statements on particular issues. For example, look at Article 40.3.3° which protects the right to life of the unborn:

> The State acknowledges the right to life of the unborn and, with due regard to the equal right to life of the mother, guarantees in its laws to respect, and, as far as practicable, by its laws to defend and vindicate that right.

Compare this to sections 58 and 59 of the Offences against the Person Act 1861, which used to govern the law on abortion in this country prior to the enactment of the Protection of Life During Pregnancy Act 2013:

> 58. Every woman, being with child, who, with intent to procure her own miscarriage, shall unlawfully administer to herself any poison or other noxious thing, or shall unlawfully use any instrument or other means whatsoever with the like intent, and whosoever, with intent to procure the miscarriage of any woman, whether she be or be not with child, shall unlawfully administer to her or cause to be taken by her any poison or other noxious thing, or shall unlawfully use any instrument or other means whatsoever with the like intent, shall be guilty of felony, and being convicted thereof shall be liable to be kept in penal servitude for life.
>
> 59. Whosoever shall unlawfully supply or procure any poison or other noxious thing, or any instrument or thing whatsoever, knowing that the same is intended to be unlawfully used or employed with intent to procure the miscarriage of any woman, whether she be or be not with child, shall be guilty of a misdemeanor, and being convicted thereof shall be liable to be kept in penal servitude.

You will see that the constitutional provision is broad in its scope, unclear in its terminology and of general application, while the statutory provisions are much more precise in nature.

What does the Word 'Legislation' Mean?

In Ireland, we have two types of legislation: primary and secondary legislation.

Primary Legislation

Primary legislation comprises Acts, or statutes. These can be very long and detailed, or very short, depending on the subject matter of the legislation and its purpose. Primary legislation goes through a formal process before it can be enacted. All legislation is passed by the Oireachtas, then presented to the President for him to sign into law. Of course, as with most principles of law, there is an exception here—where a Bill proposes to amend the Constitution, it is introduced and goes through the Houses of the Oireachtas in the normal way, but then it is put to the people in a referendum for its approval. An example of this is the Twenty-Eighth Amendment to the Constitution Bill 2007, available on the Oireachtas website. You will see that there is no corresponding Act for this Bill—can you think why this might be the case?

No matter how long or short, or for whatever purpose the legislation is introduced, each Act will follow a very particular format.

Secondary Legislation

While the Oireachtas enacts primary legislation, the power to pass secondary legislation can be given to a variety of bodies, for example, Government Ministers or statutory agencies. Secondary legislation includes statutory instruments, rules, regulations, orders, schemes and bye-laws. The power to make secondary legislation comes from primary legislation. This is because the real law-making power rests with the Oireachtas, as provided for by the Constitution. When delegating the power to legislate to a particular body or Minister, the legislature cannot abdicate its constitutional duty to be the sole law-making body in the State. What this means is that the rule, or law, must be contained in the Act, while the mechanisms or procedures to enforce the law, for example, can be 'filled in' by secondary legislation. The legal term used to describe this process is that the 'principles and policies' which determine how the secondary legislation is formulated must be described in the Act.

> ■ To learn more about this distinction, go to <www.legalwriting.ie> and complete Assignment 4.1.

How does an Act of the Oireachtas Come into Being?

You will probably learn about the process of enacting legislation in more detail in other parts of your legal studies. What follows is a short and simplified summary, but with pointers to where you can learn more about what happens in the process. We will use the Planning and Development Bill 1999 as an example of a piece of legislation which went all of the way through the Oireachtas and Supreme Court before signature by the President.

A new piece of legislation generally starts life as an identified social problem. A lobby group, political party or State body (such as the Law Reform

Commission) will identify an issue as one which requires a change in the law. This may happen quickly, but usually it takes time (sometimes years or decades) and sometimes follows an extended public debate in the media. The introduction of the Gender Recognition Act 2015 followed a nearly 20-year battle by Lydia Foy to have her gender recognised by the State. She first brought her application in 1997, and despite a ruling by the High Court that the failure of the State to recognise Ms Foy's gender made its laws in this regard incompatible with the European Convention on Human Rights in 2007,[2] it was a full 10 years (and following another application taken by Ms Foy to the High Court) before the legislation was introduced.

Discussion on these issues sometimes takes place in the various specialised committees within the Oireachtas, such as Education and Social Protection, Environment, Culture and the Gaeltacht, or European Union Affairs. These include a cross-section of Teachtaí Dála and senators from a variety of parties and will often engage in very detailed examination of a particular social or economic problem. They will also occasionally draft legislative proposals. As a law student, you should read newspapers regularly so that you are aware of legal reform proposals.

In Ireland, there has been a system of planning law in place since the 1930s but it became a significant body of law in 1963 with the comprehensive Local Government (Planning and Development) Act. That legislation was amended so many times that it had become a patchwork spread across various Acts and was badly in need of tidying up. This process began in 1997.

If the issue is taken up by the political process, it will generally require the approval of the Government to progress very far. (The opposition will often put forward proposals for legislation, known as a Private Members' Bill, but these rarely succeed and are largely symbolic.) The relevant Minister will ask his or her civil servants to begin the process of drafting legislation. This may involve public consultation and should usually include a Regulatory Impact Assessment (RIA).

If you are trying to understand recent legislation, the RIA is a good place to start. This document is an overview of the choices which the Government has considered and an explanation of the purpose and principles underlying a proposal for legislation. As part of the Government's 'Regulating Better' initiative, an RIA is now required for:

(i) proposals for primary legislation involving changes to the regulatory framework (the mechanisms by which the law manages this topic);

---

[2] *Foy v An t-Ard Chláraitheoir* [2007] IEHC 470.

(ii) significant statutory instruments;
(iii) proposals for EU Directives and significant EU Regulations when they are published by the European Commission; and
(iv) proposals for legislation brought forward by Policy Review Groups.

The RIA for a particular proposal should be available from the relevant Government Department. If it is not, ask your law librarian to help you find it, or contact the Government Department directly.

Once the overall structure of the proposal is clear, it will be passed to the Office of the Parliamentary Counsel to the Government, which is part of the Office of the Attorney General. 'Heads' of a Bill are produced to be approved by the Cabinet—an early draft of the legislation, which may go through further public consultation and comment. Once the Heads are ready to be converted into a Bill, the relevant Minister will put it before the Oireachtas, in one of the two Houses (Dáil or Seanad).

Discussion and consultation on planning law reform took two years and the Planning and Development Act 2000 began as the Planning and Development Bill 1999. (There was no RIA for this particular proposal as it pre-dated the introduction of this requirement.) You will find the information page for this on the Oireachtas website at <www.oireachtas.ie/viewdoc. asp?fn=/documents/bills28/bills/1999/4699/default.htm>. Look at this page, and see if you can identify some of the key aims which the Bill sought to achieve.

The first stage is short: the House decides whether to proceed with the Bill or not. You will see that there is no additional information on the Oireachtas website about this stage, as it is straightforward.

The second is a general debate, by the House as a whole, on the merits of the Bill.

Click on the link for the first part of the second stage (which is listed as 14/10/1999) and you will see the Minister's speech introducing the proposed legislation. Read carefully what he has to say about Part V. This starts on page 804 of the report; you will see the page numbers in square brackets in the text. You can skim through much of the rest, but observe the way in which members of the House raise general questions of policy at this stage. If you are particularly interested, you can also read the second part of the second stage of the Bill, on 20/10/1999.

The third stage, also known as the 'committee stage', involves a more detailed discussion and amendment of the legislation by a small and specialised committee (or in some circumstances, by the House as a whole).

You will see links to the committee stage on the Oireachtas website, starting on 10/11/1999. Read a few of these and note the way in which the discussion becomes much more detailed. It is worth skimming through the last day (26/11/1999), as it deals with Part V.

The fourth stage, or report stage, is a general debate by the entire House. Amendments can still be made, but only minor ones.

You can see the debates for this stage taking place in the Seanad on 01/12/1999.

The fifth stage, or final stage, is a vote on the Bill by the whole House, to determine whether or not it should pass. If it has only passed one House, it goes to the other for consideration and approval.

This is what happened to this legislation; it went from the Seanad to the Dáil in February 2000 and was finally passed in June of that year. Skim through the Dáil debates to get a sense of the procedure there and the type of debate that takes place at each stage.

If it has passed both Houses of the Oireachtas, it goes to the President for his signature. He has the option to convene the Council of State and ask for advice on whether he should refer it to the Supreme Court for a ruling on its constitutionality under Article 26 of the Constitution. This rarely happens, however, and the President generally signs the Bill, at which point it becomes an Act.

If the President does refer the Bill, the Supreme Court will hear arguments on both sides of the question and make a ruling within 60 days. After this ruling is made, the Bill either goes back to the President for signature if it is found to be constitutional, or its life ends there, although the Oireachtas can choose to begin again with a fresh proposal.

The legislation we are examining was referred to the Supreme Court for a decision on its constitutionality. If you go to <www.supremecourt.ie> and click on 'Judgments', then 'Article 26 References', you will see *In re Article 26 and the Planning and Development Bill 1999* towards the bottom of the page. Open that document.

As the judgment is lengthy and detailed, and this book is not about planning law but about how to locate and understand legislation, you do not need to read it closely. Note only the procedural history of the case (pages 324–325), the central argument made by the lawyers assigned to oppose the legislation (page 336) and the conclusions of the court (from page 346 on). Finally, on the last page, you will see that the Supreme Court held that the legislation was constitutional.

If you now return to the Oireachtas website that you were at previously, you should be able to view a list of legislation signed in 2000. You can therefore check whether or not an Act has been signed into law.

Do this for the Planning and Development Bill 1999. When was it signed by the President?

Once the legislation is signed by the President, it becomes law but is not necessarily in force. Most legislation will require *commencement* by the relevant Minister by means of statutory instrument. There are two ways to check whether or not a *commencement order* has been made: the best is to use the Irish Statute Book website, which will be discussed in more detail below. The second is to go to the website of the relevant Government Department and see if it has a list of legislation available. This can be a more difficult source to navigate, but is often more up to date than the Irish Statute Book website.

Try this now for the Planning and Development Act 2000. Go to the website of the Department of the Environment, Community and Local Government (<www.environ.ie>), click on the link for Legislation at the top of the page, and then select Planning. Can you find out how and when the Act came into force?

WHAT ARE THE PARTS OF AN ACT OF THE OIREACHTAS?

Every Act of the Oireachtas follows a particular format. By understanding this format and structure, reading and understanding an Act will become much easier. Every Act will have particular parts to it.

■ To learn more about these, go to <www.legalwriting.ie> and complete Assignment 4.2.

The constituent parts of an Act are:

1. THE SHORT TITLE OF THE ACT

This is the title of the Act, and the year of the Act. This is the way you refer to an Act when you are writing about it. If you refer repeatedly to an Act in a passage, it is acceptable to refer to it as, for example, 'the Act of 2007', though you would have to make this clear in advance by use of a footnote or brackets.

> For example, 'the Criminal Justice Act 2007'³ (the Act of 2007).
> ³ Hereinafter referred to as the Act of 2007.

2. THE OFFICIAL CITATION OF THE ACT

This sets out the number of the Act and the year it was introduced, and is rarely used to cite legislation. Acts will be numbered 1, 2, 3, etc. in order of their passing each year.

3. THE LONG TITLE OF THE ACT

This will explain the reason the Act is being introduced, and sets out what the Act does.

4. DATE OF PROMULGATION

This is the date upon which the President signed the Bill into law.

5. LIST OF ACTS REFERRED TO

This will be a list of all the Acts that are referred to in the Act in question.

6. MARGINAL NOTES

These are at the side of the page opposite the start of each section. They are an easy way to establish what each section is about, without having to read through the whole thing.

7. INTERPRETATION SECTION

Most Acts will have an interpretation section to establish how particular words and phrases are to be interpreted in the Act in its entirety.

8. Repeals and the Schedules

Some Acts will repeal one section of an earlier Act and, if so, this will be set out in a particular section. For example, section 18 of the Social Welfare Act 1991 was repealed quite simply by section 32(6) of the Social Welfare Act 1992. However, some Acts are so far-reaching in their scope and repeal so much legislation that a section will be included in the Act which states that all the Acts in the Schedule to the Act are repealed.

Where do you Find Legislation?

Bills and Acts of the Oireachtas are available in a number of places. First, they are available in the library, bound according to year. In the same way that there are increasingly more cases being reported every year, there are also larger volumes of legislation coming out every year—compare the volumes of legislation from the early 1980s with those from this century.

The second official place to find legislation is on <www.oireachtas.ie>. Click 'Legislative Observatory', then click 'Legislative Observatory' again. Here you can see what a Bill looked like when it was initially presented to the Oireachtas, progressed through the various stages of the Houses, and what it looks like in its finished form. In addition, when a Bill is published, there will often be an Explanatory Memorandum attached to the Bill which sets out the reasons for its introduction and a detailed section-by-section analysis of the Bill, which can be very useful when determining the scope, purpose and definition of a particular section—though only for research purposes, as such memoranda are not used by the courts when interpreting the legislation.

The Oireachtas website is very useful for Acts from 1997, where the official version appears in PDF format, and reasonably useful for legislation from 1922–1996, where an 'unofficial' version appears (though there can be mistakes in these versions, and care should be used). However, where the official version is required for research purposes, it is best to go to the library where the printed official version will be available. Further, for any piece of legislation pre-1922, the library is the only place to find the Act in its entirety.

It is really important to note that, for both these sources, what you will find is the Act as enacted. For very recent Acts, this will probably be unproblematic, but where the piece of legislation is quite dated, it may well have been amended a number of times: if you only refer to the Oireachtas website, you may well be relying on a section or Act that is either out of date or even repealed.

For this reason, a very useful website for these purposes is <www.irishstatutebook.ie>. Here, all the Acts of the Oireachtas from 1922 are available and the site allows you to find out whether an Act has been amended after its enactment.

You should take some time to acquaint yourself with both these websites as you will use them a lot over your time as a student, and later as a practising lawyer. However, you should be aware that the Irish Statute Book website can contain errors and the contents should be checked against the printed version of the legislation before you finalise your work.

Finally, the Legislation Fastcheck service, available through Westlaw IE, provides you with a condensed list of all Acts and Statutory Instruments affected by primary and secondary legislation issued from 1993. It should have accurate and current information on whether legislation is in force or has been amended.

HAS THE ACT BEEN AMENDED?

While the Oireachtas website is useful for establishing what the Act looked like when it was published originally, Acts are constantly amended, updated and repealed by later pieces of legislation. In this context, it is important to note that the Fines Act 2010 makes amendments across the entire Statute Book in relation to fines for criminal offences: this will not appear in the Irish Statute Book website so make sure you know how this particular piece of legislation operates when seeking to establish the penalties appropriate to a particular criminal offence.

A particular example to illustrate the complexity of amending legislation in a non-codified legal system was highlighted in the legislation governing companies. There were 11 Companies Acts, known as the Companies Acts 1963–2009, all of which were to be read together, and some of which amended what was known as the Principal Act—the Companies Act 1963. Even for the most seasoned lawyer, it would have been a particularly difficult task to establish the true legal position on a particular issue if all he or she had access to were the 11 Acts in paper form.

Luckily, we do not need to engage in this process today. In order to establish whether an Act has been amended, there are a number of options. The first option is to see if the Act has been part of the Restatement Project run by the Law Reform Commission, available at <www.lawreform.ie>, where Acts are published in their most up-to-date format as a result of the Statute Law (Restatement) Act 2002. However, if you look at sections 4 and 5 of the 2002 Act, you will see that there is a serious limitation to the operation of such Acts. See if you can figure out what the limitation is by reading the sections:

Section 4: Subject to section 5, a restatement shall not have the force of law and, accordingly, shall not have effect so as to alter or otherwise affect the substance or operation of any provision to which it relates of a statute or statutory instrument.

Section 5: (1) A statement purporting to be certified under section 2 shall be prima facie evidence of the law contained in the provisions to which it relates of any statute or statutory instrument.

(2) A restatement shall be judicially noticed.

A second way to determine the current status of an Act is to see if it has been consolidated. Again, this work will not have the force of law, but it is a useful way of establishing how various pieces of legislation interact with each other. A consolidation means that someone has sat down and established what sections have been amended and how. From there, he or she will set out the updated version of the Act. For example, the Fisheries Legislation 1959–2003 is available in consolidated form from Round Hall, as well as in the library in looseleaf binders.

A third way to establish the most up-to-date version of an Act is to try and find a consolidated *and* an annotated version of the Act. With an annotation, there is a key difference: the author will explain each section and any case law which has interpreted the scope of each section. For the most part, Acts will be annotated shortly after they are published, though for some more important pieces of legislation, the process will be one of annotation and consolidation. Most annotated Acts in Ireland are published through the *Irish Current Law Statutes Annotated* series. However, as these annotations are not usually updated, the annotation remains stagnant from the moment it is published. For this reason, they are more generally useful for an explanation of an Act when it is first published, or an examination of how an Act has been applied if the annotation is published a number of years after an Act is introduced. For an example of an annotation and consolidation, see Paul Ward, *The Child Care Acts: Annotated and Consolidated* (3rd edn, Round Hall 2014).

If the Act has not been the subject of a restatement, a consolidation or an annotation, it is up to you to figure out what the current law is. Fortunately, there is an easy way to do this. If you open up <www.irishstatutebook.ie> and click into 'Legislation', you will see a further link, 'Acts of the Oireachtas'. If you click into this, you will see a list of Acts organised by date, so find the name of the Act you are searching for and click on it. This will display the text of the Act. If it has been amended, you will see a link to 'Amendments, Commencement, SIs made under the Act'. Clicking on this will bring you into a new screen where you will have the name of the Act on the left, a list of the sections of the Act appearing in the middle of the screen, and a list of the amending legislation on the right—you can click into both the original and amending sections. In terms of the abbreviations used, the most important ones are 'am', which is short for 'amended', and 'rep', which is short for repealed. The full list of abbreviations used is available here: <http://www.irishstatutebook.ie/eli/isbc/abbrev.html>.

There are two important caveats to using the Irish Statute Book website for this purpose. First, you must be aware that there are mistakes in it, so in all cases it is best to check your findings by reference to the official reports. Secondly, the chronological tables are at least six months behind, so if you suspect an amendment has been made recently (and you should always suspect such a thing!), then you will have to look through the Oireachtas website to establish if an amendment has been made.

> ■ To test your knowledge of how to use these resources, go to <www.legalwriting.ie> and complete Assignment 4.3.

Is the Act in Force?

Once a piece of legislation is enacted, it is sometimes automatically part of the law. However, with other statutes, the Act itself will provide that the entire Act, or sections of it, must be commenced by an Order of the relevant Minister. This 'commencement order' is done by statutory instrument. Sometimes, the reason for the delay is that the infrastructure, resources or funding are not in place for the Act to operate, and until the Minister sets up this infrastructure, the Act cannot work.

How should you Read Legislation to Discover its Meaning?

A good deal of your time as a lawyer will be spent looking at legislation. Reading legislation requires a particular approach. If you do not know what a particular section means, or how it is to be applied, then you cannot begin to understand the law, or advise a client on his or her legal position.

To begin with, read the section you are trying to interpret. What are the important words? Initially, you may find it useful to underline them. With practice, you will be able to pick them out without great difficulty.

Take, for example, section 37(1) of the Copyright and Related Rights Act 2000:

37. (1) Subject to the exceptions specified in Chapter 6 and to any provisions relating to licensing in this Part, the owner of the copyright in a work has the exclusive right to undertake or authorise others to undertake all or any of the following acts, namely:

  (a) to copy the work;

  (b) to make available to the public the work;

  (c) to make an adaptation of the work or to undertake either of the acts referred to in paragraph (a) or (b) in relation to an adaptation,

and those acts shall be known and in this Act referred to as 'acts restricted by copyright'.

(You might find it useful to go to the library and find the 2000 Act at this point, or display it on a computer screen if you have access to the Internet. You will find the Act at <www.irishstatutebook.ie/2000/en/act/pub/0028/index.html>.)

What are the important words here? 'Copyright' is an obvious one. 'Work', 'copy', 'make available' and 'adaption' are others. Do you know what these words mean? Do you think that they might have a different meaning if you apply them in a legal context, or in the particular context of the 2000 Act?

You may have a general understanding of the meaning of a word in a statute—for example, you know what it means to copy something, but it is important to note that a word can have a specific meaning in a particular statute. Once you have identified what the important words are, you must discover what they mean in that statute.

Most statutes will have an interpretation section, which will be the first or second section in the Act. This will define the important words in the statute. However, not all of the words will be defined, generally because the legislature prefers to leave the meaning open in case of changes in the future. For example, most statutes dealing with technology do not define the word 'computer' because a definition of a computer that might be accurate in the 1980s would not capture some of the tools that have evolved today (such as mobile phones). Another reason is that the legislature believes the meaning of the term to be so clear and precise that defining the term is unnecessary. Unfortunately, it is sometimes these 'clear and precise terms' which cause so much trouble for lawyers.

In the 2000 Act, section 2 is the interpretation section. If you have access to the legislation, see how many of the words identified above you can find in it. Only one is defined there: 'work' ('a literary, dramatic, musical or artistic work, sound recording, film, broadcast, cable programme, typographical arrangement of a published edition or an original database and includes a computer program').

Definitions may also be found elsewhere in the statute. Section 37 is an example of this, defining 'acts restricted by copyright'. Some of the other important words in section 37 are also not defined in the interpretation section: 'copying' is defined in section 39, 'making available' in section 40 and 'adaptation' in section 43. Scattering definitions around an Act like this is not ideal, and can make it difficult to determine the meaning of a word, but it can happen, so you must be conscious of it.

A whole host of interpretive rules are employed by the courts to read or interpret legislation. Because it is important for Acts of the Oireachtas to have specific meanings, and to ensure that the courts do not stray into the area of making law, which is reserved to the Oireachtas under Article 15.2.1° of the Constitution, there are particular rules which govern the interpretation of legislation. These are called the 'rules of interpretation'. Many presumptions and canons of interpretation also apply, which assist the courts in interpreting individual provisions.

LITERAL APPROACH

If the statutory provision is one directed to the public at large, in the absence of internal evidence suggesting the contrary, the word or expression should be given its ordinary or colloquial meaning. For example, the word 'cattle' in its ordinary sense would not include pigs, if construed literally and using common sense meanings.

In the case of *Inspector of Taxes v Kiernan*, the court was asked whether the term cattle in the Income Tax Act 1967 should include pigs or other animals. The distinction had important consequences for the tax liability of dealers in livestock. The Supreme Court held that the phrase included bovines only and not any other large animals or any more liberal construction.

When the word is a simple word which has a widespread and unambiguous meaning, the judge interpreting it will, and you should, draw primarily on experience of its use. Dictionaries or other sources can be used if you do not understand the word, but courts will usually only use them when alternative meanings or regional usages cast doubt on the ordinary meaning, or when there are grounds for suggesting that the meaning of the word has changed since the statute in question was passed. If the legislation is aimed at a particular class who use the word or expression in either a narrow or an extended way, or as a term of art, then it is this more limited, or expansive meaning, which will be used in the case.

Purposive Approach

This process of interpreting legislation can become complicated when the meaning that emerges from the literal approach seems ridiculous or does not make sense in the context of the Act. It is important also to bear in mind the underlying rationale of the legislation (the intention of the legislature in introducing change in the law), and ensure that the meaning given to words is consistent with this. If the literal interpretation of a statute means that the Act itself will be interpreted in a way which seems at odds with the general aim of the Act, then this creates what used to be called a 'mischievous' situation—and this is a mischief which should not be allowed. The modern version of this, the purposive rule, states that the purpose or objective of the legislative provision has to be considered in order to discover its meaning.

In the case of *Nestor v Murphy*,[3] a wife who had not signed a consent form for the sale of her family home tried to rely on the provisions of the Family Home Protection Act 1976 to get out of the sale. The Act provided that a conveyance (transfer) of a family home was invalid unless she had signed the consent form. Because she had not done so, technically, the conveyance should not have gone ahead, though it was clear from other circumstances that she did fully consent. However, Henchy J in the Supreme Court held that to allow her to rely on the literal wording of the Act would allow her to renege on the sale of the home for reasons not envisaged by the Act, when it was clear that she had consented to the sale. The purpose of the Act was to protect a spouse who did not have any ownership rights in the family home. To construe the Act literally and require a consent form in these circumstances would have resulted in an absurdity.

What this means is that when the literal rule is used and the provision does not make sense as a result, the purposive rule is used. This was initially developed by the courts in Ireland in the 1970s, but now it is set out in section 5 of the Interpretation Act 2005 which states that the purposive rule is the default rule where the literal rule results in an absurdity.

Interpreting Criminal Legislation/Taxation Statutes

There is a presumption that penal (criminal law) or revenue (taxation) statutes must be construed very strictly. This means that the courts cannot extend the meaning of criminal or taxation statutes beyond that set out in legislation. On grounds of fairness and in the interests of protecting the liberty of the

[3] [1979] IR 177 (SC).

individual, the courts will ensure that a 'narrow reading' is given to criminal or taxation statutes.

EU Law and Statutory Interpretation

Legislation based on EU directives is usually interpreted purposively or in light of its objective. This means that the Irish courts must consider what the EU legislation is attempting to achieve, even where it appears that they are straining the meaning of clear phrases and terms.

As an example, see the case of *Murphy v An Bord Telecom*.[4] This involved female employees who were paid less than male employees even though the men did work of lesser value. Here, Keane J interpreted a European law requirement of equal pay for like work as also meaning that women engaged in work of a superior value could not be paid less than men who worked in a different role.

Other Aspects of Legislation

Canons of Statutory Interpretation

There are certain rules or canons of interpretation that are used by the courts to interpret words or phrases in legislation. The most important canons of interpretation are:

1. *Expressio unius exclusion alterius*—'To say one thing is to exclude another';
   eg 'a dog ...': this would then exclude all other animals.

2. *Ejusdem generis*—'of the same genus';
   eg 'dogs, cats ...': this then might exclude a camel from the categorisation.

3. *Noscitur a sociis*—'a thing is known by its associates';
   eg 'dogs, cats, gerbils': it can be assumed that all these animals are domestic pets usually and are not jungle animals.

Presumptions Applied by the Courts to Interpret Legislation

Presumption of constitutionality

All legislation enacted by the Oireachtas after 1937, which is when the Constitution was enacted, is presumed by the courts to be constitutional. This

---

[4]   [1989] ILRM 53 (HC).

means that it is more difficult for an individual or group to successfully challenge the constitutionality of a law, as the courts will assume the constitutionality of the law until the presumption is rebutted. In the case of *East Donegal Co-Operative Livestock Mart Ltd v Attorney General*,[5] the Supreme Court stated that the 'onus rests on the challenger' to prove that the legislation is not compatible with the Constitution.

This rule does not apply to pre-1937 legislation and it is important to closely examine the date of the relevant legislation that you are considering. However, the Supreme Court stated that even with pre-1937 legislation, the onus of proof is very high on a challenger, and hinted that it might be similarly high, as with post-1937 legislation, in *A v Governor of Arbour Hill Prison*.[6]

Presumption of compatibility with EU law

All Irish law implementing EU legislation is presumed to be compatible with EU law because of the obligations of membership of the EU that Ireland has signed up for. This means that all Irish judges must interpret Irish law in a manner consistent with the aims of an EU law.

Compatibility with the European Convention on Human Rights

Since the incorporation of the European Convention on Human Rights into Irish law in 2003 by the European Convention on Human Rights Act 2003, Irish law should, where possible, be interpreted in a manner consistent with the Convention. This is provided for in section 2(1) of the Act, which states:

> In interpreting and applying any statutory provision or rule of law, a court shall, in so far as is possible, subject to the rules of law relating to such interpretation and application, do so in a manner compatible with the State's obligations under the Convention provisions.

Importantly, this applies to legislation which pre-dates the commencement of the Act, and does not just apply to legislation enacted after 2003.

The use of parliamentary debates in statutory interpretation

The use of Oireachtas debates by the courts to interpret the meaning of legislation might seem to be useful, but the reality is different. If the courts were to examine closely the statements of Ministers in such debates, which are often in a heated and political or politicised context, there is a danger that

---

[5] [1970] IR 317 (SC).
[6] [2006] IESC 45, [2006] 4 IR 88.

the courts could become too involved in political wrangles and stray outside of their constitutionally enshrined role. For this reason, the courts have not looked at such debates when construing provisions of legislation. This is called the exclusionary rule, which the Supreme Court approved in *Crilly v Farrington*,[7] even though their counterparts in the House of Lords relaxed it in the case of *Pepper v Hart*.[8]

FURTHER READING

- Dodd D, *Statutory Interpretation in Ireland* (Tottel 2008)
- Hanson S, *Learning Legal Skills and Reasoning* (4th edn, Routledge 2016), Chapter 10
- Smith ATH, *Glanville Williams: Learning the Law* (15th edn, Sweet & Maxwell 2013), Chapter 6

---

[7] [2001] IESC 60, [2001] 3 IR 251.
[8] [1992] UKHL 3, [1993] 1 All ER 42.

5   **Legal Writing**

The language of the law must not be foreign to the ears of those who are to obey it.[1]

INTRODUCTION

Words are of fundamental importance to lawyers and law students alike. They are the lawyer's raw material, the input to the intellectual mill and the output when the day's work is done. Much of your time as a student will be spent reading, writing and rearranging words. It is therefore very important to become skilled in writing.

Good legal writing is, first and foremost, good writing. A command of English will be of great benefit to you. Much of what follows is little more than general precepts of good English style, with a focus on legal writing. You can learn a great deal from books on writing, and more generally, by reading legal journals, books and judgments—soon you will be able to identify good writing and bad writing, and to learn which writing style suits you best. Some of the best writing guides are listed at the end of this chapter; buy your own copy or borrow them from your library, read them and apply them.

CLARITY

CLEAR AND CONCISE

Good legal writing is clear. The law can be complex and confusing. Your purpose as a lawyer is not to complicate matters further but to make the law clear and easy to understand. You may find that your source material (case law, statutes, textbooks and articles) is not very well-written, as it is dense, verbose and sometimes internally inconsistent. This is not an excuse for you to follow in those misguided footsteps but a challenge for you to extract the essential meaning from the texts you are working with and present the information in a way that is easy to understand, particularly if you are writing for non-lawyers. Consider the difference between these sentences:

---

[1]   Billings Learned Hand, 'Is There a Common Will?' (1929–30) 28 Michigan L Rev 46, 52.

Consequent upon a comprehensive consideration of all relevant circumstances, it is argued that the additional endeavours by the plaintiff were otiose.

If everything is taken into account, the plaintiff's extra work was needless.

Good legal writing is concise. Use as few words as you can. Verbose writing is opaque and hard to understand. If you keep your writing brief and to the point, it will be easier and quicker to read and should be easier to understand. Word limits are ceilings to avoid, not targets to reach at all costs.

'PLAIN ENGLISH'

Use plain English as much as possible. The law tends to use flowery phrases, Latin words and redundant phrases, such as 'notwithstanding the fact that', 'mutatis mutandis', or 'to the best of my knowledge, information or belief'. Some of this comes from the common law's roots, where it developed its vocabulary from the language spoken by the Normans. Some comes from the conservative nature of lawyers: if a phrase has worked for centuries, why change it? Further, if one word is enough, then two will do, for the sake of certainty.

As the name suggests, 'plain English' is a movement towards using simpler language which is easily understandable by non-specialised audiences. Lawyers have been reluctant to embrace this, largely due to the conservatism mentioned above, but you can see its influence in, for example, insurance contracts, which are now usually written in a straightforward style. While these are easy to read, they are often difficult to write, as you have to ensure that the language used, while plain, is precise, and reflects exactly what is required of the document. This means you have to work quite hard on learning how to write in a plain yet effective style.

Any notice, request, instruction or other document to be given hereunder shall be delivered or sent by first class post or by email or facsimile (in all cases to be confirmed by letter posted within twelve (12) hours) to the address of the other set out or referred to in this Agreement (or such other address as may have been notified) and any such notice or other document shall be deemed to have been served and deemed to have been received (if delivered) at the time of delivery (if sent by post) upon the expiration of forty-eight (48) hours after posting and (if sent by email or facsimile) upon the expiration of twelve (12) hours after dispatch.

> Communication between us can take place by first class post, email or FAX. If communication is by email or FAX, it must be confirmed by letter within twelve (12) hours. We must use the address given for the other in this agreement, unless we have been notified of a change. Communications will be presumed to have been received after forty-eight (48) hours if sent by post and within twelve (12) hours if sent by email or FAX.

A full discussion of plain English would be a book in itself. For general information on plain English, see <www.plainenglish.co.uk>. To learn more about plain English in Ireland, see <www.simplyput.ie>. For a discussion of plain English in the drafting of Irish legislation, see chapter six of the Law Reform Commission's *Report on Statutory Drafting and Interpretation: Plain Language and the Law*,[2] which is available on the website of the Commission at <www.lawreform.ie>.

SIMPLE SENTENCE STRUCTURE

Keep the structure of your sentences simple. Avoid multiple objects and verbs. Break long, complex sentences up into shorter ones. For example:

> In *TD v Ireland*, the Supreme Court held that the excessive authority which the High Court judge took on himself to re-consider the decisions made by the executive in deciding the allocation of resources for dealing with social problems went beyond the separation of powers and was unconstitutional.
>
> In *TD v Ireland*, the Supreme Court held that the High Court did not have authority to deal with the allocation of resources by the State. The doctrine of separation of powers meant the judge could not decide how the executive should deal with social problems. The Court found that to do so was unconstitutional.

START AT THE START AND END AT THE END

One of the most important elements of clear writing is a good overall structure. Make sure that what you write follows a clear flow from a logical starting point to a coherent end. If it is an essay which is making an argument, ensure that each element of that argument is present and builds on the previous section. If you are explaining the background to a legal problem or a proposal for reform, use the historical timeline as your fundamental structure. Do not confuse or lose your reader with needless detours, tangents or shortcuts. Guide them through from start to finish.

---

[2] LRC 61, 2000.

Formality and Legal Writing

Legal writing is inherently formal, however simplified it becomes.

Write in the Active Voice

Constructions that you will see in legal writing include 'It is argued', 'It is believed', 'It is submitted' and 'In the opinion of this author'. Avoid these. If you are the person making an argument or submission, make the statement, put forward your opinion and back it up with authority. You should not hide behind circumlocutions. Write in the active rather than the passive voice. Consider the difference between these sentences:

> The interpretation of this provision which is preferred is one which leaves the greatest flexibility to the agency concerned.
> It is better if the court interprets this provision in a way that gives the agency the greatest flexibility.

The passive voice is a construction that uses the verb 'to be' and the past participle of another verb. It places the actor in the sentence in second place and makes it difficult to figure out who is doing what. In the first example above, who is interpreting the provision? In the second example, it is clear that the court is doing this. Notice also how the agency has moved nearer to the start of the sentence, which is useful as a way of emphasising its importance.

It is easy to fall into using the passive voice. Or, to put it another way, you will find it easy to fall into using the passive voice. Watch out for this. It makes your writing less vibrant and harder to understand. Check for it by asking if it is clear who the actor in each sentence is.

Discussing and Disagreeing with Academic Material

When you are discussing the arguments of others, to begin with, it is best to refer to the writers by their surname only in the main body of the text, and to factually set out what the writers have contended in as straightforward a manner as possible: for example, 'Marshall states that ...'. Then, to disagree with the content of the statement, it is advisable to keep the level of disagreement to as objective a level as possible and to avoid personal statements or opinions as far as possible. This can be done without being vague and colourless. For example:

> Clarke J held that the requirement to obtain leave was not a barrier to the review procedure required under Art 7 of the Public Participation Directive but was part of that procedure. Given the relatively open nature of a leave application, this view is *most likely correct*. However, his conclusion that judicial review meets the Convention requirement for a substantive challenge is *more questionable*.

By using phrases such as 'this conclusion may be mistaken', 'this does not take full account of', or 'there is an alternative explanation', you are making it clear that you disagree with the opinion of the author without being personal or disrespectful. Unless you are certain, you should not say that another lawyer is 'wrong'.

Direct and indirect quotations

When referring to material written by other people, you will use what they have written in two ways: first, by directly quoting from the text, and secondly, by paraphrasing the material, or indirectly quoting from the text. Two things are important here: first, both require the same level of referencing by way of footnotes—see 'Writing Law Essays' for details on how to do this; secondly, it is important to understand the use of 'that' when directly and indirectly quoting from a text. The use of 'that' is only appropriate in indirect quotations—or, to put it even more simply, if you are using quotation marks, you should never use the word 'that' right before them.

> Material referenced: Thomas O'Malley, *Sentencing Law and Practice* (Thomson Round Hall 2006) 2: 'By the standards of the time, therefore, and certainly when compared with the situation that prevailed a century earlier, the new State inherited a reasonably humane body of sentencing law.'
>
> Direct Quotation:
> **Incorrect:** O'Malley notes that 'the new State inherited a reasonably humane body of sentencing law.'
> **Correct:** O'Malley notes 'the new State inherited a ... body of sentencing law.'
>
> Indirect Quotation:
> **Correct:** In his seminal text on sentencing in Ireland, O'Malley notes that the body of sentencing law inherited by the State was reasonably humane.

TONE AND EMOTION

As legal advice and academic writing is predominantly objective, it is inappropriate in a student essay to begin sentences with 'I think', 'I feel' or

'I believe'. It is best to write objectively and not to employ these subjective phrases. The tone of your writing should be neutral. Good legal writing rarely uses inflammatory or passionate language. While we often write in the context of a debate or a dispute, you should focus on changing your reader's mind by the logic of your legal arguments, not by the force of your language. Look at the difference between these two statements:

> The death penalty is a barbaric and inhuman way of punishing a human being.
> The death penalty is best placed in its historic context, as a penalty which is contrary to the vast majority of international human rights instruments as being a punishment which is, to use the language of Article 3 of the European Convention on Human Rights, inhuman and degrading treatment.

Both these statements mean essentially the same thing, but while the former uses language which would be appropriate in newspaper editorials, the latter uses language which has a legal argument at its core.

You should always avoid displays of emotion in your legal writing. You may be writing about difficult, controversial and even upsetting topics, but if you do feel strongly about the issue at hand, use that energy to marshal good research to state your case rather than hope that using emotive language will convince your reader that you are right.

TECHNICALITY

GRAMMAR

Given what has been said above about the importance of language to a lawyer and the obvious need for precision in the use of words, it should not be necessary to stress the importance of good grammar to a law student.

If you make a minor mistake on some obscure rule in an examination script, the person marking it will probably forgive you. However, mistakes in a printed essay, written over a number of weeks, are more difficult to excuse. For a lawyer, grammar mistakes are as serious as miscalculations are to an engineer or mis-measurements are to a scientist.

This book does not provide a detailed overview of English grammar. If you feel you need one, your lecturer or law librarian can direct you to appropriate texts. It is important not to rely on a 'spell check' or worse, 'grammar check' on your computer as a failsafe way of ensuring your writing is accurate. These tools, while useful, can often create absurdities and are best used cautiously. They will not, for example, notice the difference between 'human rights' and 'human tights', although your reader may.

JARGON

One simple step towards a simpler style is to avoid the use of legal jargon. Some specialised language is inevitable, and often common words have a distinctive meaning in legal writing, but resist the temptation to overuse obscure or Latin phrases, particularly if you are unsure as to what they mean.

You will find that you have to use certain terms of art or legal Latin: for example, it is difficult to write about the doctrine of precedent without mentioning ratio decidendi or about contract without mentioning contra proferentem. These are terms of art that are well-understood, at least by lawyers, and it would be odd to say 'the reason for the decision' or 'construe against the grantor'. However, do not use Latin phrases unless it is necessary and never deliberately seek out obscure phrases in a mistaken attempt to impress the reader.

Examples of phrases to avoid include:

Jargon	Plain English
Notwithstanding	In spite of
Heretofore	Before now
As to	About
Instant case	This case
In the event that	If
Pursuant to	Under
Prior to	Before
Subsequent to	After
Thereafter	Later
Aforementioned	Previously mentioned

> ■ For an exercise in simplifying jargon, go to <www.legalwriting.ie> and complete Assignment 5.1.

FREQUENTLY MISSPELT WORDS

There are some legal words which are commonly misspelt. You need to watch for these. If you are not certain of the spelling of a particular word, or if you think there are different words with similar spellings, get a dictionary and check. One to be particularly careful about is 'judgment' rather than 'judgement'. The first spelling refers to the decision of a court; the second is used in other contexts.

These are some other commonly confused words. Find a dictionary and learn the difference between them:

- advice/advise
- affect/effect
- assent/ascent
- council/counsel
- censure/censor
- ensure/insure
- immoral/amoral
- offence/offense
- practice/practise
- precedence/precedent
- principal/principle
- their/there/they're

> ▓ To test your knowledge of these, go to <www.legalwriting.ie> and complete Assignment 5.2.

PUNCTUATION

In order to write well, you must know how to punctuate properly. Many students are unclear about the details of punctuation. It is worth learning the basics and keeping an eye open for how good writers use punctuation as a way of breaking up and enlivening text.

When you need to put a footnote at the end of a sentence or phrase, the footnote mark should always go after the punctuation. A footnote mark should rarely be inserted into the middle of a sentence with no punctuation.

Where you are quoting text, and the sentence ends at the end of the quote, then put the full stop inside the closing quotation mark. If the sentence that you are quoting continues but the sentence you are writing ends, then put the full stop outside the quotation marks.

Full stops

A full stop is one of the basic tools in your punctuation cabinet and one which you should be familiar with already. Generally speaking, it is used to end a sentence. While it may seem obvious, make sure you have enough full stops in a paragraph—very few sentences you write should be more than two lines long.

Always make sure that when you put in a full stop, you are ending a proper sentence and not just a collection of words or a sentence fragment (which has no verb). For example:

> **Incorrect:** The Oireachtas must therefore fill this gap. Because similar cases will inevitably arise again in the future.
>
> **Correct:** 'The Oireachtas must therefore fill this gap, as similar cases will inevitably arise again in the future', or 'The Oireachtas must therefore fill this gap. It is inevitable that similar cases will arise again in the future.'

You may also encounter full stops in the form of an ellipsis '...' which is three full stops together. It is used to signify that some text is missing. In modern informal writing, the ellipsis is often used to indicate irony, to link between sentences or concepts or to indicate a rhetorical statement. It is not acceptable to use the ellipsis in these ways in formal legal writing.

Commas

The comma is used to separate two phrases in the same sentence or to punctuate a list. It is not a substitute for a full stop.

> **Incorrect:** The Oireachtas must therefore fill this gap because similar cases will inevitably arise again in the future, the consequences of this for children in danger could be disastrous.

Serial commas and lists

The serial comma is used before the last item in a list and its coordinating conjunction ('and', 'or', sometimes 'nor'). Whether or not you use the serial comma is a stylistic choice. It is not right or wrong. It is more common in American English but some publishers on this side of the Atlantic also prefer it. It can sometimes help to avoid ambiguity, but if you use it once in your writing, you should use it throughout. However, when you are listing words or terms, you should always use a comma between the terms.

> **British English:** The three branches of government are the legislature, the executive and the courts.
>
> **American English:** The three branches of government are the legislature, the executive, and the courts.

Colons

A colon can be used as a substitute for a full stop, when the next sentence follows closely and logically from the preceding one, to introduce a list of items or to introduce a quotation.

It is therefore clear that the planning authority acted without legal authority: the original application was invalid, which makes the entire procedure void.

There are three branches of government in Ireland: the legislature, the executive and the courts.

As Byrne and McCutcheon state:
Popular perceptions of the law are derived from a variety of sources.

Semi-colons

A semi-colon can be used as a substitute for a full stop when two sentences are closely linked and you want to emphasise that link. Do not confuse it with a comma: there must be a verb on both sides of the semi-colon and each side should be a full sentence in its own right. Do not confuse it with a colon, which is a very common mistake; it cannot be used to introduce a list. However, it can be used to separate the items in a list, particularly when they are long.

The Oireachtas makes the law; the courts interpret it.

There are three branches of government in Ireland: the legislature, which is made up of the Dáil and Seanad; the executive, which is also known as the government; and the courts, which include the High and Supreme Court.

Exclamation marks

Exclamation marks are used to emphasise a statement. They should be used rarely, if ever, in formal writing and have no place in technical legal documents. F. Scott Fitzgerald said that using an exclamation mark is like laughing at your own joke.

Question marks

A question mark, as the name implies, indicates that a question is being asked. It can be used in formal writing, but sparingly. If it is already clear from your text that you are asking a question, you should not use a question mark.

The question to be asked is whether we need a referendum on children's rights.

This leaves two issues: does the bank holiday give an additional day for the submission of objections, and can the objectors rely on the oral assurances of the planning authority staff?

Hyphens/dashes

Hyphens or dashes can be used to separate clauses and phrases in your sentences, in the same way as commas and semi-colons, but should be used sparingly. They are best used for interjections and to add urgency, but too many will leave your reader feeling breathless and rushed. Note the difference between three different types of dashes. These are the hyphen, en and em dash, which have different widths: -, – and —. A hyphen is used to hyphenate words, an en dash is generally used to separate ranges of numbers and dates, while an em dash is used to separate phrases.

At that point, a new issue arose in relation to the full-time student—whether the essay was ever submitted.

Possessive

Indicate the possessive case (that a particular thing belongs to a particular person) with an apostrophe and the letter s. The apostrophe here is used where the term 'of' is understood, so 'The decision of the court' becomes:

The court's decision

If the noun representing the owner is a plural and thus already ends in s, use an apostrophe by itself.

The judges' robes

If a proper name ends in s, use an apostrophe and the letter s to indicate possession:

Thomas's book

You will also see the preceding rule applied to proper names:

Thomas' book

This is more common in American English. Whether it is correct or not is often debated. Choose an approach that you and your lecturer are happy with and be consistent about it.

It is incorrect to use an apostrophe to form a plural.

Correct: Both parties agreed a fresh set of contracts.
Incorrect: Both parties agreed a fresh set of contract's.

You will often see this mistake made. Do not repeat it. It is also incorrect to use an apostrophe to form the plural of an abbreviation or after a range of years (although it is used in this fashion in American English):

John took the CDs.
During the 1960s, the Supreme Court expanded the scope of constitutional rights.

Its/It's

One common mistake is to confuse 'its' and 'it's'. This is understandable, as these constructions do not exactly follow the rules above.

'Its' is the possessive form of 'it'.

The company and the shareholders are not one and the same. It is not correct to say that its property belongs to the shareholders.

'It's' is a contraction of 'it is'. As a contraction, it should not be used in formal or legal writing.

Capitalisation

Only capitalise proper nouns (people, legal entities, named buildings and places and so on). Do not capitalise words because they seem important. Lawyers often fall into this error, perhaps because it is common in contracts. In that context, the important terms should be defined in the contract and there is therefore some validity to capitalising them. It is not correct elsewhere.

Correct: If the Insured Person does not return the completed Claim Form to the Insurer within fourteen (14) days, the claim will lapse.
Incorrect: The Judiciary rarely appear on television or radio.

Sometimes, lawyers will capitalise words because they think they are important, though they should not. Only capitalise a term when you are referring to a specific named thing. Generally speaking, when you refer to the Constitution, you will mean the Constitution of Ireland 1937, and so you should usually capitalise the word. The exception is where you are referring to constitutional principles, or constitutions generally.

Correct: The Criminal Justice Act 2007 was a Bill in the Houses of the Oireachtas.
Incorrect: When commencing an Act, a Minister will promulgate a commencement order.

■ To check whether you properly understand the rules of punctuation, go to <www.legalwriting.ie> and complete Assignment 5.3.

The Irish Language

If you are researching and writing about Irish law, you need to be aware of some issues that arise with regard to the Irish language. Although it is the first national language, the unfortunate reality is that very little real use is made of it in government or legal administration. Nonetheless, you will encounter it from time to time, and it is important to deal with it correctly.

First, a practical note: writing text correctly in Irish requires the use of accents. Modern Irish spelling only uses the '*síne fada*' (commonly referred to as the '*fada*'), which is the accent over the letter 'i' in '*síne*' and which (as the name implies) lengthens the sound of the vowel. A *síne fada* is only used on a vowel. Omitting it is a serious mistake, as you risk causing confusion. For example, '*fear*' (without a fada over the e) means 'man'; '*féar*' (with a fada over the e) means 'grass'.[3]

Although those who are not used to writing in Irish will often not know how to produce these accents while typing at a computer, it is generally quite simple to do so. If you are using Windows, and your computer's keyboard is configured as Irish, holding down the 'Alt Gr' key while typing the vowel should work. If it does not, try holding down 'Alt' while pressing the apostrophe key, releasing both, then typing the vowel. On a Mac, holding down the 'Alt/ Option' key while typing the vowel should work.

Very few primary legal texts are prepared in the Irish language. The most likely context in which you will have to work with Irish is when interpreting the Constitution. If you do need to use Irish, and you are not familiar with or comfortable in that language, ask a friend or colleague who is more knowledgeable to review what you have written and your interpretation of words before you submit your work.

However, you will almost certainly have to deal with bodies with Irish names. One example is the planning appeals board, which has only one name, An Bord Pleanála (see section 3 of the Local Government (Planning and Development) Act 1976). Confusingly, the English language text of the legislation refers to this body as 'the Board'. However, it is incorrect to speak of the 'Planning Board' or any similar English name. (If you should do this in legal proceedings, you may find that your paperwork is rejected.) With some bodies, you need to be very careful, as the English title is in common usage: for example, the body known generally as the Higher Education Authority has only one legal name, An tÚdarás um Ard-Oideachas (see section 2 of the Higher Education Authority Act 1971). If you are unsure about the proper name of a state or semi-state body, check the establishing legislation. Note

---

[3] Investigating the difference between 'cáca' and 'caca', and the possible adverse consequence of omitting the fada, is left as an exercise for the reader.

also that the lower house of the Irish Parliament is the Dáil (not Dail) and that the plural of garda is gardaí. The organisation to which gardaí belong is An Garda Síochána, sometimes shortened to AGS. Neither individual members nor the organisation itself should ever be referred to as 'Guards' or 'the Police', though it is acceptable to refer to members as 'police'.

You also need to be careful about individual names. If a name has different spellings in Irish and English, verify from a reputable source (such as his or her own writings) what version the person uses. A person who prefers to be called 'Mícheál' is not likely to be happy to be referred to as 'Michael'. Using 'Micheal' is simply wrong. Sometimes the difference between the Irish and English versions of a name are slight: 'Ultan' and 'Ultán' look very similar but are pronounced differently.

Be particularly careful with surnames. Many Irish surnames begin with Ó (in Irish) or O' (in English). Check which version a person uses. Do not mix the two forms: either use the fada or the apostrophe, not both. It is not uncommon to see an abomination like Ó'Dalaigh CJ, which is wrong on two counts, as it mixes English and Irish and omits the fada over the first a.

Finally, bear in mind that Article 4 of the Constitution provides: 'The name of the state is Éire, or, in the English language, Ireland.' The name of the state is not 'Eire' and it is incorrect to use Éire when writing in English. The Irish Free State was called 'Saorstát Éireann' in Irish. It is not correct to use 'Éireann' by itself.

GENDER NEUTRAL WRITING

If you read Articles 12, 13 and 14 of the Irish Constitution, you will see that, while the President of Ireland was a woman for over two decades, any reference to the office-holder refers to a man. Article 12.3.1° provides:

> The President shall hold office for seven years from the date upon which he enters upon his office, unless before the expiration of that period he dies ...

While it may have been considered highly unlikely that there would ever be a female President when the Constitution was written, in contemporary writing, the use of gender neutral language is preferred to avoid both confusion and offence.

For this reason, when you are writing, you should always try and write in a gender neutral way. When you are referring to individuals of an unspecified gender, write your sentence to avoid the need for a pronoun. When referring to a particular office, try to use gender neutral terms: rather than using 'the policeman' you should use 'the police officer'. The term 'garda' is itself gender neutral, and should be preferred when referring to policing in this jurisdiction, as the term 'bangarda' is no longer used. The one apparent exception to this rule is when we refer to an 'ombudsman'. This term derives from Swedish, and is gender neutral in itself, though on occasion you may see reference to an 'ombud'.

On occasion, it sometimes makes a nonsense of a sentence to try and write it in a gender neutral way. Think about how confusing this sentence, written in gender neutral language is:

> According to the Constitution, once a Bill is passed by the Houses of the Oireachtas, the Taoiseach goes to Áras an Uachtaráin to meet the President. Once there, they ask them to sign the Bill and they do so unless they wish to consider referring the Bill to the Supreme Court under Article 26.

It is unclear from this sentence who is asking who to sign the Bill, who signs it, or who can refer the Bill to the Supreme Court. There are two ways of re-writing this sentence. The first is to use the name of the office-holder repeatedly through the sentence:

> According to the Constitution, once a Bill is passed by the Houses of the Oireachtas, the Taoiseach goes to Áras an Uachtaráin to meet the President. Once there, the Taoiseach asks the President to sign the Bill and the President does so unless the President wishes to consider referring the Bill to the Supreme Court under Article 26.

This solution can be a little wordy, however, and would be very cumbersome when writing a lengthy essay, comparing the role of the Taoiseach and the President under the Constitution. In situations such as this, it is considered acceptable to assign a particular gender to a particular individual or group of individuals, and to use this assignation throughout the piece of writing. This must be made clear at the beginning of the piece, and is usually done so in a footnote or in the foreword to the text. If we assign the female gender to the President, and the male gender to the Taoiseach, the sentence begins to make sense again, but flow better:

> According to the Constitution, once a Bill is passed by the Houses of the Oireachtas, the Taoiseach goes to Áras an Uachtaráin to meet the President. Once there, he asks her to sign the Bill and she does so unless she wishes to consider referring the Bill to the Supreme Court under Article 26.

The choice of gender is your own, but make sure that you choose useful ones. In an essay such as that described above, it would make little sense to assign the female gender to both parties.

Examples of common assignations would be:

President: female	Taoiseach: male
Garda: female	Defendant: male
Judge: female	Counsel: male
Doctor: female	Patient: male
Teacher: female	student: male

If you do choose to use this device in your writing, ensure that you do not use it to the point of absurdity. For example, when writing about medical consent in pregnancy, it would be silly to use the convention of referring to the patient as male.

AUDIBILITY

DEVELOP YOUR OWN VOICE

As you develop as a writer, develop your own voice. All the advice offered on good style here is just that: advice, not a strict set of rules. Read widely and discerningly, find styles that you like, and draw inspiration from them. (Do not simply copy someone else's style.) A good writer has a distinctive way of expressing his or her thoughts. This variety can make reading enjoyable. Again, the best way of doing this is to read legal texts—journals or books— after which the process of developing your own style will come naturally over time. It is not necessarily something you have to sit down and think about in an academic way. If you read a lot, and practise legal writing frequently, your own personal writing style will develop over time.

KNOW YOUR AUDIENCE

Part of having your own voice is knowing who you are writing for. Choose and vary your writing style depending on your audience. Know also what you can leave out and what you must include. A particular assignment may ask you to write as if you are working in a specific context, such as a memorandum for a judge or an article for an academic journal.

Word limits will also impact on the way in which you write. If you are writing to a tight word count limit, you may have to leave out certain fundamental material and assume that your reader will know it. If you are writing a longer essay, you will need to cover this ground, to show that you do know these basics.

Each of these will require a particular approach, which you will have to learn by reading and by practice.

FURTHER READING

- Butt P and Castle R, *Modern Legal Drafting* (Cambridge 2006)

  This book provides a good overview of the move towards 'plain English' in legal drafting. The examples and case studies used focus on drafting in practice, and so this book will be more useful to the qualified lawyer than to the undergraduate student.

- Foster S, *How to Write Better Law Essays: Tools and Techniques for Success in Exams and Assignments* (2nd edn, Longman 2009)

  This book is a thorough and attractively presented guide to legal writing for the undergraduate, covering both essays and examination technique. It is aimed at UK undergraduates, but the content is largely relevant to Irish students also.

- Garner B, *Legal Writing in Plain English: A Text with Exercises* (Chicago 2001)

  This is a thorough, thoughtful and clear text on legal writing, with plenty of exercises. Unfortunately for an Irish undergraduate audience, it is aimed at American law students, whose education includes a great deal more practical drafting, so not all of the examples and exercises are useful, but there is a great deal to be learnt from this book.

- —— *The Elements of Legal Style* (2nd edn, Oxford 2002)

  Although perhaps a little too oriented towards American examples and usage for an Irish audience, this book is very useful because its style recommendations are well thought out and specific to the law.

- Gowers E, *The Complete Plain Words* (Sidney Greenbaum and Janet Whitcut, eds, 3rd edn, Penguin 2004)

  Originally written for the British Civil Service, this is a classic text containing many words of wise counsel.

- Strong SI, *How to Write Law Essays and Exams* (3rd edn, Oxford 2010)

  This book instructs the reader in the use of the CLEO (Claim, Law, Evaluation and Outcome) framework, which is similar to the ILAC method discussed in chapter 7. There are also some general tips on English style. The book is useful as an alternative perspective on how to tackle essays and exams.

- Strunk W and White EB, *The Elements of Style* (4th edn, Longman 1999)

  This is a classic, although controversial, text on the fundamental rules of writing in English, including basic style rules, principles of good essay composition, and common mistakes. Whether you agree with it or not, there should be a copy in any library of style books.

- Zillman D and Roth E, *Strategic Legal Writing* (Cambridge 2008)

  This book is aimed at American legal practitioners rather than undergraduate law students on this side of the Atlantic and is of limited use to the latter audience.

6 **Writing Law Essays**

There are two things wrong with almost all legal writing. One is its style. The other is its content.[1]

INTRODUCTION

Sitting down to write a law essay for the first time can be a daunting prospect. It requires skills that are different to those which you apply when preparing for and writing in exams, and those skills you will have learned writing essays before entering law school (although there is some crossover between the two).

When you are assigned an essay to write in law, you will usually be asked to discuss a particular aspect of the law, or to analyse a particular viewpoint. What is most important at the outset is that you know exactly what you are being asked to do. Lecturers are always disappointed to receive an excellently written, clearly argued and concisely formulated essay on a topic entirely unrelated to that which was assigned. So first: read the question you are asked, and make sure that you know exactly what is being required of you.

Generally speaking, when you are writing a legal essay, you need to be able to clearly identify the law, analyse it and draw your own conclusions on it. Often 'your own conclusions' may simply be agreeing with another academic writer on the issue at hand—this is completely acceptable, as you are not being asked to develop your own theory on, for example, the appropriateness of the postal rule to the modern business environment.

Over time, you will develop your own personal approach to the task of writing an essay, but there are some basics that you can continue to apply and refine as you develop your skills.

To make it easier to explain, the process of research is presented here as divided into distinct phases. The reality is much less neat. These phases will blend into each other and you will often find yourself having to go back and revisit or repeat an 'earlier' phase.

---

[1] Fred Rodell, 'Goodbye to Law Reviews' (1936) 23 Virginia Law Review 38.

HOW TO THINK, WRITE AND CITE

If you are studying law in combination with another subject, such as sociology, at the beginning of your other subjects you will have been introduced to, instructed in, and engaged with, research methods and methodologies. Typically, this is not something that is done in law school, and students generally learn the 'how' and 'what' of legal research by reading scholarly articles and judgments. Thus, while students engage in legal research and utilise research methods subconsciously, often at an advanced level, they are often not given any formal instruction on the subject, and are regularly unable to articulate why the approach to the research question is appropriate and justifiable. This short section is not an exhaustive description of legal research methods, but rather is intended to introduce you to the language and processes which are used in legal research. It will probably be unnecessary for undergraduate research unless you are engaged in a large project, but at a graduate level, you will be expected to be conversant in the language of legal research methods.

There are two points to consider when seeking to understand legal research methods. First, if you have taken courses on research methods in other disciplines, it is worth remembering that the language that is used in describing legal research methods is often similar to that used in other disciplines, but can have different meanings. Secondly, and relatedly, while it is certainly possible, and expected, that you will engage in some or all of the methods and methodologies listed below, be aware of your abilities and limitations in this regard—for example, using historical sources in the elaboration of a legal principle can be considered quite a different process to engaging in historical research, or utilising the historical method.

Doctrinal Legal Research

The doctrinal approach is by far the most common approach to research you will use at undergraduate level. Indeed, you have been learning how to use it without realising it: it is what is described in chapters 2 and 3 of this book, and most, if not all, of your lecturers will have been using this method for understanding and explaining the law without explicitly naming it. You should find it immediately familiar.

Doctrinal analysis involves the processes which have been described in detail earlier in this book: locating the relevant authoritative primary legal texts; reading them carefully to identify the rules which they articulate; and finally trying to identify the unanswered questions or conflicting principles which they contain. While this sounds straightforward, it is in fact quite a complex and sophisticated process. The reader must be aware of possible differences in

WRITING LAW ESSAYS

the meaning attached to particular words and phrases by different Acts or judgments. The rules will often be incomplete, and sometimes very closely tied to 'material facts', which are quite subjective and will vary from judge to judge. Clearly identifying the ratio decidendi is not always easy.

In using this method, what you are seeking to construct is a comprehensive and coherent understanding of the law, which you can then criticise or suggest improvements to. For some, this is quite a limited goal and there are many criticisms of doctrinal research as being conservative, mere research rather than scholarship, and always providing an incomplete picture of the reality of 'law in action'.

Nonetheless, it is a completely acceptable research method, particularly for undergraduate students and for much graduate work. It is how judges and practising lawyers work, and must be properly understood in order to engage with the legal system in any meaningful way. While a socio-legal or critical approach has many advantages and attractions, it is vital to master doctrinal research before adopting these other tools.

THE COMPARATIVE APPROACH

Next to the doctrinal methodology, a comparative approach is one which will perhaps be most instinctively utilised by law students. The size of the jurisdiction (and the resulting amount of case law), combined with its legal heritage, means that when analysing a particular legal principle or doctrine, we will often look to other jurisdictions for assistance. Most commonly we will ask, what is the law in England and Wales?[2] We will also often look to case law and legislative practice in other common law jurisdictions such as Australia, New Zealand and Canada. The one primary exception to this is in the context of constitutional law, where we will often look to the United States, as well as Canada, less commonly South Africa, and where the jurisprudence of the European Court of Human Rights is often illuminating.

However, simply because we ask 'what is the law in England and Wales?' or 'what does the legislation say in Northern Ireland?' does not mean that we are necessarily engaging in a comparative analysis. Comparativists would tell you that there is a lot more to the comparative method than simply borrowing principles or analysis from another jurisdiction—though that is probably all they agree on. The fundamental question to be asked is what can be learned from examining alternative approaches. Does the law of another country provide a

---

[2] Naturally, being careful not to conflate the position in England and Wales (not just England) with that of Great Britain (England, Wales and Scotland), or worse, the United Kingdom (England, Wales, Scotland and Northern Ireland), unless you are clear which jurisdiction(s) you are referring to; and of course understanding that our 'closest neighbour' is not in fact England and Wales but rather Northern Ireland.

source of inspiration for law reform in Ireland, or highlight particular practical or ideological choices in Irish law, or provide support for the appropriateness of Irish law because it is similar to its comparator? Always have a reason for a comparative approach.

In writing an undergraduate essay, you will not necessarily need to articulate why the country you are examining is relevant to the analysis in any great detail, but you need to be aware why, for example, in choosing a jurisdiction to look to in an effort to explore the right to silence, you chose to look to America rather than Armenia. If you are looking at two jurisdictions—Canada and New Zealand, for example—and prefer one approach over the other, are there any reasons for your preference which could be based in the comparative method? Finally, in looking to non-English speaking countries, unless you are fluent in the language of that country, be cautious about your use of translated materials, or materials produced in English in relation to the legal principle under discussion. How accurate is the translation? How do you know that the analysis you discovered in English is accurate, or representative?

THE HISTORICAL APPROACH

Again, the historical method, once described and understood, is generally instinctively familiar to law students. The links between the disciplines of law and history are often clearly evident: at the very early stages of your legal training you will have been instructed on the historical context to the Irish legal system; the system of precedent means that scholarly research and textbooks are littered with historical material.

Thus, in researching a particular legal principle or issue, you often cannot avoid placing the subject matter in its historical context. However, this does not necessarily constitute a utilisation of the historical method as understood by some legal historians. This approach will often simply involve examining the evolution of a rule or principle, rather than placing and understanding it in its historical context.

In examining some of the pitfalls and dangers with utilising the historical method, Cahillane observes how it can be used to demonstrate the conditions of emergence of a particular law or practice in order to better understand it, or to demonstrate how thinking might have changed on an issue, or to highlight an injustice.[3] She cautions, however, that we must recall the dangers of removing meanings from their original historical setting. Lawyers, essentially, are not historians.

[3] Laura Cahillane, 'The Use of History in Law – avoiding the pitfalls' in Laura Cahillane and Jennifer Schweppe (eds), *Legal Research Methods: Principles and Practicalities* (Clarus Press 2016).

Socio-Legal Studies

A relatively new, and often very interesting, approach to thinking and writing about legal questions is socio-legal studies. This is often understood as a style of research which is very much in contrast to doctrinal analysis. Its proponents have criticised the latter and sometimes portray conventional legal analysis as very much on the way out. It takes a perspective which is very much external to legal traditions, texts and institutions, and asks how society as a whole, or particular sub-sections of it, view, understand or are affected by aspects of the law.

This broader contextualisation of the law is often based on very different ideological foundations to doctrinal analysis. It includes critical legal studies (which seek to challenge unspoken and often unconscious assumptions about power), often using the frameworks of important schools of thought such as Marxism, feminism, race, queer theory, and post-colonialism. While these are radical forms of socio-legal studies, it can also take a conservative approach, with much of law and economics scholarship being quite supportive of the idea of the free market.

Socio-legal studies are sometimes linked to empirical legal research, which is discussed in more detail below. It is true that gaining a good understanding of alternative conceptions of the law can involve gathering individual viewpoints through interviews or surveys, but it is not necessary. It is perfectly possible to conduct very good socio-legal work from desk- or library-based research: simply re-reading legal texts through the prism of an alternative frame of reference can be quite illuminating.

It is also quite possible to engage in socio-legal research as an element of a larger project. References to policy documents, statements by politicians, or public surveys are forms of socio-legal studies, and many essays and articles will include an element of this. This can be quite beneficial, and can be done without having to extensively research or justify the use of a particular theoretical perspective. However, you should know what socio-legal research is, watch for it as you read, and if you discover that your work is leaning more in that direction than towards doctrinal analysis, make this a conscious choice which you justify and fully adopt in your writing. It is very acceptable to mix and match different styles of research and analysis in your work, but if you do not reflect on the choices you are making, and why, you risk producing text which is weakened by a confused approach.

Empirical Legal Research

Finally, you will hear or see the term 'empirical research' used with increasing frequency in legal research. It is highly unlikely that you will be engaging in empirical legal research at an undergraduate level, but again, it is useful to understand what it constitutes.

First, what is empirical legal research? The Nuffield Foundation defined it as 'the study through direct methods of the operation and impact of law and legal processes in society'.[4] What this means is that the research is not doctrinal or theoretical in its nature, but rather involves an element of experiment and/or observation. Most commonly, it is understood as utilising some form of qualitative (eg interviews) or quantitative (eg surveys) research techniques.

While you may unwittingly engage in other forms of research without necessarily understanding what you are doing, or why you are doing it, it is highly unlikely that you will engage in empirical legal research unknowingly. If, however, you do intend to utilise empirical methods, it is most important that you seek and secure ethics approval from your institutional, faculty or departmental ethics committee prior to doing so. You should also ensure that you have adequate education and training in the tools and analysis techniques that you intend to use.

General Advice on Assignments

Increasingly, law students in Ireland are being assessed in a variety of different ways. In legal skills modules, particularly, law lecturers seldom rely solely on a written final examination in order to evaluate their students. Instead, students are required to complete a number of progressively more demanding assignments, such as case briefs and legal research and citation exercises.

This form of assessment is ideal in skills modules, given that assignments more closely replicate the work you will be doing in legal or law-related careers. Furthermore, it is to your advantage as, generally speaking, your final mark in any continually assessed module is arguably a better and fairer reflection of your overall performance than an examination, which is, by comparison, a mere snapshot taken over the course of two or three hours on one day.

Indeed, the conclusion that continuous assessment is the ideal method of examining is borne out both by a number of academic studies and by student surveys that almost always express a preference for more assignments. Sometimes students say they want more continuous assessment, but when the time comes to complete the work, they either do them poorly, or submit assignments late, or fail to submit them at all.

---

[4] Hazel Genn, Martin Partington and Sally Wheeler, 'Law in the Real World: Improving Our Understanding of How Law Works – Final Report and Recommendations' (Nuffield Foundation 2006).

To avoid these pitfalls, and to make the most of continuous assessment—both in terms of your own learning and your achieving the best possible result—some tips for completing assignments follow.[5]

Start Early

Most assignments in law, as you will soon discover (if you have not already), are labour-intensive and time-consuming. Some require a considerable amount of research and time in the library; others require that you read a tremendous amount of material that usually is not easy to fully comprehend and analyse. As such, and even though it goes against the natural tendency to procrastinate, you should commence work on them as soon as possible upon receiving them. Academic terms go by fast and deadlines creep up very quickly. It can be tough to motivate yourself, but nonetheless: START EARLY!

Ask Questions

The only caveat to the foregoing rule of thumb is that you should not dive into an assignment if you do not fully understand precisely what your lecturer is looking for you to do. These assignments can be challenging—they are meant to be—and often require that you obtain clarification about some of the finer details. As such, most law lecturers encourage and welcome questions from students as to what exactly they need to do. Many lecturers find it exasperating when they deliberately set aside time for questions from students in the knowledge that there must be some uncertainty in the often large groups they are teaching, but no one asks any. The bottom line is that students should not be shy about asking questions about assignments—whether in a lecture, in an email or during a lecturer's office hours. It can make all the difference between doing well and doing poorly.

Research and Citation

As law students, you have access to a wide array of both high-powered, costly legal research databases and an incredible, ever-expanding volume of legal materials on freely available websites, as well as law libraries with huge holdings of primary and secondary legal sources from around the world. There is also a much greater emphasis on the teaching of legal research skills and methodologies. Accordingly, where your assignments call for you to undertake legal research, you should ensure that you search thoroughly for relevant materials from this jurisdiction and internationally. Reliance

---

[5] Some of these tips are drawn from the abundance of useful information for law students that can be found on the excellent website, The Student Lawyer (<thestudentlawyer.com>).

upon what is contained in your reading lists will typically prove insufficient; many assignments mandate that you undertake your own independent investigation. Moreover, the primary and secondary materials you unearth in your investigation must be cited in accordance with the OSCOLA Ireland style of citation (contained in the Appendix).

Review and Proofread

A senior judge in the United States once commented that there is no such thing as good writing; there is only good revision. While procrastinating is a tendency that many of us struggle with, it is advisable that you always endeavour to give yourself time to review any assignment you work on and eliminate all substantive and stylistic errors. If there is someone you know who writes well, whose opinion you trust and who is generous spirited, it would be beneficial to ask her to proofread your more involved assignments. A fresh pair of eyes can often catch things that escape an author's notice. Two pairs of eyes are even better.

Follow all Directions Carefully

It goes without saying, but there are always students who read directions incorrectly and get poor marks on assignments as a result. Assignments typically have a specific purpose and are tailored in a certain way. Make sure you do what is asked, and if directions seem unclear to you, make sure that you ask your lecturer to clarify matters.

Getting Started

Managing the Research Process

Perhaps the most important skill, but one which many law students do not learn until late in their careers as researchers, is an ability to manage the actual process of research. It is not wise to rush an essay.

Any significant piece of research and writing also needs careful planning; you need to work backwards from the due date and calculate how much time you will need in order to do the basic research, gather your thoughts, write up and then revise your work, and submit in good time.

As you become a more experienced researcher, you will get a better understanding of how long it takes you to research and write about a particular topic. Break a large essay down into its component parts and estimate how much work each involves. Apply this knowledge to make the planning and execution of the research project smoother, simpler and less stressful.

Find Relevant Material

The most difficult phase of research is the initial few steps. You may be given a title by a lecturer, or have an idea that you want to explore yourself. You may not know where to start. Sometimes, the way forward is clear as you know of a good textbook or article dealing directly with the topic. However, research is not always straightforward and sometimes you have to cast about for a while until you discover a good lead.

There are perhaps half a dozen good starting points for your research. A student textbook should give you the basics. However, for real depth of analysis, you should try to locate a monograph—a book written by a scholar for other scholars. There may also be good academic articles published in legal journals. If the topic is one of general public importance, there may be a government report examining it and recommending changes to the law. It may also have been dealt with by the Law Reform Commission. Finally, there is the internet. The chapter on legal research contains some pointers to useful sites, but although the internet makes research easy, it is not always a good place to start as you can get overwhelmed quite easily. Do your groundwork in the library and use the internet later to make sure that your sources are comprehensive. If you are particularly stuck, as a last resort, speak to the person supervising your research, generally your lecturer, and ask him or her for pointers.

From the initial material that you find, you need to start branching out. That first article or book will cite other material: cases, legislation, articles and other secondary material. Find those and read them. Look to see if there is any commentary on the primary materials that you are working with. Read all the articles and book chapters that are relevant. (Bear in mind that not everything that you come across will, in fact, be relevant and sometimes it is a better use of your time to stop reading something that proves unhelpful for your essay.) You will find that each relevant source should lead you to others. Now that electronic databases are so easy to use, after some digging, you will probably find yourself with more material than you can possibly cope with and you'll be wondering why you thought this topic was difficult to research.

When you get to this point, it is time to stop researching and move onto the next stage. You need to consolidate what you have found and begin to work out what you are going to write. This does not mean that you are done with library and internet research. As you progress through the essay, you will continually find that you need to go back and fill in gaps.

Taking Notes

It is very important to begin to structure what you are learning. Take notes on the materials that you are reading. As these begin to take shape, you should begin to see the structure of the topic as a whole. Remember that individual authors and articles will each have their own perspective, and will not always agree with each other. It can be very useful to identify these differences of opinion, as they will help to suggest how your own writing should develop and decide what you want to focus on in your essay.

There are many different ways to take notes—summaries, outlines, mindmaps—and no one method is better than the other. You are probably already familiar with summaries: as the name implies, this is a very truncated note of an article, book or judgment. You will find one technique for taking a summary of a case in the chapter on 'Reading Judgments'. An outline is a comprehensive overview of a topic, perhaps highlighting particular themes, debates or a chronology of events. A mindmap is a diagram which uses the arrangement of items on a page to highlight the hierarchy and connections between them, and can be enhanced by including images.

This is an example of an outline:

Misrepresentation
False statement of fact by A that induces B to contract with A
Doran v Delaney and Greene

Elements of Misrepresentation
1. Must be statement of fact, not
   * Sales talk
   * Law
   * Intention (*Edgington v Fitzmaurice*)
   * Opinion
        Bisset v Wilkinson
        Esso Petroleum v Mardon
        Doheny v Bank of Ireland
2. Statement of fact must be untrue
3. Must be a statement (not silence)
        Stafford v Keane Mahony Smith
Note
        uberrimae fidei
        change of circumstances (*With v O'Flanagan*)
        half-truths (*Nottingham Patent Brick and Tile Co v Butler*)
4. Must be reliance on misrepresentation
        Grafton Court v Wadson Sales

Find a system or combination of systems that works for you, and vary it as required.

STRUCTURING YOUR ESSAY

When you are writing your essay, you need to keep in mind that you are answering a single question and that you are building your argument throughout. There are some techniques that can be used to ensure that your essay flows in a logical way, and where each paragraph builds on the previous one. Again, it is important to remember that these techniques are not rules—and you certainly should not use them dogmatically. They are simply intended as ways to help you learn how to write in a clear way.

Legal writing should follow a logical structure. Before you start writing, have a plan for your work. The plan may change as you go along, but if you have some idea as to how your writing will be structured, this will help your research process enormously.

Before you start writing as such, brainstorm your ideas. Scribble whatever you think you will deal with in your essay down on a piece of paper. Get your ideas out of your head and on paper, so that you can work with them.

Now, take those ideas and re-arrange them into a logical, coherent plan. What background does your reader need to know about the topic? What argument are you going to make? What are the steps in your argument? What is your conclusion?

Use this plan as the basis for your writing. You may find that as you write, you discover gaps or flaws in your plan. Just change it—the cutting and pasting functions on your computer are your friend, as is the delete button. When you are finished, read over the essay as a whole. It is best to do this on paper, not on a computer screen, and after taking a long break, preferably overnight, from writing. Does it flow? Does it make sense? Do any of the sections need to be moved from one place to another? Should any of it be removed? Is there anything you need to add?

It is also particularly useful to ask someone else to give you feedback on whether your approach seems logical. This can be a classmate, a friend or a family member. If they are not a law student, that does not matter. In fact, it may be better, as your ideas should be clear even to a person without a grounding in the topic. Ask him or her to sit and listen to you talk through your structure for 5 or 10 minutes while taking notes. If he or she identifies any gaps, disconnections or unanswered questions, you know where you need to focus your attention.

These are three different structures for an essay on the same topic, comparing constitutional and statutory interpretation.

While the rules relating to statutory interpretation are strict and mechanical, the rules for constitutional interpretation are much more fluid. Discuss.

Outline 1: This first outline will result in an essay which is quite basic, but will contain all the relevant information. The conclusion will be a relatively simple one: that is, that the two methods of interpretation are different due to the different type of texts in question.

> Introduction
>
> What is a Constitution? Why is a Constitution different to a piece of legislation?
>
> Rules for constitutional interpretation
>
> Rules for statutory interpretation
>
> Conclusion: Justification of difference due to difference in nature of two texts

Outline 2: This second outline will result in an essay which has more of a law reform emphasis: here, the movement from the old approach in statutory interpretation to a more rigid one will be compared with the increasingly fluid approach by the courts to constitutional interpretation. Recommendations by Kelly for a dual approach to constitutional interpretation will be referred to, and approved of.

> Introduction
>
> Historical background to statutory interpretation: movement from literal/ mischief and golden rules to literal and schematic: why?
>
> Outline of various methods of constitutional interpretation, highlighting the problems which exist with this pick 'n' mix approach.
>
> Recommendations by Kelly re: dual approach which would bring it closer to statutory interpretation
>
> Conclusion

Outline 3: This third outline will result in a more theoretically based essay, which will ask what the purpose of judges is, and whether it is appropriate that they interpret the basic law of the country without any real guidance on how to do so. This essay will have a more critical edge, though will ultimately also have a law reform focus.

> Introduction
>
> Outline of rigid nature of statutory interpretation
>
> Outline of variety of approaches taken by courts to constitutional interpretation
>
> Criticisms of this type of judicial activism by Hogan etc.; recommendations for clearer guidance to judges on constitutional interpretation
>
> Conclusion

Headings and Sub-headings

Good use of headings and sub-headings can make your essay easy to follow, as these expose the structure of your argument to the reader. Try not to be too simplistic with these: headings such as 'Introduction', 'Overview', 'Analysis' and 'Conclusion' are good starting points, but you should expand on these with additional explanation ('Overview: The Development of Work-Related Stress Claims', 'Analysis: Incomplete Protection for Employees in Tort Law', etc.), or with sensible sub-headings. Avoid lengthy headings and sub-headings, which you will sometimes see in American writing, and always ensure that your text will read well without the headings—do not assume that the reader will actually read them. At the same time, it is important not to overuse headings—there is absolutely no need, for example, for there to be a heading for each paragraph. Most essays will have between three to five key points in them—these will be set out in your introduction. Use these key points as your headings.

Roadmaps

One of the easiest ways to make your writing clear is to provide roadmaps to what you have to say. In the introduction to your essay or answer, provide a summary of what is to follow. In the conclusion, summarise what has gone before. In each of the main sections, do the same thing.

In the introduction to a long essay, the roadmap may be a few sentences or even a paragraph or two. In each section, the roadmap will be shorter: probably just one sentence. There is no strict rule—what matters is that the reader is clear about what you are going to discuss or what you have just discussed, and how it all links together. This can significantly aid comprehension, or at least reduce frustration.

This essay will examine the question of statutory interpretation from a critical perspective. It will ask what the purpose of judges is, and whether it is appropriate that they interpret the basic law of the country without any real guidance on how to do so. It will begin with an outline and discussion of the rigid nature of statutory interpretation. It will then examine the variety of approaches taken by courts to constitutional interpretation. Building on this, the essay will then explore academic criticism of this type of judicial activism, and will conclude with recommendations for clearer guidance to judges on constitutional interpretation.

Linking Sentences

Another simple trick is to connect from paragraph to paragraph by linking sentences, using words that refer back to what was just dealt with. The word 'another' at the beginning of this paragraph is an example of that. It goes back to the word 'one' at the beginning of the previous section, and reminds the reader that this is a list of tips.

This can be a very effective device for maintaining the flow of a piece of text, and also helps to keep your own mind on track as you write. If you cannot connect from one paragraph to the next, perhaps the ideas you are writing about do not belong together.

Other linking words are:

'On the other hand ... '
'While ... '
'By comparison ... '
'In addition ... '
'Similarly ... '
'Finally ... '

TOPIC SENTENCES

Finally, another way in which you can make the structure of your essay clear to your reader is to use 'topic sentences' to open each paragraph. These simply state the principal purpose of the paragraph. They make it easy for the reader to know what the paragraph is about, to skim through the text if they are in a hurry or just want to get the gist of it, and to build your argument in a coherent way.

This section will describe the rules which apply to statutory interpretation ...

Unlike the rules relating to statutory interpretation, those concerning constitutional interpretation are much less formal and mechanical.

Academics have been very critical of judicial activism in the context of constitutional interpretation ...

WRITING YOUR ESSAY

A large part of good writing is the application of simple tools and techniques. If you remember a few of these, they will always be useful and, with practice, you will become very comfortable with using them. In time, they will become second nature.

HOW TO INTRODUCE A CONCEPT

A good deal of legal writing deals with abstract concepts. You will therefore need to introduce and explain these. Sometimes these concepts have very different meanings in law to their day-to-day meanings: for example, the notion of 'mistake' in contract. If you need to introduce a concept in your essay, assume that your reader knows very little about it.

Start from its foundations, which may be historical, philosophical or legal, or some combination of these. Where does this concept come from, and how has it changed over time? For example, the idea of the nation-state is something that developed in the 1800s. The perception of the morality of killing is not static. The list of external constituencies which a company must take into account continues to develop as 'corporate social responsibility' gains wider acceptance.

If the concept has a legal definition, give that definition. Are there problems with that definition? Is it complete or still appropriate? What do legal academics have to say about it? Are there writers who challenge or contest it? How might the definition be improved or updated?

How to Cover the Legal Issues

If you are writing an essay for a legal module, you have to deal with the law. The amount of 'law' that you will need to deal with will vary depending on the particular subject area and your approach to the topic. However, it must be there to some degree and you must cover the law comprehensively.

To be ready to do this, re-read and reflect on the chapter on legal thinking. Be sure you identify the legal issues which are (reasonably) clear and the unanswered questions. Reading the academic literature can help you with this.

Once you have a clear inventory of the difficult issues involved, either answer them (which will help you to structure the remainder of your essay) or state that they are outside of the scope of your essay, perhaps because you are not exploring that aspect of your overall topic or because of lack of space. Do not simply ignore or pass over obvious questions. Your reader will see these gaps and you may lose marks as a result.

Methods and Methodologies

It is not usually necessary in an undergraduate essay to include a section on the research methods and methodologies that you used in your research and analysis. However, you should at least be *aware* of the approach that you have taken. Is it a purely doctrinal approach, or a socio-legal one? Is there a comparative element to the piece? If so, you might consider explaining what jurisdictions you have chosen to consider in this regard, and why they are appropriate to your research. By being cognisant of the methodological approach you have chosen, this will assist in your research planning, analysis and structuring your essay.

Building an Argument

It is very likely that your essay will involve some sort of argument, probably for reform or improvement to the law. If you are writing this type of essay, you need to be careful to ensure that you build that argument as you go. If you have identified the legal issues correctly, this will help a great deal in ensuring that your argument is well-structured. If you are writing a doctrinal analysis, you should build your argument around the legal issues.

To build your argument well, you need first to state your thesis clearly and concisely. You need to set out the context and the evidence that supports your point of view. This may be primary legal material, research from another discipline such as economics, or academic commentary. You must also deal with any counter-arguments fairly and either refute them or show that they are not relevant to your specific thesis. If there is a case that points in a different direction, you have to mention it. Similarly, you must deal with studies that do not support your argument. You may find that your opinion changes as you do this. This is generally a good thing.

The legal definition of ... is not up-to-date because ...

The gap in the definition causes difficulties because ...

Some authors have argued that this gap is not significant in practice but ...

The definition must be improved by amending the law to provide ...

Coming to a Conclusion

At some point, the writing must end. You need to arrive at some overall conclusion. You probably had this conclusion in mind when you started writing, but do not be afraid to change it as you go. It is these unexpected turns that make research such an interesting journey. If the state of the law or your analysis directs you to a different end, you should follow this.

Craft your conclusion carefully. It will probably be the last thing that the person marking your essay will read before coming to his or her conclusion on your work. He or she may also re-read the first paragraph, so you should pay attention to that also. It is sometimes wise to write your introduction after writing your conclusion. This is good practice, as you may not know what will be in your introduction until you have finished writing the whole essay.

The conclusion may require a summary of the essay as a whole. The longer and more complex your writing, the more advisable a summary is. There should certainly be a definite statement of your overall argument and your recommendations, whether they are to leave things be, reform the law or conduct further research. Leave your reader in no doubt about where you stand and what you propose to do.

Revise and Abandon

As mentioned above, research is a process. You need to give your reading time to settle in your mind. Once you have written a draft, put it aside for a day or two, then re-read it through with a fresh perspective. You will probably find many things in it that can be improved. You should allow time in your schedule for at least one round of revision and two or three if you can manage. It is time well-spent, particularly when you come to the end. It is easy to forget that the reader will sometimes not know the topic as well as you do, and may not understand things that seem obvious when you are in the middle of writing about it.

However, every piece of writing has to be abandoned at some stage, or it will never see the light of day. You need to submit your essay in order for it to be graded, and you need to do this in time to avoid being penalised. You also have other coursework to complete. You never really stop revising a good piece of work, you simply abandon it. Knowing when to do this is something that you will have to learn through experience.

Proofreading

The last thing you should do before submitting your essay is proofreading. This is a different process to redrafting. At the proofing stage, you are not interested so much in the content of the work, but rather the grammar, punctuation and, most importantly for a law essay, the referencing. Go through your essay with a fine-tooth comb and make sure that each reference is accurate and that all references are consistent with each other. Ensure that you have page numbers on the document and that your bibliography, if you need one, is in the right style. Finally, look once more at the instructions your lecturer gave you on the submission process and any stylistic requirements.

Using Technology

As your research progresses, you will find yourself using computer and information technology throughout. This is a great advantage which you have over previous generations of researchers: the experience of research today is very different to what it was 20, 40 or 60 years ago. Information technology is useful to you at a number of stages in the process (all of which are covered in various parts of this book): in identifying suitable materials, in getting access to those materials quickly and easily, and in citing and referencing these. As you progress through successive years of your programme, you may find it useful to store your electronic references in some sort of research-oriented database system, of which there are a number available.

You will also be using electronic tools to prepare the final essay which you will be submitting. You will write up your essay using a word processor and you will probably submit the final result online, both for the convenience of your lecturer and also to enable it to be checked for plagiarism (a topic which will be covered below). In the same way as a good carpenter familiarises himself with his tools, you should become very familiar and comfortable with your word processor or web browser. If your institution offers training courses, you should take advantage of these to the fullest extent possible.

KEEPING BACKUPS

One thing to bear in mind when you are using electronic tools is that they are not as reliable as they might seem. Computers can fail, sometimes at the worst possible moment. You can lose days, weeks or months of valuable research in an instant because of some technical problem. This can be avoided if you back up your data properly.

Small portable drives are now increasingly popular and very easy to lose or accidentally break. It is therefore vital that you take backups of all of your work at regular intervals. (A backup is a copy of your work on another disk drive, which is stored apart from your main working copy, preferably in another location.)

This can be done in a number of ways. The easiest way is to ensure that you always save your work in two places—if you get into this habit early in your career, it will become second nature. Saving to your computer and to a portable drive is one way of ensuring you do not lose your work, but be sure you do not accidentally lose track of where the latest version is.

Another simple method is to email your work to yourself at the end of each working day. If you own your own computer, it may come with automated backup software.

There are also internet-based services which allow you to upload your documents to a file which you can access from any computer in the world. All of these methods have their benefits and drawbacks, but each should ensure that you have your work in more than one place. Figure out which method works for you, and get into the habit of using it after each working day.

TYPOGRAPHY

Before you submit your essay, you should make sure that it is well presented. Modern computer technology makes this easy; it also makes it easy to present yourself badly. Your essay will be marked for its content, but the easier it is to identify what the content is, the better.

Paying some attention to the basics of layout and typography will help you with this. For more details on this topic, including advanced topics like kerning and letter spacing, please see the website 'Typography for Lawyers' at <www.typographyforlawyers.com>.

The tips below are only guidelines. The person who is grading your work has the final say on what he or she will accept, and will sometimes give very specific guidelines on how to present your work; you should consult with your module coordinator if you have any questions.

Cover page

Make sure that your essay has a clear cover page, which includes all the essential information required by the person marking: the module name and institutional code, title of the essay, your name (if your institution does not have anonymous marking), your identification number, word or page count (if there is a limit on these), date of submission and any other essential information. There is really no need to bind your essay, unless this is required by the module coordinator—usually, simply stapling the essay on the top left-hand corner is more than adequate.

Not too many typefaces

Resist the temptation to mix (and mis-match) a large number of typefaces in your essay. Modern word processors make it quite easy to use a variety of fancy fonts in printed work. One or two carefully selected (and relatively sober) fonts work much better. If you are not an experienced graphic designer, you risk creating a document with clashing visual styles which is difficult to read.

Serif and sans serif

One thing to be aware of is the difference between serif and sans serif typefaces. Serif fonts are those like Times New Roman which contain small 'hooks' at the end of the letter shapes. These hooks help to guide the eye from place to place and are thus easier to read in body text.

Times New Roman is an example of a serif typeface.

Sans serif fonts, such as Arial, have clean outlines, without any direct decorative features. They work best for titles, headings and other text that will be read in larger sizes (such as notices).

Arial is an example of a sans serif typeface.

Also resist the temptation to use cursive type, which is very difficult to read and distracting for the reader.

This typeface, for example, is much less clear than Times New Roman.
This is particularly the case when it is not in a large size.

Finally, styles such as Comic Sans are used regularly for material which is widely distributed—do not use them for formal writing, as they make your writing appear immature.

No matter how serious the topic, this font looks childish.

Readable typeface sizes

Be sure that your text is printed in a reasonable size. A point size of 12 works well with most typefaces. Anything smaller may not be readable on the printed page. Anything larger will begin to look childish. Your headings should be in a larger size than the body text, but not excessively so. If you are given a page limit, rather than a word limit, the temptation might be to use a larger point size to use up space. Resist this.

Line spacing

Many institutions will require double-spaced essays, although modern word processing software can easily produce more legible layouts, such as 1, 1.15, and 1.5 spacing. If you find that this is more readable, check whether or not it is acceptable and use it if you can.

Avoid underlines

Underlining does not belong in printed work. It is a hangover from manual typewriters. It is a very sensible thing to do when handwriting, as a form of emphasis, but in print it cuts across the 'descenders' (the portions of some letters such as y and g which lie below the line) and makes the text less readable. Use **bold** and *italics* as a means of emphasis instead, but do not overuse these or use them both together unless there is a good reason to do so.

Lots of whitespace

You should ensure that the finished document has plenty of white space, which makes the text seem less intimidating and is easier on the eye. You can do this by leaving space between paragraphs (your word processor can probably automatically do this, so that the space can be less than a full line) and by leaving space around headings. If your document is long, consider having a page break after each principal section or chapter. Giving your text space to 'breathe' will make a significant difference to its readability.

CITATIONS

WHEN AND WHY DO LEGAL WRITERS CITE?

Legal writers cite for two primary reasons: 1) authority, and 2) attribution. In academic or essay writing, they cite using footnotes.[6] You might think that you only need to include citations and footnotes where you have directly quoted language from another source. This, however, is not the case. In fact, you should avoid excessive quotation, bearing in mind the writer's maxim that language should be quoted only where it 'says something so beautifully that it bears repeating', and instead paraphrase the source. If you paraphrase a source, be it a case, an article, a book, a blog or a newspaper, you must always cite the place from which you take your information.

1) Authority: Legal writing is extensively documented. Virtually all propositions of fact or law must include a citation to a source that provides authority. These citations will typically be to primary sources (ie constitutional or treaty provisions, statutes and case law). In some essays, this may mean a footnote to almost every sentence. You must back up every statement except those that are very widely accepted.

In a seminal English case, the appellant purchased and drank a portion of a bottle of ginger beer in which she ultimately discovered the remains of a small snail and subsequently suffered shock and gastro-enteritis.[31]

[31] *Donoghue v Stevenson* [1932] AC 562 (HL), 566.

In Ireland, there is a constitutional right to marital privacy.[45]

[45] *McGee v Attorney General* [1974] IR 284 (SC).

There is no authority required for the following statements:
In Ireland, there is a written Constitution.
There are seven days in the week.

The first example demonstrates that, when facts are taken from a case and referred to in legal writing, the relevant case and specific page number on which they appear must be cited. The second example demonstrates that every statement of law—even if it seems obvious or self-evident—must be supported by reference to the primary legal source from which it originates. The only exceptions to this rule are statements of pure, original argument, general common knowledge and concluding comments.

---

[6] See generally, Elizabeth Fajans and Mary Falk, *Scholarly Writing for Law Students* (2nd edn, West Publishing 2000). Much of this discussion is adapted from that text, where these issues are explained in greater detail, though from an American perspective.

In terms of what is common knowledge, a good rule of thumb is that if the 'man on the Clapham omnibus' would be aware of it, then it is common knowledge. Thus, the fact that we have a Constitution in Ireland would be common knowledge; the fact that there are 26 counties in Ireland is common knowledge; and the fact that we have a President is common knowledge. Any information which engages more substantially with the issue requires a reference: thus, the fact that the State is required to provide a residence for the President under the Constitution would require a reference to that constitutional provision.

2) Attribution: In addition to needing citations to primary authorities, scholarly works typically build upon and advance ongoing legal debates and are likewise crucially important to legal writing. As such, you are expected to rely on and to engage with scholarly writing—books and, perhaps more importantly because of their tighter focus and more frequent release, journal articles—in your own writing.

You need to include citations to scholarly works whenever you borrow, refer to or engage with the ideas contained in them. When you do this, you may agree, disagree or take a nuanced view of the arguments advanced by the previous writer. Regardless, when the ideas are introduced for the first time, whether by way of quotation or paraphrasing, you must cite them and thereby provide appropriate attribution to the previous author's own original thoughts and ideas.

Some observers have argued persuasively that the reticence of the current Irish Supreme Court to recognise and enforce socio-economic rights is rooted in a conservative or neo-liberal ideology.[23] Although compelling, their analysis overlooks the strong argument articulated by many judges that the Constitution has been designed so that socio-economic rights are to be enforced by the legislature, not the judiciary.[24]

[23] Shivaun Quinlivan and Mary Keys, 'Official Indifference and Persistent Procrastination: An Analysis of Sinnott' (2002) 2 Judicial Studies Institute Journal 163, 183.
[24] Ronan Keane, 'Judges as Lawmakers: The Irish Experience' (2004) 4 Judicial Studies Institute Journal 1, 15–16.

The example demonstrates how writers can, and should, use the ideas contained in scholarly works in their own writing to justify their own arguments. Be careful about when you cite reference material, such as encyclopaedias: these can be used to explain the consensus on a topic but are not necessarily definitive. Be particularly careful about citing web-based resources such as Wikipedia; although often high-quality and very useful starting points for your research, these are not reliable and should not be cited in your work.

Footnotes can be useful to include additional explanatory information that might not be relevant enough to warrant inclusion in the main text, but provide valuable supplementary information. One example might be to include a brief recitation of facts from a case cited as authority for a proposition of law in the text. You should be careful, however, not to overload footnotes with extraneous and unnecessary information, or to use them as a way to evade word count limits. (Most lecturers will not count text in footnotes towards a word count unless you attempt to use this leeway to sneak large amounts of extra text into the essay.)

One of the key ways of conducting legal research is to 'follow the footnote'. When reading an article, your primary aim is to understand, analyse and contextualise what the author is arguing. However, when legal writers make arguments, they rely on other sources to reinforce those arguments. The secondary aim, then, is to identify which of the sources are relevant to your own research. It is these sources that you will 'follow'. Sometimes when you read the article, you will quickly realise that it is not relevant to your own work. Sometimes, however, you will find that by 'following the footnote', you have discovered a new way of analysing the issue.

When you conduct research in this way, there are a number of important points to understand. The first is that you should never simply rely on what the original author wrote about the piece, even if there is an extensive quote. When we write, we write with an aim, and if you take a quotation out of context in this way, it may not make sense for what you are writing. For this reason, you must always read the article or source that you are following. There are two exceptions to this general rule. The first is where you are writing about the first author's opinion of the second piece. Here, it is acceptable to say, 'Smith utterly rejects Jones' argument that the Constitution should be amended to protect the individual rights of children.' In order to conduct thorough research, however, you should read Jones' piece to understand what her arguments were, and why exactly Smith rejected them (and if Smith properly understood what Jones was saying). The second exception is where you simply cannot locate the second source. This will happen infrequently—you should be able to locate the source through your library (or on inter-library loan) or on the internet. Occasionally, however, you will come across a source which you simply cannot locate. This could be an unreported case from the 1960s or an out-of-print book. (Reported cases and journal articles, no matter what the jurisdiction, will nearly always be available). On these few occasions where you cannot locate the source, but you wish to refer to the piece nonetheless, it is important to cite the material appropriately. You should *never* cite a source you have not personally read. If you cannot locate the source, the appropriate way to cite is:

Jones, *Children's Rights and the Constitution* (Stoneage Press 1942) 15 as cited in Smith, 'Contemporary Understandings of Family Law in Ireland' (2011) 12(3) Family L 3.

GETTING CITATIONS RIGHT

For your citations to be useful to another reader, they must be correct, which means that they must be complete, accurate and consistent. For a full explanation of what is required for citations, we recommend that you use the OSCOLA Ireland style guide, which is included as an appendix to this book and is also available at <www.legalcitation.ie>. However, check with your lecturer if he or she has other preferences. What follows are some brief notes on how you get citations right. For the full details of what is required, see OSCOLA Ireland.

A complete citation provides the reader with all of the information that he or she needs to find the document that you refer to, either in a library or on the internet, and to find the particular page or passage that you rely on. To be able to provide complete citations, you need to take full notes as you research. Get into this habit early, as it will save you difficulty in large research projects.

You need to take care to ensure that your citations are accurate, particularly small details like volume and issue numbers. It is very easy to make a mistake with these. Check and double-check them.

It is also very important to be consistent in the way that you present your citations. The inconsistency can be small—sometimes giving first names, sometimes using initials only—but it will be noticed and it will cost you marks. Again, follow OSCOLA Ireland or some other recognised standard and you should not have any difficulty.

In the same way that every judgment given by a court will have a 'code' which helps readers find the case, journal articles have a similar 'code'. No matter how you source your material (online or in paper), the 'code' will be exactly the same. If you find the article on Westlaw IE, for example, it is *never* appropriate to simply have 'www.westlaw.ie' in your footnote. Every article written for a legal journal will be cited in exactly the same way. If you find the article online, cannot find other citation information and are sure that the document was not published on paper, only then should you include the full URL to the website where you found the material. Look at the OSCOLA Ireland Appendix to see how to cite this type of document.

In terms of referencing, there are two distinct types of journal. Some will have a number of editions each year, while others will have one edition each year. Yet others will have a number of editions each year, but they will be numbered consecutively, so that, for example, the first edition will start at page 1 and end at page 187, with the second edition starting at page 188.

Each of these three types of journal are cited slightly differently, but the general principle remains the same for each. Similarly, some journals are so well-known that an acronym is sufficient—though you should always list the acronyms you use in a preliminary or bibliographic section of your writing. Always indicate the first and last name of the author, including initials where the author uses them in the text itself. Ensure that you read carefully through the OSCOLA Ireland Appendix so that you are familiar with the finer details of citing these sources.

Cases

The general format for cases is:

Name of Case in Italics [year] court case-number, [year] volume report-series first-page

Name of Case in Italics [year] volume report-series first-page (abbreviation-of-court)

Therefore, a recent case from the Supreme Court of Ireland which has been given a case number and which is reported in the *Irish Reports* would be cited as:

Riordan v Ireland [2009] IESC 44, [2009] 3 IR 745

An older case from the same court but without a case number is cited with the abbreviation of the court at the end in brackets:

Doran v Delaney [1998] 2 IR 61 (SC)

A High Court case which is reported in the *Irish Law Reports Monthly* would be cited as:

Friends of the Curragh Environment Ltd v An Bord Pleanála (No 2) [2006] IEHC 390, [2007] 1 ILRM 386

It should always be clear to the reader which court the decision comes from.

Articles

The general principle is:

Name of Author, 'Name of Article' (Year) Volume of Journal (Edition of Journal) Name of Journal (or Acronym of Journal) Page number

Thus, this article by Dickson would be cited as follows, as the NILQ has consecutive page numbering:

Brice Dickson, 'Positive Obligations and the European Court of Human Rights' (2010) 61 NILQ 203

or

Brice Dickson, 'Positive Obligations and the European Court of Human Rights' (2010) 61 Northern Ireland Legal Quarterly 203

An article in the Judicial Studies Institute Journal, which restarts page numbering with each issue, would be cited as follows:

Peter Charleton, 'Employment Injunctions: An Over-loose Discretion' (2009) 9(2) JSIJ 1

or

Peter Charleton, 'Employment Injunctions: An Over-loose Discretion' (2009) 9(2) Judicial Studies Institute Journal 1

Books

Books follow the following format:

Name of Author, *Title of Book* (Edition, Publishing House, Year of Publication)

Where the book is in its first edition, or there is no edition specified, then it follows the following format:

Name of Author, *Title of Book* (Publishing House, Year of Publication)

Examples of these are:

Bryan McMahon and William Binchy, *The Law of Torts* (3rd edn, Butterworths 2000)

Eoin Carolan, *The New Separation of Powers: A Theory for the Modern State* (Oxford University Press, 2009)

Edited collections are cited as follows:

Eoin O'Dell (ed), *Leading Cases of the Twentieth Century* (Round Hall Sweet & Maxwell, 2000)

Again, ensure that you read carefully through the OSCOLA Ireland Appendix so that you are familiar with the finer details of citing these sources.

> ■ To test your ability to cite correctly, go to <www.legalwriting.ie> and complete Assignment 6.1.

GETTING QUOTATIONS RIGHT

When you cite directly from another source, you must get the citation exactly right. If you discover a mistake, misspelling or American usage, you should reproduce the statement exactly. If you believe that the mistake requires some clarification, then you should make this clarification in the footnote.

HOW TO TYPESET QUOTATIONS

Follow the instructions in section 1.5 of OSCOLA Ireland when typesetting quotations.

BIBLIOGRAPHIES

For some essays, you will need to provide a bibliography. This is a list of all of the works that were consulted during the research. It is not always required, but you must check with your lecturer before you start. It can be quite time-consuming to prepare. Do not leave it all to be done just before you hand your work in.

You should include all of the books and articles that you read and found useful, even if you did not directly cite them. Your lecturer may prefer to see these divided into categories of documents. You may also need to include a table of cases, legislation and other primary materials that were relevant, although this is rare.

Do not include a general vague citation to a website. <www.google.com> does not belong in a bibliography. You may have found material through that search engine, but that information is no use to the reader. You can cite web-based documents (OSCOLA Ireland includes full guidelines for this) but these citations need to be very specific, so that other researchers can find your references easily.

If you can cite a printed version of a document that is available online, use the printed version in preference. It is not as likely to change. Assume that your reader will know that the document is available online and will use electronic services if that makes more sense to him or her.

REFERENCING PREVIOUSLY CITED MATERIAL

One of the aspects of legal citations that is distinctive is the use of back-references. Lawyers will cite extensively but also like to refer back to a previous citation rather than repeat it in full. See section 1.2 of OSCOLA Ireland for full instructions on how to do this. To avoid mistakes, when you are writing include full details in all footnotes and review when you have finished writing, or use bibliographic software to automate the generation of back references.

As you read for your essays, you will encounter what OSCOLA calls 'Latin gadgets' such as supra, infra, ante, id, op cit and loc cit. These were once very common but are now used less and less. Except for ibid, do not use them unless your lecturer requires you to. They make it difficult to decipher a citation and, without footnote numbers, tracking down the information required to find a document can involve careful reading of all of the preceding footnotes. The most common 'Latin gadgets' are set out below, so that you can understand them when you encounter them.

Latin phrase	Meaning
supra	Above, usually with a footnote number
infra	Below, usually with a footnote number
id	The same
ibid	In the same place
op cit	In the work cited
loc cit	In the place cited

AUTOMATING REFERENCING

One of the key advantages of using computer technology is that it can help to make tedious tasks manageable and sometimes very easy. This is particularly the case with referencing. The citation guide presented in this book is based on a UK standard known as OSCOLA. As this is now widely used in the UK and Ireland, many software tools are developing the ability to cite using the OSCOLA formats. This means that you do not have to worry about your footnotes being correct, and the software will automatically generate a bibliography for you. In the early stages of your career as a law student, this may not seem that important, but as you move on to writing substantial pieces with lengthy lists of references, the saving in time and heartache can be considerable. It is therefore worth putting the effort in to learn how to use these tools and make them a consistent part of your workflow.

Software develops and changes at a rapid pace, and therefore a full discussion of how to use these tools would be both very long and quickly out-of-date. However, your law librarian or instructor may know more about these tools and other options, and may be able to provide training.

If you would like to try these tools on your own, a very good place to start is the OSCOLA website page devoted to software tools at <www.law.ox.ac. uk/content/oscola-styles-endnote-latek-refworks-and-zotero>. This contains information on, and links to, styles that can be used with EndNote, LaTeX, and RefWorks. It also mentions Zotero, but at the time that this book is written, this information is somewhat out-of-date. Some information is also available on <legalcitation.ie>.

EndNote is a popular commercial reference management package which can interface directly with online databases and with your word processing software. RefWorks is a web-based tool with similar functionality to EndNote. Both of these require payment but your institution may have a site licence. Ask in your library to find out if they are available.

LaTeX is a type-setting program rather than a word-processing package. It has a long history and a wide range of 'packages' which provide advanced functionality. It is very technical and not easy to learn, but can produce beautiful and complex documents once you master it. If it interests you, there is a wealth of information available at <www.latex-project.org>.

Zotero is a free tool which can manage references, documents and interface with some online databases. You can learn more about it at <www.zotero.org>. There is a special version of Zotero for lawyers, which used to be known as Multi-Lingual Zotero (or MLZ) but is now known as Juris-M. At the time this book is written, Juris-M is still under active development, but by the time you read this, a stable version should be available at <juris-m.github.io>. Although it has some rough edges, this tool offers a much cheaper and easy-to-use alternative to the software mentioned above.

Finally, ReadCube is a tool which provides similar functionality, and supports citations using OSCOLA Ireland, with both free and paid-for versions. If you want a simpler computer-based approach to OSCOLA citations, try <www.citethisforme.com/oscola>.

PLAGIARISM

As you work on essays throughout your career as a law researcher, you must be particularly careful to avoid plagiarism. This is probably the most serious offence that you can commit in an academic context. There are many different definitions of what constitutes plagiarism. Your institution should have a plagiarism policy which will contain a definition. You should read this before continuing further.

At a basic level, all of these definitions and policies mean: do not claim other people's work as your own. There are two general types of plagiarism: *overt*, which is copying word for word; and *disguised*, which is basically bad referencing. This means that you must be careful to provide proper references for any information that you rely on.

Simply copying another person's text word-for-word in your essay is intellectual dishonesty, can lead to disciplinary proceedings, and you should never contemplate it. Excessive paraphrasing, or summaries that are not properly attributed, are a symptom of lazy or sloppy research habits. If you are making summaries of material that you read as you research, be sure to take full and complete notes of the sources that you were working on, so that when you are finally writing up your essay, you do not accidentally mix in text written by someone else. This is good practice generally; otherwise you may end up with an excellent quote, argument or piece of information that you cannot use in your essay because you have not recorded the source.

In the context of modern information technology, it is easy to copy and paste from other sources, particularly websites, but this also constitutes plagiarism (and is also a risky strategy because not all the information found on the web is reliable). Be very careful to avoid plagiarism as it can have serious consequences for your career, during and after your time in education. Many institutions do use specialised software to detect it.

Sample Essays

As an appendix to this chapter, there are three sample essays. These are intended to be representative of the types of essays that you might write in first, second and third year of a law degree. You should regard them as sources of inspiration rather than a model to slavishly copy. There are many ways to approach writing an essay and you are not required to follow all of our suggestions. You should also note that the essays are not perfect and could be improved upon.

Further Reading

- Cahillane L and Schweppe J, *Legal Research Methods: Principles and Practicalities* (Clarus Press 2016)
- Foster S, *How to Write Better Law Essays* (2nd edn, Pearson Longman 2009)
- Gowers E, *The Complete Plain Words* (2nd edn, Pelican 1973)
- McConville M and Chui WH, *Research Methods for Law* (Edinburgh University Press 2007)
- Strunk W and White EB, *The Elements of Style* (3rd edn, Macmillan 1979)

Sample Essay: Should the Supreme Court of Ireland Follow a Strict Rule of Stare Decisis?

> This is an example of a short essay, without extensive citation, which might be written as an introductory exercise in legal research.

Introduction

This essay considers the application and operation of stare decisis in the Supreme Court of Ireland. It explores its advantages and disadvantages. It concludes that the Court's liberal policy is the most appropriate middle ground and should be continued without changes.

> The essay begins with a clear 'road map' for what is to come. The reader is clear about the argument that will be made, how it will be approached and the conclusion that the author will reach. Academic essays should not contain surprises or plot twists.

Stare Decisis

Precedent is how the common law develops. Unlike civil law systems, which are rooted in written codes intended to cover all circumstances, the common law is based on general customs. Judges built these into a relatively coherent body of law. This involved drawing analogies between different situations so that the law developed in a rational, consistent and predictable manner.

> The essay then makes a general statement about the subject matter. This is a good way of setting the context for the discussion that is to come.

Application and Operation

An old case that is similar to a current one is known as a precedent. Precedent can be either binding, which must be followed, or persuasive, which can be followed at the judge's discretion.

> Another good way to begin, as is being demonstrated here, is with a definition. This makes it clear to the reader what the author understands the topic under discussion to be and helps make communication clear.

When considering how binding a precedent is, a judge must consider two things. The first is how close an analogy she can draw with the previous case. This turns on the reason for the decision (or ratio decidendi) in the previous case. A precedent is authority only for the legal principle based on the facts of the case which both is a necessary part of the decision and which is treated as such by the original court. Everything else is a comment 'by-the-way' (or obiter dictum) and is not binding on later courts.

Also, precedent operates within a hierarchy of courts. Confusingly, the Latin phrase stare decisis ('let the decision stand') is used here with two meanings. First, for precedent operating *vertically*: Supreme Court decisions bind the High Court and so on down.[1] Second, for precedent operating *horizontally*: judgments from the same court may be binding on that court in the future.

> Note the use of 'two things', 'Also' and 'First'/'Second' as linking phrases, to keep the reader oriented and interested, so that it is easy to follow the chain of topics.

STARE DECISIS IN THE SUPREME COURT

The most important aspect of the operation of stare decisis in the Court, therefore, is the extent to which past decisions are binding. A strict policy means that the Court cannot change or overturn its own decisions, as was the case in the English courts until well into the 20th century and here until the mid-1960s.

In *The State (Quinn) v Ryan*,[2] the Supreme Court held that s 29 of the Petty Sessions (Ireland) Act 1851 was unconstitutional despite having already upheld it in two previous decisions.[3] The Court declared that it was free to decide its own policy on stare decisis and to apply it less strictly than the English House of Lords if it wished.

Although *Ryan* was a constitutional case, *Attorney General v Ryan's Car Hire*[4] made it clear that the relaxation of stare decisis was not limited to these cases. In *McNamara v Electricity Supply Board*,[5] the Court indicated that it would overrule past decisions if it felt that changes in social circumstances or legal understanding made that necessary. However, in *Mogul of Ireland Ltd v Tipperary (North Riding) County Council*,[6] the Court said that it must be clearly of the opinion that the old case was wrongly decided and that if a decision was widely accepted and relied upon, it might not be overruled. This was affirmed by Keane CJ in *O'Brien v Mirror Group Newspapers Ltd*,[7] although Denham

---

[1] See, for example, the comments of the Supreme Court in *The People (DPP) v Rock* [1994] 1 ILRM 66 (SC) at 72, which make it clear that the Circuit Court is bound by decisions of the Court of Criminal Appeal even where there are conflicting High Court decisions.

[2] [1965] IR 110 (SC).

[3] *The State (Dowling) v Kingston (No 2)* [1937] IR 699 (SC) and *The State (Duggan) v Tapley* [1952] IR 62 (SC).

[4] [1965] IR 642 (SC).

[5] [1964] IR 269 (SC).

[6] [1976] IR 260 (SC).

[7] [2001] 1 IR 1 (SC).

and Keane JJ indicated in *SPUC v Grogan (No 5)* that there may be more latitude in constitutional cases.[8]

Here the author engages in doctrinal analysis, tracing the development of a legal principle through a number of cases and showing how a rule has been clarified by later decisions. Note how each case is mentioned by name and full references are given in the footnotes.

ADVANTAGES AND DISADVANTAGES OF STARE DECISIS

Advantages

A strict policy has four advantages:
- *Stable development*: Because past decisions are not overturned, the law develops in a measured way.
- *Predictability*: Because lawyers can be confident that the courts will follow past decisions, they can give clear advice to their clients.
- *Equality*: Because similar cases are decided in the same way, all persons are treated equally by the courts.
- *Efficiency*: The courts do not have to consider every issue in a case in detail as they can apply previously-accepted rules.

Disadvantages

It also has four disadvantages:
- *Preventing change*: Because past decisions cannot be overruled, the law cannot change quickly even though society may require this.
- *Forcing legislative intervention*: Thus, legislation is the only way to deal with changing social circumstances or opinions.
- *Causing injustice to individuals*: Out-of-date precedent may lead to injustice in individual cases, particularly if society has changed.
- *Over-distinguishing of cases*: Sometimes judges will limit the applicability of a precedent by *distinguishing* it, claiming that the circumstances are different to the case they are deciding. This is sometimes used to quietly overrule a case. These disguised changes make it hard to understand the law.

Note how the author uses a list to set out the two sides to an argument in a clear fashion. Some readers may not like this, as it makes the document read less fluidly. Whether or not you adopt it is a choice for you. There is no one correct way to write, and you should develop your own style.

---

[8]   [1988] 4 IR 343 (SC).

Conclusion

The Supreme Court has moved from a strict policy of stare decisis to a more flexible one. While it is clear that continuity of judicial decisions is vital for the stability of the legal system, it is important that a court of final appeal can overrule its past decisions where they are clearly wrong. This helps it to avoid injustice and protect constitutional rights. Therefore, the Supreme Court's current policy is the correct one and should be continued.

The essay ends with a summary of the argument, to ensure that the reader remembers what was said. This is perhaps not necessary for a short essay, but it is a good habit to develop. The essay also comes to a clear conclusion which directly responds to the title.

Bibliography

Byrne R and McCutcheon P, *The Irish Legal System* (6th edn, Butterworths 2014)

Note that the bibliography contains only secondary materials—none of the case law cited in the essay is listed—and lists a book that is not actually cited in the footnotes for the essay. The book was a key source when researching the essay and should therefore be acknowledged in the bibliography.

Sample Essay: The Preamble of the Constitution has no Place in a Modern Secular Democracy. Discuss.

Introduction

The Preamble to the Constitution of Ireland is a product of its time. In the context of today's Ireland, there are two main problems: first, like the rest of the Constitution it is gendered and could be interpreted as misogynistic; second, it is explicitly Christian, which is not appropriate in a multicultural secular democracy.

> In the first paragraph, the author outlines her basic understanding of the question, and how she intends approaching the question.

In discussing the problematic aspects of the Constitution, this essay will consider these issues under three broad themes: first, what function or purpose a Preamble has in a Constitution; second, whether the Preamble has any legal significance; and finally, what the views of the Constitution Review Group were in this regard. It will conclude by arguing that, given the society in which we live today, the Preamble to the Constitution could be viewed and interpreted as exclusionary and divisive, and thus has no place in the Constitution.

> In this second paragraph, the author provides a simple summary of the article, and what she will do.

What is the Purpose of a Preamble?

> The Constitution Review Group will be used a lot through the essay: for this reason, the author includes an acronym in brackets that will be used instead of the full name of the group.

The Constitution Review Group (CRG) noted that a Preamble is not essential to a Constitution—indeed, the only part of it that has any formal significance is the enactment phrase, 'We, the People, enact this Constitution'.[1] While it has no formal purpose, the CRG noted that it:

> is intended to express a sense of national identity and destiny and to include invocational, commemorative, exhortatory and aspirational elements.[2]

---

[1] Constitution Review Group, *Report of the Constitution Review Group* (1996), 1.
[2] ibid.

Certainly, at the time of the enactment, the Preamble most likely did fulfil these criteria, clearly expressing a sense of national identity ('the rightful independence of our Nation') and aspirational elements ('true social order attained, the unity of our country restored').

Note here how the author backs up her statement by reference to the primary text. It shows how, in one sense, the Preamble fulfils its purpose.

However, if we look at the Ireland of today, the Preamble cannot possibly be understood to express a sense of national identity. First, it is exclusionary of women, referring only to 'actions of men' and 'our father'; and, as with the rest of the Constitution, uses a binary understanding of gender out of place in Ireland today. Second, in a multicultural society and a secular democracy, the Constitution could be seen to be immediately exclusionary, with the first eight words of the text reading, 'In the Name of the Most Holy Trinity'; further, an entire paragraph of the Constitution reads, 'Humbly acknowledging all our obligations to our Divine Lord, Jesus Christ, Who sustained our fathers through centuries of trial...' In 1972, references to the 'special position' of the Catholic Church in Article 44 were removed by referendum as an acknowledgment that no one religion should be preferred over another.[3]

Note here how the author places the specific issue in a broader context.

Forde and Leonard state that, so far, 'the more heterodox religious make-up of the Irish has not given rise to major constitutional difficulties.'[4] While they may be, strictly speaking, correct, the absence of any problematic litigation is not a justification for an exclusionary Preamble which is intended to, and expected to, express a sense of national identity. Indeed, in *Norris* O'Higgins CJ stated:

> It cannot be doubted that the people, so asserting and acknowledging [in the Preamble] their obligations to Our Divine Lord Jesus Christ, were proclaiming a deeply religious conviction and faith and an intention to adopt a Constitution consistent with that conviction and faith and with Christian beliefs.[5]

---

[3] Gerard Hogan and Gerry Whyte, *JM Kelly: The Irish Constitution* (4th edn, Lexis Nexis 2003) 2034.

[4] Michael Forde and David Leonard, *Constitutional Law of Ireland* (3rd edn, Bloomsbury 2013) 634.

[5] *Norris v Attorney General* [1984] IR 36 (SC) 64.

This, of course, raises the question of who this definition of 'the people' includes and excludes.[6] A comparison of the census data from 1936 and 2011 shows, first, that the people of Ireland were not universally Christian or Catholic then; and second, that they have become much more diverse with the passing of time, with many denominations which are now numerous simply unrecorded in the past.[7]

	1936	2011
Total	2,968,420	4,588,252
Catholic	2,773,920	3,861,335
Church of Ireland	145,030	134,365
Muslim		49,204
Orthodox		45,223
Presbyterian	28,097	24,600
Apostolic or Pentecostal		14,043
Hindu		10,688
Buddhist		8,703
Methodist	9,649	6,842
Jehovah's Witness		6,149
Lutheran		5,683
Evangelical		4,188
Atheist		3,905
Baptist		3,531
Agnostic		3,521
Jewish	3,749	1,984
Pantheist		1,940
Latter Day Saints		1,284
Quaker		925
Baha'i		520
Brethren		336
Other	8,005	56,558
No religion		269,811
Not stated		72,914

---

[6] Garrett Barden, 'We, The People ...' (2012) 48 Irish Jurist (ns) 323.
[7] Central Statistics Office, *Census 2011 Profile 7 Religion, Ethnicity and Irish Travellers – Ethnic and cultural background in Ireland* (2012) 47.

The use of demographic, economic or other statistical data is somewhat unusual in law essays, but it often helps to strengthen an argument. If you have a good grounding in research from another discipline, by all means use that when it seems appropriate.

DOES THE PREAMBLE HAVE ANY LEGAL SIGNIFICANCE?

While a Preamble is not *required,* the next question to ask is, when one is included in the Constitution, if it has any legal significance. In this context, a question that has arisen is the value of the Preamble in determining questions of law.

Note that here, the author links to the previous section.

Hogan and Whyte observe that the Preamble cannot in and of itself be the basis upon which litigation is founded, but rather than the text can add to the understanding and interpretation of other aspects of the Constitution:

> On no occasion has a decision been based solely on [the Preamble], but it has been used to lay the ground for the deployment of later parts of the Constitution, or to underpin judgments rhetorically and emotionally.[8]

There are a number of examples of this. O'Byrne J stated in *Buckley v Attorney General*:

> These most laudable objects [expressed in the Preamble] seem to us to inform the various Articles of the Constitution, and we are of opinion that, so far as possible, the Constitution should be so construed as to give them life and reality.[9]

Davitt P in *Attorney General v Southern Industrial Trust* stated:

> ... the justice or otherwise of any legislative interference with the right has to be considered in relation, *inter alia*, to the proclaimed objects with which the Constitution was enacted, including the promotion of the common good.[10]

In *Magee v Attorney General*, Henchy J used the Preamble to ensure a marital right to privacy. The case concerned the question as to whether an

---

[8] Hogan and Whyte (n 3) 53.
[9] [1950] IR 67 (SC) 80–81.
[10] (1960) 95 ILTR 161 (HC) 168.

Act prohibiting the importation of contraceptives was in breach of an alleged right to marital privacy. He stated that the Act was indeed unconstitutional in light of the right to marital privacy he found to exist, and went on to state that the position the plaintiff found herself in was contrary to the Preamble, which 'proclaims as one of its aims the dignity and freedom of the individual'.[11]

Problematically, and in a judgment which used the Preamble in an exclusionary manner, in *Norris v Ireland*, O'Higgins CJ stated:

> ... the preamble indicated an acceptance of Christian values which militated against the conclusion that in adopting the Constitution the people rendered inoperative laws which had existed for hundreds of years prohibiting unnatural sexual conduct which Christian teaching held to be gravely sinful.[12]

In addition, writing extra-judicially, O'Hanlon J based his explicitly Catholic theory of constitutional rights and statutory interpretation on the reference to the Holy Trinity in the Preamble.[13] While this conclusion was criticised by academic commentators,[14] the controversy shows how a text that seems initially to be without legal force can powerfully shape the development of the law.[15]

SHOULD THE PREAMBLE BE AMENDED?

The CRG asked whether the Preamble should be amended. It noted that there are four possible approaches that could be adopted:[16]

1. Leave the Preamble as it is.
   The CRG felt that the language was overly-reflective of 1930s' language, the Roman Catholic ethos, and too nationalistic and gender-biased in nature.
2. Insert an explicit provision in the Constitution declaring the Preamble to be the historical introduction in 1937 to the Constitution, with the corollary that it would also be declared no longer cognisable by the courts.

---

[11] [1974] IR 284 (SC) 326.

[12] [1985] IR 36 (SC) 64.

[13] Roderick O'Hanlon, 'Natural Rights and the Irish Constitution' (1993) 11 Irish Law Times (ns) 8.

[14] Tim Murphy, 'Democracy, Natural Law and the Irish Constitution' (1993) 11 Irish Law Times (ns) 81 and Desmond M. Clarke, 'The Constitution and Natural Law: A Reply to Mr Justice O'Hanlon' (1993) 11 Irish Law Times (ns) 177. There is a response in Roderick O'Hanlon, 'The Judiciary and the Moral Law' (1993) 11 Irish Law Times (ns) 129.

[15] Eoin Daly, *Religion, Law and the Irish State* (Clarus Press, 2012) 28.

[16] Constitution Review Group (n 1) 2–4.

3. While adopting 1 or 2, leave amendment of the terms of the Preamble to a future inspirational political context.

   While this would be a good idea, most members thought that the Preamble should be amended anyway in the near future, which is the fourth option.

4. Amend the Preamble

   The majority thought that this should happen, and noted that there were two options open:

   A   Confine the Preamble to the words of enactment 'by the people of Ireland'.

   Favoured by the majority, who felt that the substantive elements of the Preamble were expressly provided for in the various articles of the Constitution. 'The recitation of such desiderata in the Preamble tends to be both selective and superfluous.'

   B   If it is felt that a revised version of the Preamble should be prepared, the essentially political nature of a Preamble should be kept in mind and care taken to avoid divisiveness and to recognise, instead, diversity of traditions, ideals and aspirations.

Reflecting on these proposals, Professor Richard Barrett highlights how increased clarity around the role of the Church in public life could assist rather than damage that significant institution.[17]

CONCLUSION

While the Preamble to the Constitution does not have the legal weight of the fundamental rights provisions (Articles 40–44), it is nonetheless significant: it sets the scene and tone for what follows, and has therefore been used by the courts as a guide to interpretation. Given its explicitly patriarchal and religious language, it excludes women and non-Christians. It was arguably not appropriate for the Ireland of 1937, which was more diverse than was generally acknowledged at the time, and is certainly no longer appropriate for the Ireland of today, which is much more secular, pluralist and open to women. The best option is that put forward by the CRG, to amend the text to reflect this new conception of Ireland as no longer dominated by one religion or gender.

Note how the essay finishes with a strong and definite conclusion. The reader is left in no doubt about how the author thinks about the issue, the reasons for her argument or what the author would like to see happen as a result.

---

[17] Richard Barrett, 'Church and State in Light of the Report of the Irish Constitution Review Group' (1998) 20 Dublin University Law Journal 51, 71.

Sample Essay: Extra-judicial Comment by Judges

This is an example of an essay that embodies many of the principles discussed above. It is based on an article published at (2005) 5(1) Judicial Studies Institute Journal 199. The preceding essays have contained additional notes to highlight the stylistic choices being made. This essay does not contain this level of detail, so that you can search for and find these points yourself.

Introduction

The issue of what judges may say (or write) when they are not on the bench is an important one but one that is rarely considered in Ireland. This is probably so for a number of reasons. The primary reason for this is that there are no rules governing such conduct, which makes it difficult to begin dealing with it. The lack of judgments and academic writings on the topic means that there is little clarity in the area. In addition, judges have traditionally been very reticent off the bench, something which is slowly changing.

Perhaps this reticence means that the limits to extra-judicial speech or comment by judges are not of great moment in Ireland. Nonetheless, there have been some significant controversies involving remarks by judges here and in neighbouring jurisdictions in recent times. Given the possible establishment of a Judicial Council with responsibility for regulating judicial conduct and ethics,[1] it is perhaps time that we looked at the topic in the Irish context.

This article looks at recent occasions where extra-judicial speech has been an issue of public comment in Ireland. It then examines case law from other jurisdictions, focusing on examples from common law countries and looking in some detail at the American experience where formal rules have been drawn up and applied to a large number of cases. It attempts to distil these into a theory of how extra-judicial comment should be limited and to provide practical guidance.

Why should Judges Speak off the Bench?

By speaking publicly, judges expose themselves as liable to accusations of bias and perhaps to having their decisions overturned on appeal. The boundaries of what they should and should not say or write when they are not on the bench are not clear. As a result, many judges prefer not to speak

---

[1] The *Report of the Committee on Judicial Conduct and Ethics* (Pn 9449, Stationery Office 2000) called for the establishment of a Judicial Council which would deal with judicial salaries and working conditions, education and discipline.

or write extra-judicially and follow the convention that judges should not make public pronouncements or statements when they are not sitting.

On consideration, however, if judges were to take this stance, they would deny public access to a considerable body of expertise built up from a particularly important perspective within the justice system. From their unique vantage point, judges have much valuable experience to share with others and can begin or make vital contributions to debates on issues central to our democracy.[2] It could be argued that judges have a duty to work for the improvement of the administration of justice,[3] and it was once customary for English judges to meet regularly and provide recommendations for reform.[4] There are, therefore, certain topics on which it is appropriate for them to comment, although the manner and means must be carefully chosen.

EXTRA-JUDICIAL SPEECH BY IRISH JUDGES

There are, of course, many examples of judges engaging in public comment in Ireland. Several judges are respected authors of legal textbooks. Judges commonly write articles for legal periodicals such as the 'Bar Review' and the 'Irish Jurist'. The Judicial Studies Institute's own Journal has published articles by judges. Autobiographical writings by judges, however, are rare and avoid commentary on points of legal controversy.[5] It is interesting to note that it is common for American judges to teach in universities[6] but Irish judges almost never do.[7] This is probably because there is a greater divide between academia and practice here and because of the prohibition on a judge holding a position of emolument in Article 35.3 of the Constitution.

Judges also speak publicly, to conferences, university students and other bodies, with relative frequency. These speeches are sometimes very topical. For example, in March 2001, the Chief Justice gave a paper to UCC Law Society on 'The Irish Legal System in the 21st Century: Planning for the

---

[2] Steven Lubet, 'Professor Polonius Advises Judge Laertes: Rules, Good Taste and the Scope of Public Comment' (1989) 2 Georgetown Journal of Legal Ethics 665, 674–677.
[3] Robert B McKay, 'The Judiciary and Nonjudicial Activities' (1970) 35 Law and Contemporary Problems 9, 21.
[4] David Pannick, *Judges* (Oxford University Press 1987) 182–183.
[5] See for example Thomas F O'Higgins, *A Double Life* (Townhouse Press 1996). In America, there are 'increasing numbers of articles and speeches by judges, especially Supreme Court Justices ... in which they discuss all sorts of issues that seem likely to come before them and discuss also the views and foibles of their colleagues'. Andrew L Kaufman, 'Judicial Ethics: The Less-Often Asked Questions' (1989) 64 Washington Law Review 851, 867.
[6] Sometimes, it seems, due to economic necessity—see Kaufman (n 5) 870.
[7] It does occasionally happen in the United Kingdom. Shimon Shetreet, *Judges on Trial: A Study of the Appointment and the Accountability of the English Judiciary* (Elsevier 1976) 326.

Future', in which he was critical of the operation of the courts. Although the paper was widely reported at the time (and was subsequently published in the 'Law Society Gazette', the 'Bar Review' and the 'Judicial Studies Institute Journal'), there were no suggestions that the remarks were inappropriate.

Some extra-judicial writing has, however, brought with it considerable controversy. In 1993, Mr Justice O'Hanlon publicly disagreed with the Supreme Court decision in *Attorney General v X*,[8] in effect saying that any attempt to amend the Constitution or pass legislation to legalise abortion would be contrary to natural law.[9] The Government of the time was committed to just such a course and purported to terminate his appointment as President of the Law Reform Commission. He challenged the validity of this termination but simultaneously withdrew from the position.

In recent times, some remarks of Mr Justice Carney have attracted controversy. In a paper delivered to the National University of Ireland, Galway, he suggested abolishing the distinction between murder and manslaughter on the basis that it would greatly reduce the length of lists in the Central Criminal Court (due to the mandatory life sentence, murder defendants have no incentive to plead guilty).[10] Professor Finbarr McAuley, a member of the Law Reform Commission, criticised these comments on the grounds that it was inappropriate for a sitting judge to offer an opinion on such a controversial topic.[11] It was interesting to note that Mr Justice Carney's remarks were subsequently defended by Lord Lester of Herne Hill in a letter to *The Irish Times* in which he said:

> British judges frequently make proposals for law reform whether in their judgments or in public lectures. It has not been suggested in recent times that this is in any way against the public interest. To the contrary, their contribution is valued both by the British Law Commissions and by the wider public.[12]

In early 2004, Mr Justice Carney was due to speak at a conference in Dublin on the criminal justice system. His paper commented on the sittings of the Central Criminal Court in Limerick in late 2003. The Chief Justice, who was

---

[8] [1992] 1 IR 1 (SC).

[9] Rory O'Hanlon, 'Natural Rights and the Irish Constitution' (1993) 11 ILT 8.

[10] Carol Coulter, 'Judge Calls for Single Charge of Unlawful Killing: Area of Contest Hinges on Manslaughter or Murder' *The Irish Times* (Dublin, 30 October 2003). The paper was subsequently published in the 'Bar Review': see Paul Carney, Decriminalising Murder? (2003) 8 Bar Review 254.

[11] Suzanne Breen, 'Issue is for Politicians not Judges, says Reform Commission' *The Irish Times* (Dublin, 30 October 2003). Professor McAuley subsequently clarified that he was speaking in a personal capacity and was not representing the Commission.

[12] Anthony Lester, 'Murder or Manslaughter' *The Irish Times* (Dublin, 1 November 2003).

chairing the conference, was not prepared to attend the conference if the paper was delivered as drafted. According to *The Irish Times*:

> Mr Justice Keane objected to three elements in the paper: the fact that it referred to matters in the recent past or still current; the fact that these matters may present themselves before the courts in another form; and his concern that judges should not talk in public about cases they had presided over.[13]

Mr Justice Carney did not speak at the conference.

Practical Examples

Case law can give some guidance in sketching the parameters for appropriate comment. Unfortunately, relevant common law decisions are scarce. There does not seem to be any Irish case law on the issue. There is some from neighbouring jurisdictions but even the United States, with a much more numerous judiciary, does not have a proper body of law on the topic.[14] On the other hand, in civil law jurisdictions, where judges are often civil servants and subject to explicit codes of conduct, there is a large volume of commentary and decisions,[15] but the different context makes these of limited relevance here.

Great Britain

In Great Britain, there are some cases where extra-judicial comment went beyond the boundaries of what is acceptable. Perhaps the most striking example is *Hoekstra v HM Advocate*.[16] In this case, four defendants were convicted of drugs offences in Scotland on 13 March 1997. Appeals were lodged in the Appeal Court, grounded partially on the European Convention on Human Rights and Fundamental Freedoms, but eventually rejected on 28 January 2000. Leave to appeal to the Privy Council was refused on 31 January 2000 and it was directed that a further stage of the appeal was to be heard on 6 March 2000.

---

[13] Carol Coulter, 'Limerick Trial Outcomes Cited in Carney paper' *The Irish Times* (Dublin, 1 March 2004). See also Carol Coulter, 'Chief Justice Worried About Judges Airing Cases' *The Irish Times* (Dublin, 1 March 2004): 'What the controversy reveals is the lack of any forum where the judiciary can decide collectively what should and should not be commented on publicly, and the mechanisms for maintaining any agreement arrived at.'

[14] Steven Lubet, 'Professor Polonius Advises Judge Laertes: Rules, Good Taste and the Scope of Public Comment' (1989) 2 Georgetown Journal of Legal Ethics 665, 667.

[15] See for example Michael Bohlander, 'Criticizing Judges in Germany' in Michael K Addo (ed), *Freedom of Expression and the Criticism of Judges* (Ashgate 2000) 67–68.

[16] [2000] UKHRR 578, 2000 JC 387.

One of the judges on the Appeal Court, Lord McCluskey, formally retired on 8 January 2000 but was appointed to sit as a retired judge in accordance with section 22 of the Law Reform (Miscellaneous Provisions) (Scotland) Act 1985. On 6 February 2000, the first of a series of three articles written by the judge appeared in the Scotland on Sunday newspaper. Part of this article was critical of the European Convention on Human Rights and Fundamental Freedoms and its adoption into domestic Scots law.

On 6 March 2000, at the further hearing, a motion was lodged asking the bench comprising the Court of Appeal to disqualify itself 'on the basis that justice cannot be seen to have been done in the past or be seen to be done in the future'. The case then went before a differently constituted court. Counsel for the appellants did not argue that actual bias could be detected in the original opinion of the Court of Appeal but

> ... that the Appeal Court could not be regarded as being or as having been impartial, when judged by an objective test, since there was a legitimate reason to fear a lack of impartiality in view of the terms of the article written by one of its members.

After considering the relevant tests in English and Scots law and the language of the article, the court concluded

> ... that the article, published very shortly after the decision in the appeal, would create in the mind of an informed observer an apprehension of bias on the part of Lord McCluskey against the Convention and against the rights deriving from it, even if in fact no bias existed in the way in which he and the other judges had actually determined the scope of those rights in disposing of the issues in the case.

Of particular interest for our purposes is the next paragraph of the judgment:

> We stress that, in reaching this conclusion, we attach particular importance to the tone of the language and the impression which the author deliberately gives that his hostility to the operation of the Convention as part of our domestic law is both long-standing and deep-seated ... [W]hat judges cannot do with impunity is to publish either criticism or praise of such a nature or in such language as to give rise to a legitimate apprehension that, when called upon in the course of their judicial duties to apply that particular branch of the law, they will not be able to do so impartially.

In England, the position was dealt with by the Court of Appeal in *Locabail Ltd v Bayfield Properties*,[17] which was a series of cases heard together. This case is well-known for the following quotation:

> We cannot, however, conceive of circumstances in which an objection could be soundly based on the religion, ethnic or national origin, gender, age, class, means or sexual orientation of the judge. Nor, at any rate ordinarily, could an objection be soundly based on the judge's social or educational or service or employment background or history, nor that of any member of the judge's family; or previous political associations; or membership of social or sporting or charitable bodies; or Masonic associations; or previous judicial decisions; or *extra-curricular utterances* (whether in textbooks, lectures, speeches, articles, interviews, reports or responses to consultation papers); or previous receipt of instructions to act for or against any party, solicitor or advocate engaged in a case before him; or membership of the same Inn, circuit, local Law Society or chambers.[18]

One of the series of cases involved was *Timmins v Gormley*. Here, a recorder at Liverpool County Court had given an award to a plaintiff in a personal injury action. The recorder was a prolific writer. From some of the articles which he had written, the Court concluded that the recorder had 'pronounced pro-claimant anti-insurer views' and allowed an appeal and retrial on the grounds of bias. The Court made this observation on extra-judicial comment:

> It is not inappropriate for a judge to write in publications of the class to which the recorder contributed. The publications are of value to the profession and for a lawyer of the recorder's experience to contribute to those publications can further rather than hinder the administration of justice. There is a long-established tradition that the writing of books and articles or the editing of legal textbooks is not incompatible with holding judicial office and the discharge of judicial functions. There is nothing improper in the recorder being engaged in his writing activities. It is the tone of the recorder's opinions and the trenchancy with which they were expressed which is challenged here … It is always inappropriate for a judge to use intemperate language about subjects on which he has adjudicated or will have to adjudicate.[19]

Of course, not all inappropriate comment ends up in court. For example, Lord Hewart, then Lord Chief Justice of England and Wales, published *The New*

---

[17] [1999] EWCA Civ 3004, [2000] 1 All ER 65.
[18] ibid 77–78. Emphasis added.
[19] ibid 90.

Despotism in 1929. This attacked administrative lawlessness and accused the civil service of deliberately seeking to infringe the liberty of the citizen. It 'was not generally accepted as appropriate for a work by a judge [then] and its equivalent would certainly not be acceptable now.'[20]

In the United Kingdom, therefore, judges are permitted to comment on matters of public importance but this commentary should be moderate, not trenchant. Above all, it should not create an apprehension in the mind of a reasonable observer that a judge would be biased or have overly fixed views on topics that are likely to come before her for judicial consideration. The test is objective; it is enough if the apprehension would be created, even if the decision itself seems free from bias. This is likely to be the test in Ireland also.

The European Convention on Human Rights

It is interesting to note that a Swiss judge who was reprimanded for distributing a political leaflet (which severely criticised the authorities and called for pending prosecutions to be withdrawn) brought an application to the European Commission on Human Rights alleging a breach of Article 10 of the Convention (the right to freedom of speech). The Commission held that the judge had, in common with any other citizen, a right to freedom of speech. His particular situation and the duties and responsibilities attaching to his position, however, meant that 'the interference suffered by the applicant in the exercise of his freedom of expression is justified in this case as being necessary in a democratic society for maintaining the authority and impartiality of the judiciary, within the meaning of art 10 para 2 of the Convention.'[21] The application was found to be inadmissible. It seems, therefore, that while judges have the right to freedom of speech, that right can be limited but only to the extent 'necessary in a democratic society'.

THE THEORY

It is not easy to distil any coherent set of principles from the foregoing case law. It is clear from *Hoekstra* and *Locabail* that it is appropriate for judges to comment on issues of public importance with a view to improving the administration of justice. They have a particular expertise in terms of court organisation and practice and temperate commentary on this topic should be welcomed.

All such remarks are circumscribed, however, by the risks that they run. The most important is bias. As *Hoekstra* illustrates, this is not simply real bias, where a judge has publicly made a statement which directly prejudices the outcome of a case before her, but also an objective apprehension of

---

[20] Shetreet (n 7).
[21] *E v Switzerland* (1984) 38 D & R 124.

bias—saying something which implies that the judge has a point of view which would lead a reasonable person to believe that she will not approach a particular issue with an open mind. Judges are as subject to prejudices and misunderstandings as any other person but should attempt to put these frailties to one side when sitting on the bench. To take a fixed position on an issue is likely to lead litigants and observers to lose confidence in the judge's fairness.

This leads to another risk, that of loss of confidence in the judiciary as a whole. The public are not likely to trust judges who express strong views on topical subjects. In a democracy, it is important that those who are called upon to resolve issues of law and fact stay out of the arena of public debate unless they have a particular contribution of special importance to make.

This is particularly important because of the tenure which judges enjoy. Under Article 35.4 of the Constitution, judges can only be dismissed for stated misbehaviour or incapacity and by a resolution passed by both Houses of the Oireachtas. Judges occupy a position of particular importance and respect in Irish society. Their comments are generally taken seriously by the media. A judge could abuse this position as a pulpit from which to make controversial statements on matters of public importance. This type of 'political' behaviour would be quite inappropriate for a judge and reflect badly on the judiciary generally:

> … there must be limits on what judges may say and do. For example, a judge must not campaign on behalf of a candidate for political office. To do so would detract from the perceived neutrality of such a judge.[22]

The context of the comment may also have some bearing on its appropriateness. A justice of the Supreme Court of Louisiana has suggested four factors which should be borne in mind:

1. the subject-matter;
2. the degree of present public interest or controversy concerning the topic;
3. the forum; and
4. the audience.[23]

There is clearly a difference between a judge speaking at or participating in a learned symposium on a legal topic and appearing on a television chat show,

---

[22] Ed Ratushny, 'Judicial Independence and Public Accountability', Appendix B to the *Report of the Committee on Judicial Conduct and Ethics* (n 1) 67. Professor Kaufman suggests that such abuse of status could lead to a loss of self-regulation by the judiciary—Kaufman (n 5) 870.

[23] Albert Tate, 'The Propriety of Off-Bench Judicial Writing or Speaking on Legal or Quasi-Legal Issues' (1978) 3 Journal of the Legal Profession 17, 22–23.

or between a judge writing a paper for a learned journal and writing a column in a tabloid newspaper. This is not to say that it would necessarily be improper for a judge to do any of these things, but the context can be as important as the content of the message.

Judges should choose their fora for comment and debate with care: the wrong event, publication or audience can make innocuous remarks seem quite inappropriate. In the United Kingdom, the 'Kilmuir Rules', set down in 1955 by Lord Chancellor Kilmuir, codify guidelines for judges' interactions with the media.[24] These rules have been somewhat relaxed since 1989. Here, there are no such rules, largely because the rule was simple: judges did not talk to the media.[25] That position is changing somewhat and if this continues, there will be a need for rules in the future. This will obviously require careful consideration and is outside the scope of this short piece. If the Judicial Council is established, it is something which it will have to concern itself with. As with any of the rules and procedures which the Council may establish, particular thought will have to be given to the proper role of ordinary citizens, professional bodies and other branches of government in this process.

Conclusion

While judges have much of value to contribute to public discourse and debate on the law and the legal system, they should be careful that when they are speaking or writing off the bench, they are both sensible and sensitive. Careless judicial comment leaves the judge open to allegations of bias and, if particularly thoughtless, could lead to very damaging controversy.

Taking this theory and applying it to practical situations is not straightforward. There are some things which are clearly inappropriate. For obvious reasons, comment on pending cases, either in one's own court or in another judge's, is very inappropriate,[26] as is commenting adversely on other judges or on other judges' decisions or explaining one's own decisions.[27] Commenting on matters of political controversy (unless the judge has very particular expertise in the area) is also inappropriate.[28]

---

[24] Pannick (n 4) 173.

[25] Raymond Byrne and Paul McCutcheon with Claire Bruton and Gerard Coffey, *Byrne and McCutcheon on the Irish Legal System* (5th edn, Bloomsbury Professional 2011) 168–171.

[26] William Ross, 'Extrajudicial Speech: Charting the Boundaries of Propriety' (1989) 2 Georgetown Journal of Legal Ethics 589, 597–601.

[27] ibid 601–612. It is interesting to note that in Hugh O'Flaherty, 'Democracy, the Judiciary and the Constitution' in *Justice, Liberty and the Courts* (Round Hall 1998) 44–48, a Supreme Court judge explains some controversial decisions of that court.

[28] Ross (n 26) 637–640.

It is appropriate and useful for a judge to comment (in a restrained fashion) on matters relating to the courts and law in general. Judges may write articles and textbooks on legal matters.[29] Commentary on non-political issues (for example, arts, culture or history) is generally acceptable, provided no particular agenda is being promoted.[30] They should be careful not to take a fixed or dogmatic position in any writings or speeches, as although they are obviously not binding on the individual judge, they are likely to be of considerable persuasive authority even if they are not cited in court.[31]

It is not possible to lay down rigid rules, however, and the best guide is the judge's own conscience. In the last analysis, the judge must determine for himself whether the good he is attempting to do for the law and society is outweighed by the disrespect he may create for the judiciary in some or in many people, either because the substance of his expression is distasteful to them or because they perceive him less as an impartial and disinterested judge and more as an active political candidate.[32]

---

[29] It seems that the prohibition on the holding of a position of emolument in Article 35.3 of the Constitution does not prevent the judge from receiving royalties: Gerard Hogan and Gerry Whyte, *Kelly: The Irish Constitution* (3rd edn, Butterworths 1994) 550.

[30] Ross (n 26) 640–641.

[31] See Tate (n 23) 19–22 for a discussion of some practical examples.

[32] ibid 25.

In examinations those who do not wish to know ask questions of those who cannot tell.[1]

INTRODUCTION

One of the keys to success as a law student is exam technique. There are three principal types of questions that you will encounter in your examinations. Essays are a form of question that you should be familiar with from previous studies, but need to be dealt with in a particular way in law exams. Problem questions are particular to the law, and you have probably never encountered them before. You may also be asked role-playing questions, in which you are asked to assume that you are a researcher or legal advisor in a government department or some other body and asked to reply to a query, write a position paper or advise on the legal options open to a decision-maker. The last type is simply a more focused version of an essay question and is not discussed in detail here.

> Outline the history of legal regulation of online services, particularly the internet. What are the challenges facing policy-makers and law-makers in this area in the future?
>
> Susan has worked for a telemarketing company for two years. Although her performance at work is good, she suffers from debilitating allergies that mean that she is often absent from work. She is therefore consistently below her sales targets, although her sales per day are above average. She becomes pregnant and informs her employer of this and of her intention to take maternity leave. Three weeks later, she is summoned to a meeting with the human resources manager. At this meeting, she is informed that because of her consistent underperformance, the company will no longer employ her. She is quite concerned about the impact this loss of income will have and comes to you for advice.

---

[1]   Walter Alexander Raleigh, 'Some Thoughts on Examinations' in *Laughter from a Cloud* (Constable and Co Ltd 1923) 120.

You work as legal advisor to the Minister for Foreign Affairs. A rebellion breaks out in the small Asian country of Mampang. The rebels rapidly seize control of most of the geographical territory, except for the capital, which remains in the hands of the government. The rebels seek to be recognised by the international community as the legitimate government of Mampang. Advise the Minister on the relevant legal principles.

GENERAL EXAMINATION TIPS

AVOID THE 'SHOTGUN APPROACH'

The shotgun approach leads to answers in which the student either writes down everything under the sun in the hope that the correct answer can somehow be found somewhere, or where the student's answer is a long, rambling discourse that shows no structure or forethought. To further the analogy, the first type of shotgun answer is akin to 'spraying fire' on the paper in the hope that something will be on target. The second type of shotgun answer is where, like a runner, the student hears the starting gun and starts writing impulsively without thinking in advance. You should read exam questions carefully, take a few minutes to plan and structure a response *to the question asked* and then, and only then, begin writing your answers.

Remember that you will only get marks for relevant material—do not waste your time writing if you are not sure you have correctly identified the topic of the question.

WATCH THE TIME

You are usually only given a limited time to complete examinations—generally two or three hours. The time allocated passes extremely quickly. Therefore, it is essential that you do your very best to stay within the time allotted to each question. By way of illustration, a student who, on a three-question examination, spends too much time on two questions and cannot answer a third, will inevitably perform poorly. Even if the student performs exceptionally well on the two questions he answers fully, his incomplete response to the third will severely affect his overall mark on the examination. For example:

Question 1 (worth 100 marks)	75/100
Question 2 (worth 100 marks)	70/100
Question 3 (worth 100 marks)	30/100
Total grade: 175/300 x 100	58%

Unfortunately, staying within time limits is not as easy as it sounds, especially under the pressures of an examination. Nonetheless, you must strive to do so. Work out how much time you have, how many minutes a mark is worth and how many marks each question will earn you. Remember to allow time to read the paper before you start and to read over your script before you finish. If you have a three-hour examination, and have to do three questions which are worth equal marks, then a time breakdown would look something like this:

Total Time:	180 minutes
Reading paper, choosing questions	5 minutes
Planning time	20 minutes
Question 1	48 minutes
Question 2	48 minutes
Question 3	48 minutes
'Finishing up' time	10 minutes

Adequate preparation and careful planning are the best means of combating the natural tendency to run over the time allocated to each question.

Planning your Answers

The best way of avoiding the 'shotgun' approach outlined above is to take 20 minutes at the beginning of the exam to meticulously plan your answers. While you might think at the beginning of the exam that you have all the information required at your fingertips, by the time you start your third question, that information may well have gone. In this 20 minutes, make sure you do the following. It might seem like a long time to spend on this exercise, but it will show dividends at the end.

1. Make sure you know what is being asked of you in each question you have chosen. Students sometimes see the word, 'President', 'Invitation to Treat', or 'Provocation' and immediately start writing their essay on that topic. Imagine, however, if the question reads, 'Aside from the defence of provocation, human emotions or motivations are rarely considered in the context of the criminal law. Discuss this statement with reference to the legal understanding of intention in the criminal law.' If a student wrote a perfect, well-written and well-referenced essay on the law of provocation, he would get a zero grade. Aside from such blatant misreading of questions, look for the subtleties in the question—what facts are included, what are excluded? Who are you being asked to advise?
2. Make sure you plan your answer. Jot down the key cases, facts, journal articles and books that you plan on referring to in your answer. Outline a plan of how you propose to answer the question which is asked of you.

Present yourself Well

Remember that your examiner will probably have dozens of scripts to correct. Make it easy for her to give you marks by making your answer clear and easy to read.

In an examination, you should be able to obtain all of the paper that you need. Use it—do not cramp your answers into a page or two. Ask for rough work paper to plan your answer, which you can use for jotting down thoughts as they come to you.

Use paragraphs when you are writing your answers. Make sure that the paragraphs are not too long, and that each paragraph contains one key point.

Leave space after each paragraph, so that it is easier to read and so that you can add to your answer if something additional occurs to you. Leave space after each answer. Write part of the answer and leave a few blank pages if you get stuck. Work on an easier question; your brain will continue to think over the first earlier problem.

Use headings and sub-headings to make the structure of your answer easy to follow. It may be useful to highlight the names of cases and other legal authority by using different coloured pens or underlining, but don't get carried away and check with the person who will be marking the paper before doing this, as not all lecturers like it. Use the best possible handwriting you can manage under pressure.

Finally, some students think that they should not refer to original sources in their exams—they could not be more wrong. While you do not need to artificially try to create footnotes on the page, a well-written exam answer might read as follows:

Under the Minimum Notice and Terms of Employment Acts 1973 to 2005, the normal terms of notice are:

- Service less than two years: one week
- Service of two to five years: two weeks
- Service of five to ten years: four weeks
- Service of ten to fifteen years: six weeks
- Service over fifteen years: eight weeks

If Susan feels that her dismissal is not valid, she can seek to claim for wrongful or unfair dismissal. Wrongful dismissal is a common law remedy, and involves a dismissal in breach of contract. This will normally involve dismissal without proper notice or in breach of disciplinary procedures (*AIB v Lupton*) or constitutional rights (*Meskell v CIÉ*) or fairness (*Glover v BLN*). Damages are the usual remedy and can include lost earnings and reputation.

Essay Questions

Essay questions are primarily a test of your ability to develop and present a logical and coherent argument. Many students tend to prefer this type of question, believing these questions to be somehow easier. This is true only in a superficial way—it is much easier to present a memorised answer to an essay question than to a problem question. Such an answer, however, will only obtain a mediocre mark at best, because it answers a question different to the one that actually appears on the examination paper. In fact, essay questions are in many respects more difficult to answer well because they require some degree of creativity from students, as well as a thorough understanding of the area.

Essay questions are not concerned with application of the law; rather, they require students to explain the law. They test your understanding of the law and its underlying principles and philosophy. This kind of question does not limit you to the law as it stands and you are often expected to comment on, and critically analyse, the law. Reasoned opinions are especially important here and you should be able to argue persuasively that the current state of the law under consideration is either good or bad and, more importantly, *why*, by reference to secondary sources.

Essay questions are typically open-ended and may evoke lengthy responses. As such, it is extremely important that you structure your answers—with a clearly defined 1) introduction, 2) discussion and analysis of the legal issue(s) at hand, and 3) conclusion. In the introduction, you should make clear what the question means to you, what you will consider, and any ancillary topics that you are excluding. The legal issues should be considered as described in the chapter on essay writing. The conclusion should state your overall answer to the question (if such is possible), summarising your reasons for it.

Additionally, essay questions require that students, wherever possible, make explicit reference to relevant primary and secondary sources of law. You should never hesitate to cite relevant constitutional provisions, legislation, case law or secondary sources. Such citations demonstrate that you have engaged with required and suggested readings and they inherently enhance the quality of your answer.

You will find more advice on how to write essays in law in the relevant chapter of this book. Of course, not all of that chapter will be helpful in an examination, where you will be working under particular time constraints, but much of what is said about methods of analysis can be adapted as necessary.

PROBLEM QUESTIONS

Problem questions present you with a hypothetical situation where two or more people have some conflict or dispute that involves one or more legal issues. You are asked to advise one of the parties to the dispute.

The key to success in problem questions is correctly identifying the issue. If you do not know what the question is about, do not attempt to answer it. Sometimes the question will make it clear what advice is needed ('Advise John whether his contract is enforceable'). In other instances, the situation will be obviously similar to a case that you studied in your course. Sometimes, the examiner will not make it obvious what is required.

You then need to determine the relevant facts. The examiner will sometimes mention information that does not matter. Sometimes something that you need to know is not stated (you can point this out in your answer). If you know what the issue is, you will know what is relevant and what is not. Do not spend any time discussing extraneous facts (except perhaps to say something like 'The fact that the document was not signed does not matter, because the contract is clearly evidenced by other means'). However, sometimes a key fact will be omitted, or it will be unclear what the factual situation is—if this is the case, make it clear what this is and why it matters.

> There is no indication whether or not there was a notice at the car park excluding the liability of the operator. If there was, and it was clearly displayed before the entrance, this exclusion clause would be incorporated by prior notice. Further information on this question is required.

The method required to answer a problem question is to state the law and apply it to the facts. There are many different ways to structure an answer which does this, but one suggested structure which will ensure that you do this is ILAC (sometimes called IRAC):

- Issue
- Law (or Rule)
- Analysis (or Application)
- Conclusion

You should bear in mind that ILAC should be viewed as train tracks rather than a straightjacket. Effective use requires practice. Do not use it in a mindless fashion. It can be a very useful tool for ensuring that your learning is presented in a clear and logical fashion, but if you are too rigid or simplistic in your approach, you risk going seriously astray, missing the point(s) of the

WRITING LAW EXAMS

135

question, or being too shallow in your answer. Tailor your approach to the legal issue(s) raised and the preferences of the lecturer concerned. What is important is to show that you have an ability to engage with the law and to show that you have learnt how to apply it to new situations.

Issue

In the issue section, state the legal issue in the question. This should be no more than one or two sentences. It should be a clear question, generally with a 'yes' or 'no' answer:

Is John's contract enforceable?

Is Helen liable for the damages to Michael's car?

Is Thomas guilty of the offence of criminal damage?

Be specific here—it is not good enough to say 'The issue here is the law relating to criminal damage'. Be specific and relate the issue to the facts: 'The issue here is whether Thomas is guilty of the offence of criminal damage.'

If the issue section is longer than this, you have probably missed the point of the question or you are not clear on the law. If you cannot state the issue in a clear question, you are not clear on what you are being asked. Refine the issue until it is simple and clear. Otherwise, your answer will ramble.

That said, bear in mind that there may be more than one issue. Do not assume that there is only one. However, most questions will not contain more than two or three. Do not tie yourself in knots trying to find more and more issues.

Law/Rule

Now, state the law that governs the area. This section will be the longest portion of the answer. Structure your answer before you write it, so that the material is presented in a logical fashion. Cite proper legal authority (the Constitution, legislation, case law) in your answer, in as complete a way as you can. The more specific you are, the better; giving the full names of cases and giving the number and text of sections of statutes is ideal. If you cannot remember the name of a case, give enough facts to show that you know what the case was about. Almost every lawyer has difficulty remembering the names of cases, and will forgive a momentary lapse of recollection in an examination hall—what is important is the legal rule which the case is authority for. Full citations (name of law reports and page numbers) are not required in examinations.

Analysis/Application

Next, apply the law to the facts. If you have correctly stated the law, this should be a relatively mechanical process:

> For John's contract to be enforceable, the four elements listed above must be present. However, the element of consideration is missing.

This portion of your answer should be shorter than the law portion. You may not arrive at a clear answer, because information is missing or because the law itself is vague. If this is the situation, say so clearly, and give the various outcomes depending on the interpretation of the facts. If the law is not entirely clear in the area (in a situation where your fact pattern falls between the stools of two cases), give your opinion on how you think the case would be decided.

Conclusion

Finally, state your conclusion. This should be quite short, and is a summary of the results of your analysis. Sometimes a sentence will be enough; a more complex question will require a longer conclusion. Resist the temptation to arrive at your conclusion before you start writing. You may find that as you state the law (and remember additional details), your view of the situation changes.

> John's contract is therefore not enforceable and he cannot force Tom to pay the remaining €300.

If you are particularly confident of your grasp of the law, and want to demonstrate this to the examiner, it may be useful to discuss academic or other commentary on the law. You could, for example, explain that the state of the law in the area you have discussed is unclear or otherwise in need of reform, and highlight proposals for change:

> The Law Reform Commission has recommended ... If this were to be implemented, the outcome would be different in that ...

However, this should only be done as an extra section to an already thorough discussion of the law as it is. Do not answer a problem question only by discussing the law as it should be. As a lawyer, you must learn to work with the current state of the law, however much you might wish it was different.

EXAMPLES

JANIE

Question

Janie works as a journalist with the *Weekly News* and is quite successful. She is approached by the editor of the *Daily News*, Jonno, who offers her a better job at a higher salary. She says that she would be delighted to accept but would have to be able to continue her existing working hours of 10 am to 4 pm as this is necessary in order for her to care for her young son. Jonno assures her that this will not be a problem and she starts work soon after.

However, once she starts, she is put under pressure to come into work early and stay later. The pace at a daily newspaper is quite different to that at a weekly and she finds it difficult to safeguard her morning and afternoon time with her child. Eventually, the editor makes it clear that she will have to come in at 9 am and stay until 5 pm.

She is not happy with this and comes to you for advice on whether she has a claim for breach of contract.

Issue

The issue here is whether the editor's statement about Janie's working hours is part of her contract, and if so, whether it is a condition or a warranty, and whether it constitutes an actionable misrepresentation.

Rule

In considering the status of the statement made by Jonno, we must bear in mind the distinctions between, first, representations at the pre-contractual stage and the terms of a contract, and secondly, the two types of terms, which are conditions and warranties.

Representations are things said during the negotiations leading up to a contract that do not become part of the contract itself. If they prove to be false in some way, they do not give rise to an action for breach of contract, but the injured party can claim damages for misrepresentation.

In looking at whether a statement is a term or a misrepresentation, the courts will look at three elements:

1. How close to the conclusion of a contract the statement was made. (The closer it was, the more likely it is to be a term.)
2. Whether the statement was included in the written contract, if such exists. (If not, it is not likely to be a term.)
3. Whether the party making the statement had special skill or knowledge. (If so, it is likely to be a term.)

The terms of a contract are divided into *conditions* and *warranties*. A condition is vital to the contract. If it is breached, the injured party can rescind (terminate) the contract and possibly also obtain damages. A warranty is not as important. A breach will not bring the contract to an end, although the injured party can still seek damages.

Thus, for example, in *Poussard v Spiers*, the non-appearance of an opera singer on the opening night was held to be a breach of condition, which brought the contract to an end; whereas in *Bettini v Gye,* which involved a singer who did not attend all of the rehearsals but did attend all of the performances, the singer was only in breach of a warranty, which gave rise to an entitlement to damages only.

In some circumstances, a term can be either a condition or a warranty, depending on the seriousness of the breach. These are known as 'intermediate' or 'innominate' terms. An example is the supply of a defective telephone system in the *Irish Telephone Rentals* case, where the implied term as to the supply of services was not classified but the defects in the system were so severe as to be a breach of a condition.

Misrepresentation is a false statement of fact by one party to the contract that induces the other party to enter into the contract. The following cannot constitute mispresentation:

- *Sales talk* or advertising puffs.
- A *statement of law*, as everyone is assumed to know the law.
- A *statement of intention*, as it is too difficult to prove or disprove. However, if the intention is clearly not present, it will constitute misrepresentation, as in *Edgington v Fitzmaurice*, where the directors of a company falsely claimed that the money obtained from the sale of shares would be used to grow the company when in fact it was intended to repay debts.
- A *statement of opinion* (*Bisset v Wilkinson*), unless the maker has special expertise (*Esso Petroleum v Mardon, Doheny v Bank of Ireland*).

The statement must, of course, be untrue. There must be a statement—silence generally cannot constitute misrepresentation—although a relevant change of circumstances must be brought to the attention of the other party (for example, in *With v O'Flanagan*, the defendant should have mentioned that the medical practice which he was selling had lost value because of his illness). Half-truths are also actionable, such as in the *Nottingham Patent Brick* case, where a solicitor stated that he was not aware of any restrictive covenants on land being sold, but did not clarify that the reason for this was that he had neglected to read the relevant documents.

Finally, the injured party must have relied on the misrepresentation when entering into the contract. It does not need to be the only thing which that party relied upon but it must have been a factor in his decision. For example, in *Wadson Sales*, the plaintiff claimed that he relied on a statement that a shopping arcade would be 'high quality retail' when choosing to lease a unit there, when in fact most of the other units were already leased and it was clear that they were not 'high quality'.

Misrepresentation may be fraudulent, negligent or innocent. For the first two, the injured party may seek recission of the contract and damages. For innocent misrepresentation, the injured party can only seek one of these remedies.

Analysis

The first question to answer is whether the statement about working hours was merely a representation or whether it became a term of the contract. Unfortunately, it is difficult to give a clear answer to this question.

It is not indicated when the statement was made or whether it was entered into a written contract. Indeed, it is not clear that there is a written contract at all. However, assuming that the bargain was made when Janie met with the editor, it would seem to be a term of the contract. If there is a written contract, anything it provides regarding working hours will override the editor's statement. Further information on these points would be useful.

If it is a term, it would seem that the importance to Janie of her relationship with her son would make it a condition of the contract. She made this clear during the negotiation process. This would entitle her to end the contract and also seek damages for breach of contract.

If the statement was only a representation, the *Daily News* would not be able to claim any of the defences to a claim of misrepresentation (except perhaps intention). If it was a misrepresentation (which is unlikely), this would seem to have been negligent, leaving her entitled to the same remedies.

Conclusion

The statement regarding working hours is probably a condition of the contract. The newspaper is in breach of this, entitling Janie to sue and claim rescission of the contract (bringing it to an end) and/or damages. If the statement was only a representation, which is unlikely, she is in the same position.

Chantelle

Question

Chantelle is manager of the Holiday Hotel. On behalf of the hotel, she enters into a contract with George's Dry Cleaners to clean the hotel's curtains. She had dealt with George's Dry Cleaners on several occasions over the last five years and has always been satisfied with its service. On previous occasions when leaving the curtains in for cleaning, she had signed a disclaimer which stated that 'George's Dry Cleaners is not liable for any loss or damage to customer's property while on the premises.' This time, she was not asked to sign any document but when she brought the curtains in to be cleaned, she was given a receipt on the back of which the same clause appeared. When she came to pick up the curtains, she was horrified to discover that some of them had been badly discoloured. While they were in the store room, an employee had spilt a canister of chemicals over the curtains, causing the discolouration. George's Dry Cleaners is denying liability on the basis of the exemption clause in the contract. Advise Chantelle.

Issue

The exemption clause that George's Dry Cleaners (GDC) is relying on is clear and wide. If it does apply to this situation, Chantelle will have no remedy against it. The issue, therefore, is whether or not the exemption clause was incorporated into the contract.

Rule

As a general rule, the courts are hostile to exemption clauses. They have created two strict tests which an exemption clause must pass in order to protect the party relying on it. The first is the construction test, which looks at whether the clause covers the events involved. As this clause is broad and clear, GDC should have no difficulties in applying it to this situation.

The discussion will therefore focus on the second rule, which is whether or not the clause was properly incorporated into the contract in the first place. The clause may be incorporated in three ways.

The first is by the signature of a document which contains the clause. Once a party signs a document, she is considered to have accepted all that it contains. This applies even if she has not read it (*L'Estrange v Graucob*, where the plaintiff was bound by an exemption clause in a 'sales agreement' which she had signed, even though she had not read it). The exception would be if the signature was obtained by misrepresentation or duress, as occurred in the case of *Curtis v Chemical Cleaning and Dyeing Co*, where a customer of a drycleaners was told that an exemption clause on a receipt which she was asked to sign only applied to the sequins on a dress when it was in fact intended to apply to the entire dress. Here, the court refused to apply the exemption clause for the benefit of the drycleaners when the dress was damaged.

The second is by prior notice of the clause, such as by a notice on the wall of a business premises. This notice must be visible before any transaction is made. For example, in *Thornton v Shoe Lane Parking*, an exemption clause on a ticket issued after money had been paid was not applied. In *Western Meats Ltd*, a notice which was printed on the back of company documents which were sent to the plaintiff was not applied by the courts, as it needed to be clearly drawn to the attention of the customer.

The third is over a course of dealing between the parties. Here, the parties have dealt with each other for a period of time and are familiar with the standard terms and conditions on which they do business. The courts tend to be more protective of consumers and will demand more clear incorporation if the case involves a consumer rather than two businesses. Thus, in *J Spurling v Bradshaw*, where two businesses dealt with each other over a period of time and the exemption clause was on the back of a standard receipt, the court was willing to apply the clause. However, in *Hollier v Rambler Motors*, where a consumer had used the same garage for car repairs several times before, but on the final occasion was not given a receipt with the standard exclusion clause, the court was not willing to apply the clause.

Analysis

In Chantelle's case, the exclusion clause would have been incorporated in the previous contracts for dry cleaning, as she signed a disclaimer which contained it. On this occasion, however, she did not sign any document and so the clause was not incorporated by signature. There is no indication that there was a notice at GDC excluding its liability and so the clause was not incorporated by prior notice.

GDC must therefore rely on incorporation by a course of dealing. In GDC's favour is the fact that Chantelle has signed disclaimers with this clause in the past. In her favour, however, is the extended period of time over which she has dealt with GDC and the inclination of the courts to protect the ordinary consumer.

Conclusion

The crucial question, therefore, is whether the exclusion clause was incorporated by the course of dealings between Chantelle and GDC. Considering that she has dealt with GDC over a long period (five years) and that she was not a consumer, it is likely that the courts will incorporate the clause into the contract and Chantelle should therefore not be entitled to compensation for the damage to her curtains.

RAY AND TOM

Question

Ray and Tom concluded an agreement for the painting of Tom's house. The contract included a term providing for an immediate payment of €500 on completion of the job and a further payment of €1,000 in three months' time. When the job was finished, Tom was so pleased that he promised to pay Ray an extra €100.

Tom paid the €500 as agreed, but when the second payment became due he offered €800. He said he could not afford to pay anymore. Ray accepted this and agreed not to sue for the remainder, but he is unhappy with the arrangement and he wants to know if he can recover the outstanding €200 and the extra €100 promised. Advise Ray.

Would it make any difference if Tom relied on Ray's acceptance and undertook further work on the house?

Issue

The issue, from Ray's point of view, is whether he can still require Tom to pay the outstanding €300. This amount consists of money due under two separate arrangements. For the €200 outstanding from the agreed price for the painting work, the issue is whether the promise not to sue for it when Ray accepted €800 consists of an enforceable contract. For the extra €100, the issue is whether Tom's statement consists of an enforceable contract or a mere promise.

Rule

In order for a legally binding contract to come into existence, four elements must be present: offer, acceptance, consideration and intention to enter into legal relations.

An offer is an unambiguous statement of an intention to enter into a binding contract. An acceptance is the mirror image of this—an unambiguous statement of intention to supply the other side of the bargain.

Consideration is some benefit or detriment which a party to a contract gives or receives. Consideration must be present, except with a contract under seal. Consideration may be executed (a promise in exchange for a future act), executory (a promise in exchange for a promise) or past (a promise in exchange for a past act). Past consideration is not valid for the purposes of contract law. For example, in *Roscorla v Thomas*, a promise that a horse was 'free from vice', given after the horse had been sold, was held not to be part of the contract; and in *Re McArdle*, a promise by siblings to pay their brother for improvements he had made to the house in which he was living with their mother was held to be based on past consideration and thus unenforceable. However, if the plaintiff's actions were requested by the defendant, the courts will not let the defendant take unfair advantage and will apply an exception to this general rule. For example, in *Lampleigh v Brathwait*, the defendant asked the plaintiff to obtain a royal pardon for him and then, after his release, promised to pay the plaintiff but reneged on this. The court required him to make the payment.

Consideration must be sufficient but it need not be adequate. In other words, there must be something of value provided by both parties but it does not need to be a fair bargain. Thus in *Chappell v Nestlé*, used chocolate bar wrappers could constitute sufficient consideration.

An example of insufficient consideration is a promise to perform a pre-existing legal or contractual duty. For example, in *Stilk v Myrick*, a captain's promise to split the wages of deserters amongst the remaining crew was unenforceable as the crew did not provide any new consideration. However, in *Hartley v Ponsonby*, which was a similar situation but where the crew had to work harder to make up for the loss of crewmembers due to desertion, a promise to share the additional wages was enforceable. (This principle has been cast into doubt by the English decision of *Williams v Roffey Bros* but the Irish courts have not yet followed it.)

In the context of the payment of a contract debt, this principle means that part payment does not satisfy the obligation to pay the whole (the rule in *Pinnel's Case*). Thus, in *Foakes v Beer* the plaintiff owed £2,000 to the defendant. The defendant promised that if there was an immediate payment of £500 and the remainder in instalments, she would take no proceedings against the plaintiff. However, she claimed the right to interest. The plaintiff claimed that she was not entitled to this, but the court held that the agreement for payment by instalment was merely an arrangement, not a legally binding contract, as there was no new consideration.

A final point to note with regard to consideration is the doctrine of promissory estoppel, developed in *High Trees House*. Here, the plaintiff made a promise to reduce the rent on a block of flats during wartime. After the war, it sought to claim the unpaid rent. As there was no new consideration, it was entitled to this. However, the court held that it was estopped, or prevented, from doing so as the defendant had acted on the promise to its detriment and it would be unfair to go back on the promise. Promissory estoppel can only be used as a 'shield, not a sword'; in other words, it can only be raised as a defence, not as a cause of action in a lawsuit.

Analysis

There does not appear to be any issue regarding the offer and acceptance element of the contract between Ray and Tom. The important questions for discussion, therefore, are whether Ray's acceptance of only €800 is final and can be enforced against him; and whether Tom's promise of €100 created a binding contract.

When Ray accepted the lesser amount, Tom gave no new consideration. There is therefore no contract here and, applying the rule in *Pinnel's Case*, Ray can still sue for the remaining €200.

However, with regard to the extra €100 promised, this is simply a promise, with no consideration provided by Ray. Therefore, Ray cannot enforce this statement by Tom. If Ray had done additional work as a result, this might be seen as creating a new contract, but there is no indication that Tom offered the money for this purpose. Ray could claim promissory estoppel, but unfortunately for him, this is a shield, not a sword.

Conclusion

Ray can still legally claim the outstanding €200, but cannot claim the promised €100 'bonus'.

Legal Research

> Research is formalized curiosity. It is poking and prying with a purpose.[1]

INTRODUCTION

There are two meanings to the term 'legal research', as identified in *Glanville Williams: Learning the Law*.[2] The first refers to the task of ascertaining the current state of the law on a specific legal question at a particular time. The second explores 'some particular facet of the legal phenomenon that is being placed under the legal microscope'.[3] While it is a simpler task to figure out the state of the law (the 'what' of the law) than it is to engage in more exploratory research (the 'why' of the law), the same skills are required for both. In order to be able to say what the law is, you need to be able to find it.

This chapter offers some general tips on legal research methodology and some more specific guidelines for using the individual, subscription-based legal research databases which students must become familiar with. Examples of these are Westlaw IE, LexisLibrary and Justis. Access to some or all of these should be available through the website of the library of your institution.

The key features of the newer, freely available legal research databases are also described here. Much of the discussion of research methodology relates to the subscriber-based databases. The freely available databases are less sophisticated and their coverage more limited, more varied and, as a result, can be less reliable. However, as a consequence, their websites are generally easier to use and searching methodologies less complex.

While a certain amount of emphasis is placed on these electronic databases, the importance of wandering around the library cannot be over-emphasised. First, if you are asked to write an essay on strict liability offences, for example, your first port of call should be a textbook (aimed at students), then a monograph (which is a more scholarly exploration of the subject) and then some journal articles. The textbook should direct you to the monograph, which will indicate what journal articles are useful. All of this research can be done without even turning on a computer, and students should not forget that

HOW TO THINK, WRITE AND CITE

---

[1] Zora Neale Hurston, *Dust Tracks on a Road* (Hutchison and Co, 1942) 91.
[2] ATH Smith, *Glanville Williams: Learning the Law* (15th edn, Sweet & Maxwell 2013).
[3] ibid 210.

knowing their way around a library is a very useful skill. Wandering through the shelves can be a pleasure in itself and you will sometimes find that the shelf containing the book that you were looking for also has a number of other publications that are relevant to your search, often in unexpected ways.

The internet provides a dizzying amount of information on any conceivable topic. However, it is *vitally* important that you know the limitations to using the internet for research. Know the difference between, on the one hand, informed legal opinion, and on the other, journalism, or worse, misinformation. Wikipedia, for example, is *not* a source that can ever be cited. This is not to say that the internet is not useful, or that a well-written article on Wikipedia cannot give you a good overview of the basics of your topic, but it will give you no more than that, and it should always be verified by research in more definitive sources, whether primary or secondary.

In addition, be aware of the subjective nature of much that is written on the internet: it may be written from a particular point of view, which will not necessarily include all relevant material on the topic. You should learn to differentiate between websites. Take note of who the author is, what her affiliations are, and who is linking to her. However, do not lose sight of one of the great advantages of the internet—the way in which it enables anyone to publish. A well-researched and well-thought out document should be taken seriously regardless of the source, but do bear in mind the hierarchy of authoritative sources. Do not rely exclusively or even significantly on online sources.

At any rate, as you will discover in the course of studying law, the bottom line is that legal research is never a 'one size fits all' proposition. If you ask three of your lecturers, for example, how they go about their own research, you will probably find that they respond with three entirely different, but entirely appropriate methodologies. Each of these will be entirely effective and valid for that person and for her particular area of specialisation. Thorough and effective legal research is only learned by practice and many readers of the following may, in time, come to question or even reject some of what follows (if they have not already). This can only be a good thing because it means that they have developed their own individualised research methodology.

LIBRARY-BASED RESEARCH

With the huge amount of information available through online services, both free and paid, it is easy to forget about printed materials and the usefulness of good old-fashioned library research. However, this is not a good idea. In the same way that scientists and science students spend a large proportion of their time in laboratories, lawyers and law students often work in libraries, researching, reading and writing. Most libraries have a specialised law librarian, who will have an encyclopaedic knowledge of the law, and the resources available in a particular area. These law librarians are often more knowledgeable about 'the law' as a general subject than your lecturers, who are experts in specific areas.

You need to become familiar with the layout of your library, and what materials are available in it. You will spend most of your time in the law library, but on occasion, you might need to venture into history, politics, medicine or philosophy, so make sure you have a good idea of where each section is in the library. (Your library will probably run tours in the first few weeks of the new academic year; sign up for these if you can.) Most Irish libraries use the Dewey Decimal system of classification. Here is an outline of how the system works in terms of classification of subjects:

000 Generalities
100 Philosophy
200 Religion
300 Social Sciences
400 Language
500 Pure Sciences
600 Technology (Applied Sciences)
700 The Arts
800 Literature
900 Geography and History

Law is considered a social science for the purposes of the Dewey system, and is sub-classified as follows:

340 Law
341 International law
342 Constitutional and Administrative law
343 Miscellaneous public law
344 Social law
345 Criminal law
346 Private law
347 Civil procedure and courts
348 Statutes, regulations, cases
349 Law of individual states and nations

Each of these sub-classifications has further sub-sub-classifications, thus the place to find *Byrne and McCutcheon on the Irish Legal System* is at 349.417.

All law libraries in Ireland have an online catalogue of the books which are available in their own stocks. These catalogues are exceptionally easy to use, and you can usually search by title, author or keyword. These books will usually be either on long-term loan, in which case you can borrow the book for a number of weeks, or, where the books are in high demand, on short-term loan, where you are limited to borrowing them for a number of days, or hours. Do not forget, when you find the book you are looking for on the shelves, quickly scan through the other books in the shelf above and below—there will most likely be some more material there that will be relevant to your research. This serendipity is one of the key advantages of library research.

Sometimes you might come across a book which is not available in your own library. If this happens, you will be able to access the book on 'inter-library loan', where your local librarian will borrow the book from another library on your behalf. These loans can take anything from a couple of days to a couple of months to come through, depending on the library they are coming from, and if they are already on loan from that library. Again, the importance of being prepared and knowing what materials you will need at the early stages of the research will mean that this will not usually be a problem.

All law libraries will also have a stock of law reports from Ireland and the rest of the world. Depending on where you are doing your research, these can be very extensive, and are often the only place that you will find full collections of law reports. Do not assume that because something is not available on the internet, or on a legal database, it does not exist—your library should be the first place you look for law reports. Most will also have official versions of Acts of the Oireachtas, and these should be used to confirm any research you do on the Irish Statute Book website. Most law libraries also have an extensive array of legal journals. When you find the article you are looking for, get into the practice of browsing through older and newer editions of the journal—again, if there is something relevant in one edition of the journal, there is a good chance that it regularly publishes articles on similar topics.

SELECTED DATABASES

SUBSCRIBER-BASED DATABASES

Some or all of the following databases will be available through your university library. It is probably best to access the database through the library website, as this will automatically log you into the database. You may need to ask your librarian for details of what is available to you and how exactly you should access them. Some, which are international databases, have less information on Ireland than others: it is only through trial and error that you will be able to know which database to use when searching for a particular case or journal article.

LexisLibrary—<www.lexisnexis.co.uk>

From the main page, you should log on to the appropriate service, LexisLibrary. There, you should click on the 'Sources' tab. On the next page, set the country filter to Ireland. Click on the link for the letter 'I.' There are several searchable databases there, but the most relevant are 'Irish Reported and Unreported Cases' (all reported cases from 1950 to the present and unreported cases from 1985 to the present—no pagination) and the *Irish Reports* (all cases in the IR series dating back to 1919—with pagination). While LexisLibrary has a heavy North American bias, it does also contain useful primary and secondary sources from around the world. The large amount of legal materials from the United Kingdom may be of particular interest to you. Depending on the subscription your library has, you may or may not be able to access Canadian, New Zealand or Australian sources—check with your law librarian if this is the case.

Westlaw IE (Irish version)—<www.westlaw.ie>

Upon logging on to this database, you will see a page where a number of different items appear. The database has the *Irish Law Reports Monthly* from the mid-1970s onward and a variety of subject-specific case reports, as well as some recent unreported judgments. It also features annotated statutes, consolidated legislation and current awareness legal bulletins. Probably the most useful and unique feature of this database is the 'Journals' icon, which provides access to full text versions of a number of general and subject-specific Irish law journals. The journals go as far back as 1966 (the 'Irish Jurist') and 1983 ('Irish Law Times'). Clicking on the 'Journals' tab provides you with a list of these journals and the searching mechanisms are quite similar to LexisLibrary. One practical difficulty, however, is that the journal articles lack internal pagination, so you may have to refer back to the hard copy to ascertain the exact page number when citing an article. In some articles, the print pagination is indicated in the online version by way of asterisks in the relevant places throughout the text.

Westlaw UK (UK version)—<www.westlaw.co.uk>

On its homepage, this database features links to cases, legislation and journal articles from the United Kingdom and the European Union. The amount of sources available here is considerable. To access sources from around the world, clicking on the 'Services' tab on the top right-hand side of the home page screen and then 'International Materials' will allow you to access primary and secondary legal materials from around the world through WestlawNext. The 'World Journals' tab you will find here is particularly useful in that it enables you to search thousands of full-text journals from around the world for relevant articles. 'World Journals', given its extraordinary scope, is an ideal resource for so-called 'needle in a haystack' research—where you just cannot find anything anywhere else.

Justis—<www.justis.com>

Upon accessing this webpage, you will see a page where, if your institution is a subscriber, the sign-in details are completed and you need simply to click on 'Continue to Justis' which is just below the sign-in boxes. Having done so, you should click on 'Cases' in the centre of the page on the next screen. The next page brings up a search facility which, if you click the 'Data Sources' tab on the right, brings up 'All cases', Irish, Scottish and European options. Justis is an excellent database for Irish cases for two reasons: coverage of cases extends as far back as 1919; and the cases are PDF reproductions of the originals, which allow for pinpoint citation without having to resort to the library for a physical copy. However, it only contains judgments reported in the *Irish Reports*. Justis is best used in tandem with LexisLibrary when undertaking research of Irish case law.

The tabs situated to the left of the text of case law viewed on Justis are among its most attractive features. These tabs provide information as to where else a case may have been reported, what cases and/or legislation are cited within it and even citations to related academic commentary on the case. The most valuable of the tabs is labelled 'Subsequent Cases' and provides citations to all subsequent cases that cite the case being viewed. Crucially, it will inform you whether a case remains good law or whether it has been subsequently overturned. This can also be done via the new companion website, JustCite (<www.justcite.com>).

HeinOnline—<www.heinonline.org>

At the HeinOnline homepage, you should click on the link that says 'Log In'. As with many other databases, HeinOnline has a heavy North American bias and that is reflected on the next page. However, there are a number of journals with an international focus available if the user clicks on 'International and Non-U.S. Law Journals'. There are multiple publications from the UK, Australia and elsewhere in Europe. An increasing number of Irish publications are also featured. As with Justis, the articles contained in HeinOnline are in a very reader and citation-friendly PDF format. However, the search engine seems less comprehensive than the search engines on sites like LexisLibrary and Westlaw IE. Again, HeinOnline is probably a site best used in tandem with LexisLibrary and/or Westlaw IE whenever possible.

JSTOR—<www.jstor.org>

Accessing the content in JSTOR is very straightforward. There is a search form on the front page. However, you should bear in mind that this site contains articles from a wide variety of disciplines. You might get better results if you click on the link for 'Advanced search' and then select 'Law' in the list of disciplines on the resulting page. JSTOR does not have the wide range of content available through LexisLibrary, Westlaw IE or HeinOnline, but it is useful for accessing journals in disciplines other than law and is also notable because it contains high-quality PDFs which exactly reproduce the pages of the original publication. This can often be easier to work with than the converted versions available through LexisLibrary and Westlaw IE.

> ■ To test your ability to use these databases, go to <www.legalwriting.ie> and complete Assignment 8.1.

FREELY AVAILABLE DATABASES

Irish Legal Information Initiative (IRLII)—<www.irlii.org>

This webpage contains a wealth of Irish legal resources. Links to, for example, recently decided case law, legislation, statutory instruments and Law Reform Commission reports are all featured on this site. You should also be aware of <www.bailii.org>, the companion site to IRLII, which contains a wealth of legal resources from the United Kingdom. While IRLII features searchable databases of mostly recent Irish Supreme Court, High Court and Court of Criminal Appeal decisions, judgments of the Court of Appeal are not included at the time of writing. These can be accessed on BAILII however. These sites are part of the World Legal Information Institute (<www.worldlii.org>), which are the result of the Free Access to Law movement and are an invaluable resource for lawyers, researchers and citizens worldwide.

Legal Periodicals through IRLII—<www.legalperiodicals.org>

Among the most useful features of the IRLII site is the 'IRLII Periodical Index' link to <www.legalperiodicals.org> on the left-hand side of the screen, also available through the URL above. This allows users to search for articles on any legal topic from all Irish law journals, not just the full-text journals accessible through Westlaw IE. There are no full-text versions of journal articles through this site (except for some articles from the 'Law Society Gazette', the 'Bar

Review' and some student journals), but the citations are provided so that you may then get hard copies of relevant articles from the library or from the subscription databases. To perform a truly comprehensive search for Irish academic commentary, this site is an indispensable source in the research process. Again, however, be aware of its limitations: you are not conducting a full-text search of the articles, but rather only a search of the keywords which are linked to the articles. Browsing through the back catalogues in the library of the key journal titles in the area under consideration cannot be underestimated.

Legislation through the Irish Statute Book—<www.irishstatutebook.ie>

The Irish Statute Book has been substantially changed recently and is now known as the electronic Irish Statute Book (eISB). From the home page, clicking on the 'Legislation' centre-left of your screen will bring up three options: Acts of the Oireachtas, Statutory Instruments and Pre-1922 legislation. On choosing the Acts of the Oireachtas (likely to be the most useful of the three), you will see Acts grouped by decade and further grouped by year.

When you have selected a year, you will be brought to an alphabetised list of the Acts for that particular year. There is an option to search by the number of the Act. There is also an option to refine the search by typing in the first letters (and more, if necessary) of the Act, which will lead you directly to the piece of legislation that you are endeavouring to track down. Clicking on an individual Act will provide options to look at individual sections, the Act in its entirety and to view amendments, the date of the Act's commencement and Statutory Instruments made under the Act.

On the homepage are also tabs with links to the Constitution, some external resources and a helpful Frequently Asked Questions (FAQ) section.

Irish Law—<www.irishlaw.org>

This is a great umbrella site for Irish legal resources online. It contains links to primary and secondary Irish legal sources online, as well as some miscellaneous items, like blogs on Irish law, listings of legal professionals throughout Ireland and even a list of legal publications by subject.

Courts Service—<www.courts.ie>

This user-friendly site contains valuable practical information about the structure of the Irish judiciary and the operations of the court system. It is especially useful if you are interested in discovering more about the procedural and substantive rules of the courts. Perhaps most importantly, it houses a searchable database of judgments which is updated on a frequent basis and should be the first port of call when you are looking to find very recently issued judgments.

Houses of the Oireachtas—<www.oireachtas.ie>

The homepage of Ireland's bicameral parliament contains much useful information about the Dáil and Seanad Éireann, its membership, geographic composition, committee structure, history and so on. Its most useful aspects for you, however, are its fully searchable database containing the Acts of the Oireachtas from 1922. Its database of Dáil and Seanad Debates from 1919 is useful if you are seeking to unearth the intent behind a particular piece of legislation. The search facility for these debates is not terribly useful, however, and it seems that no matter how limited your search terms, a vast number of results will come back—if at all possible, try to limit your search by either the reference for the debate, or by date. For this, it is sometimes easier to search the relevant legislation through Google with the term 'Dáil Debates' in the first instance, which will then give you the relevant information you need to refine your search on <www.oireachtas.ie>.

Europa—<www.europa.eu>

This is a great site for beginning any research on the law of the European Union. The homepage has a list of specific links to the wide range of matters the EU deals with. Depending on which link is chosen, the new screen contains links to all relevant documents, summaries of relevant legislation and to the actual primary and secondary European legislation on the topic. A fully searchable and regularly expanding database of Court of Justice of the European Union case law is also a very useful feature

Findlaw—<www.findlaw.com/12international/index.html>

This website provides access to a wealth of legal materials from all over the world and groups together hundreds of law and law-related databases by individual jurisdiction. It is an excellent tool if you are called upon to do any research of materials from far-flung jurisdictions. It is particularly good for US legal research because it neatly classifies materials at both the federal and state levels; its US Supreme Court database, in particular, is first-class. Its grouping of Irish law and law-related websites is also quite useful.

HUDOC—<www.echr.coe.int>

To access the HUDOC site, navigate to the web page of the European Court of Human Rights. Clicking on 'Case-Law' will bring you to a database which contains the text of all of the decisions of the European Court of Human

Rights. It is a very useful resource if you are researching in this specific area. The search form allows you to bring up the text of a specific case, if you know its name or reference number, or to do a general search for text that has relevance to your topic.

The Law Reform Commission—<www.lawreform.ie>

The Law Reform Commission has published a number of consultation papers in a wide variety of areas. After the consultation process, the Commission publishes reports. When researching an area, see if the Commission has published a consultation paper or report on the topic, as this will be a useful starting point. Do not just assume that all the important information will be in the report either—the consultation papers are often longer, with consideration given to various aspects and arguments, with reports simply identifying the recommended course of action. The Law Reform Commission website also includes more than 260 Revised Acts, which bring together in one text all subsequent amendments and changes to an Act. This can be extremely useful when undertaking research on statutes.

Social Science Research Network (SSRN)—<www.ssrn.com>

The Social Science Research Network website is a very useful source of academic articles and other commentary. It contains works in progress and finished articles from researchers across the world in the general area of social science. Academics will often put their papers on the site just before or just after they have been published in a journal. Sometimes, the papers are not entirely complete, but it is nonetheless an invaluable means of making sure that your research is as up-to-date as possible. The home page includes a quick search option, in the top right-hand corner, but in order to get best value from the site, it is best to use the search form, which is accessed by clicking the search button on the navigation bar across the top of the page. Here, you can decide whether you want to search in the title of the paper only or in the title and the abstract. Finding relevant research can sometimes be difficult, as the site includes more than law articles, and you may find that you are presented with a long list of items, not all of which are relevant. However, a little persistence can pay off and it can often be useful to be exposed to research on the topic from other disciplines.

Google Scholar—<scholar.google.com>

A useful addition to your toolkit is Google Scholar. This uses the Google search engine to give you access to scholarly material that is freely available worldwide. The interface, as with many Google tools, is very simple—type in your search term and click the search button. There is also an Advanced Search form which is self-explanatory. Note that the 'Legal opinions and journals' option searches American court judgments rather than academic commentary.

From a certain perspective, it is not as comprehensive or useful as the subscription-based services, as it will often find articles but not be able to provide you with access to the full text version, which is almost always available through the paid services. However, it is in some ways more comprehensive as it indexes and searches a large volume of content. It also has some nice 'added extras', such as telling you who has cited an article, giving you formatted citation information which can be imported into a citation manager, and (if you set the preferences correctly) figuring out if your institution has access to a full-text version of a document through a subscription service.

> ■ To test your ability to use these databases, go to <www.legalwriting.ie> and complete Assignment 8.2.

USING DATABASES—SEARCHING TOOLS

The remainder of this chapter assumes that you are familiar with the basic operation of a computer and can access the internet and websites without difficulty. It also assumes that you know how to access the subscription-based databases mentioned from your particular institution. If you need assistance with any of these, please speak to your lecturer or the law librarian in the first instance and he or she should be able to direct you to where you can learn more about those topics. If you do not, you are likely to find the instructions confusing and frustrating.

INVERTED COMMAS

To ensure a precise search, you should enclose legal terms of art, or indeed any specific phrase you are looking for, in inverted commas or quotation marks. If you are looking for material on the separation of powers doctrine, that precise term, separation of powers, should be entered 'separation of powers' in the search field. Doing so ensures that the search will unearth only those materials where that exact term appears. A simple search for separation of powers without quotation marks will, of course, yield many of the same results, but may also bring up results that are not relevant.

Go to <www.westlaw.ie> and try 'invitation to treat' in the search engine. Then try the phrase without quotation marks. Can you see how using the quotation marks narrows and refines your search considerably? What was the difference in results you got from using and not using the quotation marks? Do the same with Google. Is there a difference between the results from the different search engines?

'AND' CONNECTOR

In performing legal research, it is highly likely that you will be searching for materials that contain two or more related, or perhaps distinct, concepts, names, phrases, etc. The 'and' connector limits a search by ensuring that only materials which contain both terms are unearthed by the search. For example, if you were researching the separation of powers doctrine in the context of abortion, a proper search would be:

'separation of powers' and abortion

This ensures that only materials containing both will be the object of the search. Moreover, you may often find that you want to further limit the search and might have a number of terms that will have to appear in the materials to be of use to your research query. As such, it is not at all uncommon for there to be a string of terms all linked together by repeated 'and' connectors. For example:

'separation of powers' and abortion and Constitution and 'statutory rape' and consent

Performing a search like this will unearth only materials that contain all of these terms. You may find that you start with a broad search and then use 'and' to narrow down the set of results to a manageable list.

'OR' CONNECTOR

Another connector, which is not used as much since search engines have become more sophisticated, is 'or'. As you might guess, this allows you to search for documents which mention any of a set of related terms.

murder or manslaughter

'NOT' CONNECTOR

The opposite of 'and' is the 'not' connector, which excludes words from matches. You can use this to limit the volume of documents found, which can be useful when you know that a particular case or phrase is likely to be found but you are not interested in it.

> 'language rights' not 'Irish language'
>
> abortion not 'x case'

FINDING NEARBY WORDS

In the same vein as the use of the 'and' connector, you may often wish to see how items are compared, contrasted or otherwise related to one another within the text of a case or journal article. For instance, if you are aware that the separation of powers doctrine relates to the three branches of government, and were hoping to find a lengthy or nuanced discussion of the topic, you might type in the search field:

> 'separation of powers' w/5 'three branches'

Doing so will only yield materials where these two search terms are used within five words of one another. 'w/' can be used with any such number for a word search, or as 'w/s' for two terms appearing in the same sentence as one another, or as 'w/p' for two terms within the same paragraph as one another. It is important to bear in mind that some databases may use \, rather than /, and some do not use 'w', such as Westlaw IE, where the simple '/5' is used.

WILD CARDS

The exclamation mark works quite well with root derivatives that can form the first part of many potentially helpful words. For instance, 'separation of powers' and 'government' are clearly two terms likely to be used in close proximity to one another. A search of 'Irish Reported and Unreported Cases' in LexisLibrary, for example, if phrased

> 'separation of powers' w/s government

will yield multiple cases. However, if you wish to cast the net even wider, you could phrase the search as follows:

> 'separation of powers' w/s govern!

This will call up not only those cases where separation of powers and government appear in the same sentence, but also all those cases where any word shaped by the root derivative 'govern' (eg governing, governance, governor, governed, etc.) appears in the same sentence.

This is known as a 'wild card'. The wild card characters vary from service to service. For example, on Google, it is *. Check the help pages for the service that you are using to be sure that you are using the correct syntax.

DATE RESTRICTIONS

In many instances, you will be looking for materials only from a certain period. Almost all databases offer self-explanatory point and click instructions that allow the user to make date-specific searches.

CONCLUSION

As you will come to realise, legal research is only something that can be mastered by practice and every individual will develop their own methodology in the process. The key points to be mindful of when encountering inevitable difficulties in the legal research process are to keep it basic, endeavour to search creatively and not to give up until all potential avenues have been exhausted. Subscriber-based and freely available legal research databases may both need to be used in the process. You should not seek assistance from lecturers before you have looked *everywhere*. If you become genuinely frustrated after a long, unsuccessful search or have more generalised queries about any of the above-mentioned databases, do not hesitate to ask questions and seek out individual mentoring.

Appendix

OSCOLA Ireland

Second Edition

<www.legalcitation.ie>

This citation guide is based on OSCOLA which was devised by the Faculty of Law at Oxford University and we are grateful for their permission to adapt it for the purposes of developing a standard citation style for Ireland.

Contents

Introduction. 164

1 General Notes. 165
1.1 Citations and footnotes 165
    1.1.1 Citing cases 165
    1.1.2 Citing legislation 166
    1.1.3 Citing secondary sources 166
    1.1.4 Order of sources in footnotes 166
1.2 Subsequent citations, cross-references and Latin 'gadgets'. 166
    1.2.1 Subsequent citations 166
    1.2.2 Cross-references 168
    1.2.3 Latin 'gadgets'. 168
1.3 Punctuation, ranges of numbers and years, and foreign words 168
    1.3.1 Punctuation. 168
    1.3.2 Ranges of numbers and years 169
    1.3.3 Foreign words. 169
1.4 Citing foreign materials 169
1.5 Quotations. 169
1.6 Tables and lists of abbreviations 170
    1.6.1 Lists of abbreviations 171
    1.6.2 Order of tables 171
    1.6.3 Tables of cases. 171
    1.6.4 Tables of legislation and other tables 172
1.7 Bibliographies. 172

2 Primary Sources. 173
2.1 The Constitution 173
2.2 Case law 173
    2.2.1 General principles. 173
    2.2.2 Case names 174
    2.2.3 Neutral citations 176
    2.2.4 Law reports. 176
    2.2.5 Courts. 177
    2.2.6 Pinpoints. 178
    2.2.7 Judges' names 178
    2.2.8 Subsequent history of a case 179
2.3 Primary legislation 179
    2.3.1 Names of statutes. 179
    2.3.2 Parts of statutes 180
    2.3.3 Older statutes 180
    2.3.4 Explanatory memoranda to statutes. 181
    2.3.5 Bills. 181
2.4 Secondary legislation 181
    2.4.1 Statutory instruments 181
    2.4.2 Rules of court 181
    2.4.3 Parts of statutory instruments. 182

2.5 **European Union legal sources** 182
    2.5.1 EU legislation 182
    2.5.2 Judgments of the European Court of Justice and General Court...... 183
    2.5.3 Decisions of the European Commission......................... 184
2.6 **The European Court of Human Rights** 184
    2.6.1 Judgments of the European Court of Human Rights 184
    2.6.2 Decisions and reports of the European Commission on Human Rights . . 185
2.7 **Cases and legislation from other jurisdictions** 185
    2.7.1 Cases 185
    2.7.2 Legislation 185

3 **Secondary Sources** 186
3.1 **General principles** 186
    3.1.1 Authors' names.. 186
    3.1.2 Titles.. 186
    3.1.3 Parts, chapters, pages and paragraphs 186
    3.1.4 Electronic sources 186
    3.1.5 Subsequent citations and short forms 187
3.2 **Books**... 187
    3.2.1 Authored books 187
    3.2.2 Edited and translated books................................... 187
    3.2.3 Contributions to edited books................................. 188
    3.2.4 Older works 188
    3.2.5 Books of authority and institutional works 188
    3.2.6 Encyclopaedias 188
    3.2.7 Looseleaf services 189
3.3 **Articles** 189
    3.3.1 Hard copy journals 189
    3.3.2 Case notes 190
    3.3.3 Forthcoming articles... 190
    3.3.4 Online journals 190
    3.3.5 Working papers 191
3.4 **Other secondary sources** 191
    3.4.1 General principles... 191
    3.4.2 Parliamentary reports.. 192
    3.4.3 Official publications.. 192
    3.4.4 Law Reform Commission Reports and Consultation Papers 193
    3.4.5 European Commission documents.............................. 193
    3.4.6 Conference papers... 193
    3.4.7 Theses 193
    3.4.8 Websites and blogs 193
    3.4.9 Newspaper articles.. 194
    3.4.10 Interviews.. 194
    3.4.11 Personal communications 194

APPENDIX 1

INTRODUCTION

There are two golden rules for the citation of legal authorities. One is consistency. The other is consideration for the reader. Legal writing is more persuasive when the author refers to legal materials in a clear, consistent and familiar way. When it is easy to identify and to find the author's sources, it becomes easier for the reader to follow the argument. OSCOLA Ireland is designed to help the author to achieve consistency and to make life easier for the reader. OSCOLA Ireland is based on OSCOLA, which was devised by the Faculty of Law at Oxford University.

OSCOLA Ireland does not purport to be comprehensive, but gives rules and examples for the main Irish legal primary sources, and for many types of secondary sources. As far as possible, the guidelines in OSCOLA Ireland are based on common practice in Irish legal citation, but with a minimum of punctuation. When citing materials not mentioned in OSCOLA Ireland, use the general principles in OSCOLA Ireland as a guide, and try to maintain consistency. OSCOLA Ireland is best read in conjunction with OSCOLA.

OSCOLA Ireland is a guide to legal citation, not a style guide. For advice on punctuation, grammar and writing style, use the most recent editions of *Fowler's Modern English Usage*, *The Oxford English Dictionary*, and *Hart's Rules*. *Hart's Rules* is particularly useful for information about typographical conventions, but note that the legal citation section is not always consistent with OSCOLA Ireland.

OSCOLA was originally designed for use within Oxford University, but is now used by law schools throughout the UK and in Ireland, and by a number of legal journals and publishers. Due to the absence of a consistent style guide in Ireland, we sought to adapt and amend OSCOLA to ensure its suitability for Irish students, practitioners and academics. We are, of course, deeply indebted to the editorial team at OSCOLA, and to Donal Nolan and Sandra Meredith in particular. Seth Barrett Tillman and David Fitzmaurice at NUI Maynooth University provided us with a great deal of useful feedback. We would also like to thank Hugo Kelly, Law Librarian at the National University of Ireland, Galway, for his generous assistance with obscure questions of Irish practice.

More information on OSCOLA can be found at <law.ox.ac.uk/publications/oscola. php>. More information on OSCOLA Ireland can be found at <legalcitation.ie>. If you have any comments or suggestions regarding OSCOLA Ireland, please contact us at info@legalcitation.ie.

Larry Donnelly, Elaine Fahey, Rónán Kennedy, and Jennifer Schweppe
February 2016

1 GENERAL NOTES

1.1 CITATIONS AND FOOTNOTES

When writing for an academic or professional audience, provide evidence for your claims by citing your sources in footnotes. Legal writing cites primary legal sources (cases, statutes and so on), as well as secondary sources such as books, journal articles, websites and policy statements.

OSCOLA Ireland is a footnote style: all citations appear in footnotes. OSCOLA Ireland does not use endnotes or in-text citations, such as '(Brown, 2007)'. Longer works, such as books and theses, also include citations in tables of cases and legislation, and bibliographies.

When citing any source, either directly (as a quotation) or indirectly (by paraphrasing or referring to ideas in a source), cite the reference in a footnote, in the style indicated in OSCOLA Ireland.

Indicate footnotes with a superscript number which should appear after the relevant punctuation in the text (if any). Put the footnote marker at the end of a sentence, unless for the sake of clarity it is necessary to put it directly after the word or phrase to which it relates. If the word or phrase to which the footnote marker relates is in brackets, put the marker before the closing bracket. A quotation need not be footnoted separately from the name of the source from which it is derived if the two appear in the same sentence. Otherwise, separate notes should be used.

Close footnotes with a full stop (or question or exclamation mark). Where more than one citation is given in a single footnote reference, separate them with semi-colons.

1.1.1 Citing cases

When citing cases, give the name of the case, the neutral citation (if appropriate), and volume and first page of the relevant law report, and where necessary the court. If the name of the case is given in the text, it is not necessary to repeat it in the footnote. For example:

> Although Costello J strongly approved of their use in *Wavin Pipes v Hepworth Iron Ltd*,[32] Keane J felt there must be some 'obscurity, ambiguity or potential absurdity in the relevant provisions which would justify the court having recourse to what was said in the Oireachtas in order to ascertain the legislative intention.'[33] Later, Walsh J stated in *Quilligan* that the search for intention is confined to the text of legislation: 'Whatever may have been in the minds of the members of the Oireachtas when the legislation was passed, in so far as their intention can be deduced ... it must be, from the words of the statute ...'[34]
>
> [32] (1982) 8 FSR 32 (HC).
> [33] *ACW v Ireland* [1994] 3 IR 232, sub nom *Wadda v Ireland* [1994] 1 ILRM 126 (HC) 137.
> [34] *People (DPP) v Quilligan* [1986] IR 495 (SC) 511.

The numbers at the end of footnotes 33 and 34 are called 'pinpoints'; they give the page on which the quotation can be found. It is also acceptable to include the full case reference in all footnotes.

1.1.2 Citing legislation

A citation in a footnote is not required when citing legislation if all the information the reader needs about the source is provided in the text, as in the following sentence:

> This case highlights the limited judicial role provided by the European Convention on Human Rights Act 2003.

Where the text does not include the name of the Act or the relevant section, this information should be provided in a footnote.

> Irish courts must only consider Strasbourg jurisprudence: they are not bound by it.[1]
>
> [1] European Convention on Human Rights Act 2003, s 2.

1.1.3 Citing secondary sources

If relying on or referring to a secondary source, such as a book or an article, provide a citation for the work in a footnote.

> Hart wrote that the doctrine of precedent is compatible with 'two types of creative or legislative activity': *distinguishing* the earlier case by 'narrowing the rule extracted from the precedent', and *widening the rule* by discarding 'a restriction found in the rule as formulated from the earlier case'.[34]
>
> [34] HLA Hart, *The Concept of Law* (2nd edn, Clarendon Press 1994) 135.

1.1.4 Order of sources in footnotes

When citing more than one source of the same kind for a single proposition, put the sources in chronological order, with the oldest first. Separate the citations with semi-colons, and do not precede the final citation with 'and'. If one or more of the sources are more directly relevant than the others, cite these first, and then cite the less relevant ones in a new sentence, beginning 'See also'. If citing legislation and case law for a single proposition, put the legislation before the cases, and if citing primary and secondary sources for a single proposition, put the primary sources before the secondary ones.

> [1] FH Newark, 'The Boundaries of Nuisance' (1949) 65 LQR 480; Richard Kidner, 'Nuisance and Rights of Property' [1998] Conv 267; Ken Oliphant, 'Unblurring the Boundaries of Nuisance' (1998) 6 Tort L Rev 21; Paula Giliker, 'Whither the Tort of Nuisance? The Implications of Restrictions on the Right to Sue in *Hunter v Canary Wharf* (1999) 7 Torts LJ 155.
>
> [2] *Brent v Haddon* (1619) Cro Jac 555, 79 ER 476; *Broder v Saillard* (1876) 2 Ch D 692 (Ch); *Pemberton v Bright* [1960] 1 All ER 792 (CA). See also *Torette House Pty Ltd v Berkman* (1939) 62 CLR 637, 659 (Dixon J).

Further details of how to cite **cases**, **legislation** and **secondary sources** can be found in parts 2 and 3 of OSCOLA Ireland. The appendix to OSCOLA includes **lists of abbreviations** that can be used in footnotes.

1.2 SUBSEQUENT CITATIONS, CROSS-REFERENCES AND LATIN 'GADGETS'

1.2.1 Subsequent citations

In a subsequent citation of a source, briefly identify the source and provide a cross-citation in brackets to the footnote in which the full citation can be found. If the subsequent citation is in the footnote immediately following the full citation, you can generally use 'ibid' instead.

For subsequent citations of cases, a short form of the case name is sufficient to identify the source. Subsequent citations of legislation may use abbreviations or other short forms. Subsequent citations of secondary sources require only the author's or authors' surname(s), unless several works by the same author are being cited, in which case the surname and the title of the work (or a short form of the title) should be given.

Note that it is also acceptable to give the full citation every time a source is cited, and some publishers and law schools may prefer this to the use of short forms. You should always do this if the previous citation was in an earlier chapter.

EXAMPLE of subsequent citation of a case

In this example, a citation for *North Western Health Board v W* is provided in footnote 1. As the name of the case is given in the text, it is not given in the footnote. The second citation at footnote 2 pinpoints several pages in the case with an attribution to the relevant judge in brackets. The third citation at footnote 7 gives a short form of the case name and a cross-citation to the full citation.

[1] [2001] IESC 90, [2001] 3 IR 622.
[2] ibid 673 (Keane CJ), 712 (Denham J), 738–739 (Murray J), 751–753 (Hardiman J).
...
[7] *NWHB v W* (n 1).

EXAMPLE of subsequent citation of legislation

This example shows legislation for which a short form could be used in a subsequent citation. The short form is indicated in brackets at the end of the full citation. In such cases, the short form can be used without a cross-citation to the full citation where the proximity of the full citation enables this to be done without confusing the reader. Where that is not the case, a further full citation should be provided, with the result that cross-citation is never necessary.

[32] Council Directive (EC) 93/104 concerning certain aspects of the organisation of working time [1993] OJ L307/18 (Working Time Directive).
...
[40] Working Time Directive, art 2.

EXAMPLE of subsequent citation of a book

This example shows a citation of a book which is first cited (in full) at footnote 1, cited again in footnote 26 with a cross-citation to footnote 1, and then cited again at footnote 27.

[1] James Casey, *Constitutional Law in Ireland* (3rd edn, Round Hall 2000).
...
[26] Casey (n 1) 110.
[27] ibid 271–78.

EXAMPLE of subsequent citation of two works by the same author

In this example, two different works by the same author are cited. The subsequent citation provides the author's surname and the title of the work, or a short form of the title.

[27] Andrew Ashworth, 'Testing Fidelity to Legal Values: Official Involvement and Criminal Justice' (2000) 63 MLR 633, 635.
[28] Andrew Ashworth, *Principles of Criminal Law* (6th edn, OUP 2009) 68.
...
[35] Ashworth, 'Testing Fidelity to Legal Values' (n 27) 635–37.
...
[46] Ashworth, *Principles of Criminal Law* (n 28) 73.

1.2.2 Cross-references

Cross-references direct the reader to points of substantive discussion elsewhere in your work. Avoid sending the reader off to another part of the text when a short point could as easily be restated. Never make a cross-reference that will be difficult for the reader to find, such as 'See above'. A good cross-reference takes the reader straight to the very place: 'n 109' or, within the same chapter, 'text to n 32'. Do not cross-refer to 'Chapter 6A2(c)' unless you have running headers on each page showing the sequence of sub-headings. Use 'See ...' only when you actually want the reader to look at the place indicated, for example 'See n 109'.

Pagination may change from draft to draft, especially in preparation for publication. It is therefore easiest to cross-refer to footnote markers, for example 'Text to n 107 in ch 7'. Cross-reference functions in word processors can help you keep track of changes in footnote numbers.

1.2.3 Latin 'gadgets'

Avoid the use of Latin 'gadgets' such as *supra, infra, ante, id, op cit, loc cit,* and *contra,* which are not widely understood. The abbreviation 'ibid', which is short for *ibidem,* meaning 'in the same place', can be used to repeat a citation in the immediately preceding footnote. Standing alone, 'ibid' means strictly 'in the very same place' while 'ibid 345' means 'in the same work, but this time at page 345'. It is equally acceptable to repeat the immediately preceding citation without using 'ibid': 'Ashworth (n 27) 635–37' thus does the trick even in n 28. Do not switch back and forth from one to the other. If there is more than one citation in the preceding footnote, use 'ibid' only if you are referring again to all the citations in that footnote. Note that the abbreviation 'cf' is short for *confer,* meaning 'compare'; it does not mean the same thing as 'see'. Never italicise or capitalise 'ibid' or 'cf'.

[28] Joseph Raz, *The Authority of Law: Essays on Law and Morality* (2nd edn, OUP 2009).
[29] ibid 6.
...
[32] cf Raz (n 28) 233–36.

1.3 Punctuation, ranges of numbers and years, and foreign words

1.3.1 Punctuation

OSCOLA Ireland uses as little punctuation as possible. Abbreviations and initials in authors' names do not take full stops. For example, *Irish Reports* is cited as 'IR' and the Director of Public Prosecutions is abbreviated to 'DPP'. Insert commas to separate items that may otherwise run together and cause confusion, such as runs of numbers or authors and titles.

Riordan v Ireland [2009] IESC 44, [2009] 3 IR 745

JG Fleming, 'Remoteness and Duty: The Control Devices in Liability for Negligence' (1953) 31 Can Bar Rev 471

When citing authorities from other jurisdictions, do not include full stops in the citation.

1.3.2 Ranges of numbers and years

When referring to ranges of numbers, use both figures for numbers between ten and twenty, and thereafter use as few figures as possible, but always use at least two for the final number.

1–6 11–17 21–26 22–32 121–221 1782–83 1782–812

If the range of numbers indicates years, and the years span centuries, give the final year in full.

1871–1914 1925–27 1965–75 1989–2001

1.3.3 Foreign words

In the text, italicise words and phrases in languages other than the one you are writing in, but not quotations. Provide a translation immediately afterwards in brackets, or in a footnote, if required. Do not italicise words that are in common usage in legal English, such as ultra vires, stare decisis, obiter dicta, ratio decidendi, a priori and a fortiori. Commonly used abbreviations, such as ie and eg, are not italicised and have no full stops.

1.4 CITING FOREIGN MATERIALS

When referring to foreign materials, cite primary sources as in their home jurisdiction, with the exception that full stops in abbreviations should be dropped. Guides for other jurisdictions can be found in section 4.3 of the appendix to OSCOLA. Cite secondary sources in accordance with the OSCOLA Ireland rules governing the citation of secondary sources.

1.5 QUOTATIONS

Quotations from other works, cases, statutes and so on must be faithful to the original, except where it is necessary to change quotation marks from single to double, or vice versa. Any comments on the quotation, such as 'emphasis added', should be in a footnote.

Incorporate quotations of up to three lines into the text, within single quotation marks (examples 1 and 2). Quotations within short quotations take double quotation marks. Punctuation follows the closing quotation mark, unless it is an essential part of the quotation, as a question or exclamation mark might be (example 2), or unless the whole sentence is a quotation. The footnote marker comes last, after both the closing quotation mark and the punctuation.

Present quotations longer than three lines in an indented paragraph, with no further indentation of the first line (examples 3 and 4). Do not use quotation marks, except for single quotation marks around quotations within quotations (example 3). Leave a line space either side of the indented quotation.

When a quotation begins in the middle of a sentence in the text, the first letter of the quotation should be capitalised if the quotation itself is a complete sentence, but not otherwise. When a quotation begins at the start of a sentence in the text, the first letter should be capitalised, and square brackets placed around it if it was not capitalised in the original text (example 3). When intervening text is missing from the quotation, or if it ends mid-sentence in the original text, use an ellipsis (...) to indicate that some of the original text is missing. Leave a space between an ellipsis and any text or punctuation, except quotation marks.

If a quotation is incorporated into the text, then no more than a comma (at most) is required to introduce it (examples 1 and 2). Generally, a colon is used to introduce an indented quotation (example 4).

When it is necessary to attribute a quotation or citation within a quotation to its original source, omit the footnote marker from the original text in your quotation, and give the original author's citation in your footnote (example 3). If it is not necessary to attribute such a quotation or citation because it is either implicit or irrelevant, omit the footnote markers or citations and add '(footnotes omitted)' or '(citations omitted)' after the citation in your own footnote. Similarly, if you add emphasis to a quotation put '(emphasis added)' after the footnote citation (example 4).

EXAMPLE 1

Casey explained that the terms of the Constitution 'show clearly that the President is intended to play a mainly ceremonial role'.[61]

EXAMPLE 2

Bix raises the question, 'What is the point of a dissent, after all, at least on the highest court of the jurisdiction, if the law simply is whatever the majority on that court says it is?'[22]

EXAMPLE 3

[T]he House of Lords also concluded that the civil standard of proof (on the balance of probabilities) should be applied in such a way as to be sensitive to the 'seriousness of the matters to be proved and the implications of proving them', which in effect means proof beyond reasonable doubt (ie the criminal standard).[27]

[27] Andrew Ashworth, 'Social Control and "Anti-Social Behaviour": The Subversion of Human Rights' (2004) 120 LQR 263, 276, citing *Clingham and McCann* [2002] UKHL 39, [2003] 1 AC 787 [83] (Lord Hope).

EXAMPLE 4

Walsh J in *DPP v Quilligan* stated that the search for intention is confined to the text of legislation: 'Whatever may have been in the minds of the members of the Oireachtas when the legislation was passed, in so far as their intention can be deduced ... *it must be*, from the words of the statute ...'[12]

[12] [1986] IR 495 (SC) 511 (emphasis added).

1.6 TABLES AND LISTS OF ABBREVIATIONS

A longer legal work, such as a book or a thesis, generally has a list of abbreviations and tables of all the cases, legislation and other primary legal sources cited in the work in the preliminary pages. Shorter works, such as articles and essays, generally only require footnotes. Tables should be indexed, so that each entry indicates on what page or pages the primary source in question is mentioned. The list of abbreviations should come before the tables, and the order of the tables should generally be: table of Articles of the Constitution; table of cases; table of legislation; other tables.

1.6.1 Lists of abbreviations

In an article or essay, define unfamiliar abbreviations in a footnote or in the text. In a book or thesis, define unfamiliar abbreviations in a list of abbreviations in the preliminary pages. Do not define abbreviations that are part of everyday legal usage, such as 'DPP'. For lists of common abbreviations that need not be defined, see section 4.2 of the appendix of OSCOLA.

1.6.2 Order of tables

If there is a table of articles of the Constitution, it should come before all other tables, including the table of cases. The table of cases will follow this, or come first if there is no table of articles of the Constitution. Tables of legislation and other tables, such as tables of international treaties and conventions, UN documents, official papers and policy documents, should follow the table of cases.

1.6.3 Tables of cases

In a table of cases, case names are not italicised. Unless there are very few cases, divide the table into separate sections for different jurisdictions. Cases should be listed in alphabetical order of first significant word. Thus, *Re Farquar's Estate* should be tabled as 'Farquar's Estate, Re'. Cases identifying parties by initial only should be listed under the initial, so *Re F (mental patient: sterilisation)* becomes 'F (mental patient: sterilisation), Re'. When listing cases with names such as *DPP v Smith*, or *People (DPP) v Smith* in works on criminal law, drop the 'DPP' (or 'People (DPP)') and list the case as 'Smith', but if citing such cases in a work primarily concerned with another area of law, list them by their full names, under 'DPP' or 'People (DPP)', and also do this when citing judicial review cases with the State as the first-named party.

List trademark cases and shipping cases under the full case name, but insert an additional entry in the table under the trademark or the name of the ship (again using the first significant word, so that *The MV Toledo* becomes 'MV Toledo, The'), with a cross-reference to the full name.

MV Toledo, The. *See* ACT Shipping v Minister for the Marine

If not listed separately, EU cases should be arranged alphabetically by first party name in the table of cases, with the case number following the name of the case in brackets, so that 'Case T–344/99 *Arne Mathisen AS v Council* [2002] ECR II–2905' is cited in the table of cases under 'A' as 'Arne Mathisen AS v Council (T–344/99) [2002] ECR II–2905'. If the table of cases is divided by jurisdiction, list ECJ, CFI and Commission decisions separately, in chronological and numerical order, citing the cases as in footnotes, with the case number first, but omitting the word 'Case'. If a large number of such cases are cited, it may be helpful to compile a separate table of the cases in alphabetical order.

1.6.4 Tables of legislation and other tables

A table of legislation should list every statute cited in the work, with the entry for each statute being sub-divided to show which parts of the statute (sections, sub-sections and so on) are cited where. Statutory instruments should be listed separately, at the end of the list of statutes. If there are a large number of citations of statutory instruments, it may be helpful to have wholly separate tables of statutes and statutory instruments. In tables of legislation, legislation should be listed in alphabetical order of first significant word of the title, not chronologically by date of enactment. If legislation from more than one jurisdiction is cited, it may be helpful to have separate lists for each jurisdiction.

1.7 BIBLIOGRAPHIES

In longer works, such as theses and books, a bibliography listing secondary sources should be provided after the main body of text and any appendices. It should include all such sources cited in the work and need not be indexed.

Items in bibliographies take the same form as all other citations in OSCOLA Ireland, with three exceptions: (1) the author's surname should precede his or her initial(s), with no comma separating them, but a comma after the final initial; (2) only initials should be used, and not forenames; and (3) the titles of unattributed works should be preceded by a double em dash. Works should be arranged in alphabetical order of author surname, with unattributed works being listed at the beginning of the bibliography in alphabetical order of first major word of the title.

CITATION in a footnote

[15] Robert Clark, *Contract Law* (6th edn, Round Hall 2008).

CITATION in a bibliography

Clark R, *Contract Law* (6th edn, Round Hall 2008)

If citing several works by the same author in a bibliography, list the author's works in chronological order (starting with the oldest), and in alphabetical order of first major word of the title within a single year. After the citation of the first work, replace the author's name with a double em dash. Alphabetise works by more than one author under the first author's name, but place them after that author's sole-authored works. If a first author has more than one co-author, arrange the co-authored works in alphabetical order of co-author surname, and if you are citing more than one work by the same first author and co-author, arrange the works in chronological order, repeating the co-author's name each time.

Hart HLA, *Law, Liberty and Morality* (OUP 1963)
—— 'Varieties of Responsibility' (1967) 83 LQR 346
—— *Punishment and Responsibility* (OUP 1968)
—— and Honoré AM, 'Causation in the Law' (1956) 72 LQR 58, 260, 398
—— and Honoré AM, *Causation in the Law* (2nd edn, OUP 1985)13

2 Primary Sources

2.1 The Constitution

The Irish Constitution, or Bunreacht na hÉireann, should be referred to in the same language as the surrounding text, whether English or Irish. Capitalise Constitution and Article, but not articles (unless referring to a specific set or range) or 'constitutional'. Use a degree symbol ° when referring to a sub-subsection.

> Other articles of the Constitution which protect the rights of the family ...
> We also find references to the role of the Council of State in Articles 14 and 31.
> Article 12.1 states that the President ...
> The Constitution provides in Article 40.3.3°...
> However, this does not have the status of a constitutional right ...

Art (or art) is acceptable as an abbreviation in footnotes:

[17] Art 40.3.3°.

2.2 Case law

2.2.1 General principles

The components of a typical case citation are the case name, the neutral citation and the law report. However, neutral citations are a relatively recent development, so many case citations consist only of the case name and the law report. To verify whether a case has a neutral citation, use the website of the Irish Legal Information Institute, <www.irlii.org>. Most cases decided after 1998 have a neutral citation and some cases have been given retrospective neutral citations.

Use italics for the name of the case, with an unpunctuated italic *v* to separate the names of adverse parties. Use normal text for the rest of the citation. A comma separates the neutral citation and the law report citation. There are no full stops in the abbreviations: hence 'IESC' rather than 'I.E.S.C.' and 'IR' rather than 'I.R.'.

Case citations including neutral citations

The components of a typical case citation including a neutral citation are:

> *case name* | [year] | court | number, | [year] OR (year) | volume | report abbreviation | first page

The example below indicates that the case of *Riordan v Ireland* was the forty-fourth judgment issued by the Supreme Court in 2009, and that a report of the judgment can be found in volume three of the 2009 volume of the *Irish Reports*, beginning at page 745.

> *Riordan v Ireland* [2009] IESC 44, [2009] 3 IR 745

Case citations without neutral citations

The components of a typical case citation without a neutral citation are:

> *case name* | [year] OR (year) | volume | report abbreviation | first page | (court)

As the following example shows, when the year is used to identify the law report volume, it is given in square brackets. In such cases, also give a volume number if the series in question was issued in more than one volume during that particular year, but do not do so if only one volume was issued.

Ryan v Attorney General [1965] IR 294 (SC)

Where the year is necessary to identify the volume and there is more than one volume in a year, give the year in square brackets and the volume number before the report abbreviation, as in the following example from volume four of the 1998 *Irish Reports*.

Phonographic Performance Ireland Ltd v Cody [1998] 4 IR 504 (HC)

Give the year of judgment (not publication) in round brackets when the volumes of the law report series are independently numbered, so that the year of publication is not needed to find the volume. For example, a report of *McCarthy v O'Flynn*, which was decided in 1980, can also be found in the one hundred and fourteenth volume of the *Irish Law Times Reports*, beginning on page twenty-two. The citation of this report is therefore:

McCarthy v O'Flynn (1980) 114 ILTR 22 (SC)

2.2.2 Case names

Where there are multiple parties, name only the first claimant and first defendant. Where the parties are individuals, omit forenames and initials. Abbreviate common words and phrases: use *HSE* for *Health Service Executive*, *Co* for *Company*, *DPP* for *Director of Public Prosecutions* and so on (see section 4.2.4 of the appendix of OSCOLA for more abbreviations).

Use *Re* in preference to *In re*, *In the matter of*, and so on: *Re the Companies Act 1963* rather than *In the matter of the Companies Act 1963*, and *Re Farquar's Estate* instead of *In re the Estate of Farquar*. Abbreviate *Ex parte* to *Ex p* with a capital *E* only if it is the first word of the case name. The *p* has no full stop. Do not include expressions such as *and another*, which may appear in titles in law reports. Omit descriptions such as *a firm* if the party in question is named, but if only the initial of the party is provided, then the description (such as *a minor*) should be given, at least in the first citation. Terms indicating corporate status (such as *Ltd* and *plc*) should not be omitted if included in the heading of the report.

Re A (conjoined twins) [2001] Fam 147

Re Article 26 and the Illegal Immigrants (Trafficking) Bill 1999 [2000] IESC 19, [2000] 2 IR 360

Re Bloomberg Developments Ltd [2002] IESC 56

Short forms of case names

Give the name of the case in full when it is first mentioned in the text or footnotes; it may be shortened thereafter. Thus, 'in *Wavin Pipes v Hepworth Iron Ltd*' can be shortened to 'in the *Wavin Pipes* case' (or 'in *Wavin Pipes*') (example 1). If a case name is shortened in this way, the name chosen must be that which stands first in the full name of the case. In shipping cases, the name of the ship can be used instead of the full case name (example 2). It is common in works on criminal law to see 'in *People (DPP) v Shaw*' shortened to 'in *Shaw*', even in the first citation, but less so where a small number of criminal cases are cited in a work primarily concerned with another area of law. Either form is acceptable (example 3). Popular names for cases may also be used. Give the popular name in brackets after the initial full citation, and then use the popular name in subsequent citations (example 4).

EXAMPLE 1

[14] *Wavin Pipes v Hepworth Iron Ltd* (1982) 8 FSR 32.

...

[19] *Wavin Pipes* (n 14).

EXAMPLE 2

[25] *Leigh & Sillavan Ltd v Aliakmon Shipping Co Ltd (The Aliakmon)* [1986] AC 785 (HL).

...

[45] *The Aliakmon* (n 25).

EXAMPLE 3

[11] *R v Evans* [2009] EWCA Crim 650, [2009] 1 WLR 13 OR *Evans* [2009] EWCA Crim 650, [2009] 1 WLR 13.

...

[23] *R v Evans* (n 11) OR *Evans* (n 11).

EXAMPLE 4

[12] *Mirage Studios v Counter-feat Clothing Co Ltd* [1991] FSR 145 (Ch) (Ninja Turtles case).

...

[28] Ninja Turtles case (n 12).

Judicial review applications

Before 1986, case names in judicial review applications cited the State against the body under review, on behalf of the individual involved.

The State (Turley) v Ó Floinn [1968] IR 245 (SC)

For cases from 1986 onwards, the following form is used:

Fairleigh v Temple Bar Renewal Ltd [1999] 2 IR 508 (HC)

In both cases, subsequent citations would cite *Turley* or *Fairleigh* in the text or in a footnote.

Variations in the name of a case

Where the same case is reported under significantly different names in different law reports, use the name given in the heading of the report being cited. Where two or more reports using different names are cited, the report or reports using the alternative name of the case should be introduced by the phrase 'sub nom' in roman (an abbreviation of *sub nomine*, meaning 'under the name').

ACW v Ireland [1994] 3 IR 232, sub nom *Wadda v Ireland* [1994] 1 ILRM 126 (HC)

Similarly, where a case appears under a different name at different stages in its history (that difference in the name being more than a mere reversal of the names of the parties), and both stages are being cited, the name of the case at the second stage cited should be introduced by 'sub nom'.

> *R v Monopolies and Mergers Commission, ex p South Yorkshire Transport Ltd* [1992] 1 WLR 291 (CA), affd sub nom *South Yorkshire Transport Ltd v Monopolies and Mergers Commission* [1993] 1 WLR 23 (HL)

2.2.3 Neutral citations

Transcripts of judgments with neutral citations are generally freely available on the Courts Service website (<courts.ie>). Not all judgments have neutral citations. The cases seem to be numbered consecutively through the year. Only some cases with neutral citations have numbered paragraphs—and even within a judgment, some judges will use numbered paragraphs and some will not. If no paragraph numbers are given, do not manually insert them.

Neutral citations give the year of judgment, the court and the judgment number. The court is not included in brackets at the end of a neutral citation because the neutral citation itself identifies the court. Where a judgment with a neutral citation has not been reported, give only the neutral citation, as shown in the last two examples below (note that these judgments may have been reported since OSCOLA Ireland was published). Where such a judgment has been reported, give the neutral citation followed by a citation of the best report, separated by a comma (for information about the 'best report', see section 2.2.4).

> *Gilligan v Special Criminal Court* [2005] IESC 86, [2006] 2 IR 406
>
> *Mahon Tribunal v Keena* [2009] IESC 64, [2009] 2 ILRM 373
>
> *Minister for Justice, Equality and Law Reform v McArdle* [2005] IESC 76
>
> *EMI Records (Ireland) Ltd v Eircom Ltd* [2010] IEHC 108

If a single report includes more than one judgment and therefore more than one neutral citation, list the neutral citations in chronological order, starting with the oldest, and separate them with a comma.

> *Masterman-Lister v Brutton & Co (Nos 1 and 2)* [2002] EWCA Civ 1889, [2003] EWCA Civ 70, [2003] 1 WLR 1511

As the unreported judgment is generally available online much earlier than the printed report, it is important to check all neutral citations to see if a report has subsequently become available before finalising your work.

A complete list of neutral citations for the United Kingdom is provided in section 4.1 of the appendix of OSCOLA. For up-to-date information on neutral citations in Ireland, see the case law databases at <courts.ie>.

2.2.4 Law reports

A law report is a published report of a judgment, with additional features such as a headnote summarising the facts of the case and the judgment, catchwords used for indexing, and lists of cases considered.

The 'best report'

In Ireland, there are no official law reports of any kind, but the *Irish Reports* and the *Irish Law Reports Monthly* are regarded as the most authoritative reports. These reports sometimes include the arguments of counsel.

If a case is reported in one of these two reports, this report should generally be cited in preference to any other report. Where the case is reported in both series, give the *Irish Reports* reference only, after the neutral citation (if the latter is available). Only if a judgment is not reported in one of these general series should you refer to another series, such as the *Irish Law Times Reports* or the *Employment Law Reports.*

Heavily edited reports

Where a report of a case gives only a summary or a heavily edited version of the judgment (which is the norm for reports in newspapers and some practitioner journals), cite the report only if there is no neutral citation and no other, fuller, report. When citing a case report, put the title of a newspaper in roman, not italics.

K v K (1998) 2 Irish J Fam L 25 (SC)

Unreported cases

If a case is unreported but has a neutral citation, give that. If an unreported case does not have a neutral citation (which will often be the case before 1998), give the court and the date of the judgment in brackets after the name of the case. There is no need to add the word 'unreported'.

S v Eastern Health Board (HC, 22 July 1988)

Release Speech Therapy v HSE [2011] IEHC 57

Reports using case numbers in the citation

In some specialist law reports, cases are given case numbers which run consecutively through the volumes, rather than page numbers. Examples include the *Reports of Patents Cases*, the *Criminal Appeal Reports* and the *Personal Injuries and Quantum Reports*. In such cases, follow the citation method used by the series in question.

Rozario v Post Office [1997] PIQR P15 (CA)

Thompson Holidays Ltd v Norwegian Cruise Lines Ltd [2002] EWCA Civ 1828, [2003] RPC 32

R v Kelly [2008] EWCA Crim 137, [2008] 2 Cr App R 11

2.2.5 Courts

Indicate the court in brackets after the first page of the report, and before the pinpoint if there is one. Use (SC) for the Supreme Court, (CCA) for the Court of Criminal Appeal, (HC) for the High Court, (CA) for Court of Appeal, and (SCC) for the Special Criminal Court. Citations of cases with a neutral citation do not require the court.

2.2.6 Pinpoints

A pinpoint is a reference to a particular paragraph of a judgment or page of a report.

If the judgment has numbered paragraphs, pinpoint to a particular paragraph by putting the relevant paragraph number in square brackets. If the judgment does not have numbered paragraphs and is not available in a form which allows unchanging references (such as a published version, a signed printed transcript or a PDF file), do not provide a pinpoint citation. If pinpointing to more than one paragraph, separate the paragraph numbers in square brackets with a comma. If citing spans of paragraphs, insert a dash between the first and last paragraph being cited.

> *A v Refugee Appeals Tribunal* [2009] IEHC 60 [21], [24]–[25]
>
> *Buckley v A-G* [1950] IR 67 (SC) 82–83

If a law report citation ends with the identification of the court in brackets, the pinpoint follows the closing bracket, without any comma. Where the court is not identified in this way, and you are pinpointing to a page number, insert a comma to prevent the numbers running together. Where the pinpoint reference is to the first page of the report, repeat the page number. Multiple page number pinpoints should be separated by commas.

> *The People (AG) v Bell* [1969] IR 24 (HC) 26, 29
>
> *Hoey v Minister for Justice* [1994] 3 IR 329 (HC) 345–46

2.2.7 Judges' names

Where reference is made to a judge in a case, use the judge's surname followed by the conventional abbreviation identifying his or her judicial office. Do not use honorifics such as 'the Honourable'.

A High Court or Supreme Court judge is called 'Mr Justice Murphy', or if a woman, either 'Mrs Justice Murphy' or 'Ms Justice Murphy', according to her preference (abbreviated 'Murphy J'). To verify the correct form, use the Courts Service web site (<courts.ie>). Forenames are not used unless there are two judges with the same surname, in which case both the forename and surname of the junior judge of the two is given (for example, 'Roderick Murphy J').

The Chief Justice is abbreviated to 'Murphy CJ', and the name of the President of the Court of Appeal, High, Circuit, and District Courts abbreviated as 'Murphy P'.

Circuit Court judges are referred to as 'His/Her Honour Judge Murphy', with no abbreviation. District Court judges are 'Judge Murphy', with no abbreviation. (Before the coming into force of section 21 of the Courts Act 1991, District Court judges were known as 'justices'.)

If a judge was elevated to a new appointment after the decision in the case you are citing, use the title of the judge at that time; there is no need to add the words 'as he then was'. If referring to more than one judge of the Supreme Court, the Court of Appeal, the High Court, the Court of Criminal Appeal, or the Special Criminal Court in the short form, follow their surnames with JJ. When pinpointing to a particular passage in a judgment, add the judge's name in brackets after the pinpoint. Do not use *per*.

EXAMPLES *in the text*

Kennedy CJ rejected this argument because ...

This is evident from the decision in *Ryan,* in which Ó Dálaigh CJ said ...

Hardiman and Fennelly JJ were of the opinion that ...

As Lynch J pointed out in ...

EXAMPLES *in footnotes*

[101] *Howard v Commissioners of Public Works* [1994] 1 IR 101 (SC) 140 (Finlay CJ); *DPP v McDonagh* [1996] 1 IR 565 (SC) 570 (Costello P); *In re National Irish Bank Ltd* [1999] 3 IR 145 (HC) 164 (Shanley J); *An Blascaod Mór Teo v Commissioners of Public Works (No 2)* [2000] 1 IR 1 (HC) 4 (Budd J).

2.2.8 Subsequent history of a case

The subsequent history of a case may be indicated after the primary citation by abbreviating 'affirmed' to 'affd' and 'reversed' to 'revd'. These abbreviations refer to the decision in the primary citation.

Ó Beoláin v Fahy [1999] IEHC 161, revd [2001] IESC 37, [2001] 2 IR 279

2.3 PRIMARY LEGISLATION

2.3.1 Names of statutes

Cite an Act by its short title and year in normal text, using capitals for the major words, and without a comma before the year.

Interpretation Act 2005

European Convention on Human Rights Act 2003

If you are referring to a particular Act a number of times in short succession, it is usually possible to use an abbreviated form of the title in the footnotes, without a cross-citation, provided the reader has been warned in advance. The abbreviation is usually the initials of the main words in the title, and should always include the year (so that, for example, the Criminal Justice Act 2006 becomes 'CJA 2006' and not just 'CJA'). In the text, it is acceptable in such circumstances to refer without any prior warning to 'the 2006 Act', but only where this short form is sure to be understood.

[12] Criminal Procedure Act 1993 (CPA 1993), s 3(1).

...

[15] CPA 1993, s 2(1)(a)(ii).

If several jurisdictions are discussed in a work, it may be necessary to add the jurisdiction of the legislation in brackets at the end of the citation.

Civil Liability Act 1961 (Irl)

2.3.2 Parts of statutes

Statutes are divided into parts, sections, subsections, paragraphs and subparagraphs. In addition, the main text of the statute may be supplemented by schedules, which are divided into paragraphs and subparagraphs. The relevant abbreviations are:

part/parts	pt/pts
section/sections	s/ss
subsection/subsections	sub-s/sub-ss
paragraph/paragraphs	para/paras
subparagraph/subparagraphs	subpara/subparas
schedule/schedules	sch/schs

Use the full form at the beginning of a sentence, or when referring to a part of a statute without repeating the name of the Act. Elsewhere in the text, either form can be used, though when referring to subsections or paragraphs it is conventional to use the short form. Use the short form in footnotes. In footnote citations of parts of Acts, insert a comma after the year, and a space but no full stop between the abbreviation and the initial number, letter or opening bracket.

Sale of Goods and Supply of Services Act 1980, s 2

If specifying a paragraph or subsection as part of a section, use only the abbreviation for the section. For example, paragraph (a) of subsection (2) of section 5 of the European Convention on Human Rights Act 2003 is expressed as follows.

European Convention on Human Rights Act 2003, s 5(2)(a)

EXAMPLES in the text

... section 4(1)(a) of the Criminal Law (Insanity) Act 2006 ... OR ... the Criminal Law (Insanity) Act 2006, s 4(1)(a) ...

... by virtue of section 2(1)(b)(i) of the Prohibition of Incitement to Hatred Act 1989...

... as provided by sections 1(2) and 7(2) ...

Subsection (1) does not apply to ...

... as sub-s (3) shows ...

EXAMPLES in footnotes

[34] Planning and Development (Strategic Infrastructure) Act 2006, ss 32(1) and 157(1).
[35] Sustainable Energy Act 2002 , s 6(c).

2.3.3 Older statutes

For older statutes, it may be helpful to give the regnal year and chapter number.

Crown Debts Act 1801 (41 Geo 3 c 90)

In this example, the information in brackets indicates that the Act was given royal assent in the forty-first year of the reign of George III. The abbreviation c stands for chapter. The Crown Debts Act 1801 was the ninetieth Act to receive royal assent in that session of Parliament, and so is chapter 90. Citation by chapter number must be used for older statutes without short titles.

2.3.4 Explanatory memoranda to statutes

When citing explanatory memoranda to statutes, precede the name of the statute with the words 'Explanatory Memorandum to the …'. As the explanatory memorandum is attached to the Bill rather than to the Act, ensure that you refer to the Bill, followed by the full title of the enacted legislation. When pinpointing, cite the page number(s).

Explanatory Memorandum to the Student Support Bill 2008 (Student Support Act 2011), 3.

2.3.5 Bills

Cite a Bill by its title, the house in which it originated, the year of presentation, and the number assigned to it. When a Bill is reprinted at any stage it is given a new number.

title | Dáil Bill | number OR title | Seanad Bill | Year | number

The rules for referring to parts of Bills mirror those for referring to parts of statutes (see section 2). 'Clause' and 'clauses' may be abbreviated to 'cl' and 'cls' in the text and should be so abbreviated in footnotes.

Communications Regulation (Postal Services) Seanad Bill (2010) 50

Planning and Development (Amendment) (No 3) Dáil Bill (2004) 49, cl 4

2.4 Secondary legislation

2.4.1 Statutory instruments

Statutory instruments (orders, regulations or rules) are numbered consecutively throughout the year. The year combines with the serial number to provide an SI number that follows the abbreviation 'SI' and which is used to identify the legislation. Before the Statutory Instruments Act 1947, secondary legislation in Ireland was known as statutory rules and orders, for which the abbreviation SR&O should be used. When citing a statutory instrument, give the name, year and (after a comma) the SI number.

Planning and Development Regulations 2008, SI 2008/235

National School Teachers' Superannuation Scheme 1934, SR&O 1934/23

As with statutes (see section 2.3.1), where the same statutory instrument is cited a number of times in the same work, an abbreviated form can be used in the footnotes (such as 'EPB 2006' for the European Communities (Energy Performance of Buildings) Regulations 2006), provided due warning is given with the first full citation.

2.4.2 Rules of court

The Rules of the Superior Courts (RSC), the Rules of the Circuit Court (RCC) and the Rules of the District Court (RDC) may be cited without reference to their SI number or year. Rules of court are divided into Orders (Ord) and rules (r). Cite all other court rules in full as statutory instruments.

> RSC Ord 27, r 9
>
> RCC Ord 15, r 2

Practice Directions (PD) are referred to simply by number, as listed on the Courts Service web site.

> PD HC48
>
> PD CC01

2.4.3 Parts of statutory instruments

The rules for referring to parts of statutory instruments mirror those for referring to parts of statutes (see section 2). As with statutes, in the text use the full form at the start of a sentence, and either the full or abbreviated form elsewhere. Use the short form in footnotes. In addition to those given above for parts of statutes, use the following abbreviations:

regulation/regulations	reg/regs
rule/rules	r/rr
article/articles	art/arts

When referring to parts of the rules of court, do not insert a comma before the pinpoint.

> European Communities (Greenhouse Gas Emissions Trading) Regulations 2004, SI 2004/437, art 4

2.5 EUROPEAN UNION LEGAL SOURCES

Official notices of the EU are carried in the *Official Journal of the European Communities* (abbreviated to OJ). The OJ citation is given in the order: year, OJ series, number/page. The letter 'L' denotes the legislation series (the 'C' series contains EU information and notices, and the 'S' series invitations to tender).

2.5.1 EU legislation

When citing EU treaties and protocols, give the title of the legislation, including amendments if necessary, followed by the year of publication, the OJ series and the issue and page numbers. Older treaties were published in the C series. With notable exceptions, such as the Lisbon Treaty, legislation is now published in the L series.

> legislation title | [year] | OJ series | issue/first page

> Protocol to the Agreement on the Member States that do not fully apply the Schengen acquis—Joint Declarations [2007] OJ L129/35
>
> Consolidated Version of the Treaty on European Union [2008] OJ C115/13

Cite Regulations, Directives, Decisions, Recommendations and Opinions by giving the legislation type, number and title, followed by publication details in the OJ. Note that the year precedes the running number in citations to Directives, but follows it in citations to Regulations.

legislation type	number	title	[year]	OJ L issue/first page

Council Directive 2002/60/EC of 27 June 2002 laying down specific provisions for the control of African swine fever and amending Directive 92/119/EEC as regards Teschen disease and African swine fever [2002] OJ L192/27

Council Regulation (EC) 1984/2003 of 8 April 2003 introducing a system for the statistical monitoring of trade in bluefin tuna, swordfish and big eye tuna within the Community [2003] OJ L295/1

Short forms and pinpoints

Give EU legislation its full name on first citation. In subsequent citations, a short form of the title may be used (provided warning is given in the first citation) and in a footnote you may also just give the document type and number (using 'Reg' and 'Dir' as abbreviations). Pinpoints indicating articles (abbreviated 'art' or 'arts') or paragraphs follow the OJ citation and a comma. For more information about subsequent citations, see section 1.2.1.

Older EU legislation

For the years 1952–72 (when there was no English edition of the *Journal Officiel*), refer where possible to the Special Edition of the OJ.

Council Regulation (EEC) 1017/68 applying rules of competition to transport by rail, road and inland waterway [1968] OJ Spec Ed 302

2.5.2 Judgments of the European Court of Justice and General Court

Since 1989, EU cases have been numbered according to whether they were registered at the European Court of Justice (ECJ) or the General Court (GC), and given the prefix C– (for ECJ cases) or T– (for GC cases). The General Court was called the Court of First Instance (CFI) until 2009. Judgments from the Civil Service Tribunal, which was established in 2005, are prefixed F–. Do not add a C– to pre-1989 cases.

Give the case registration number in roman and then the name of the case in italics, with no punctuation between them. Give the report citation in the same form as for Irish cases.

case number	*case name*	[year]	report abbreviation	first page

Where possible, refer to the official reports, which are cited as ECR. ECJ cases are reported in volume one (ECR I–) and GC cases are reported in volume two (ECR II–). The volume number, which is in roman numerals, attaches to the page number with a dash. If an ECR reference is not available, the second best report is usually the *Common Market Law Reports* (CMLR).

For an unreported case, cite the relevant notice in the OJ. If the case is not yet reported in the OJ, then cite the case number and case name, followed by the court and date of judgment in brackets. (Please note that unreported cases given here as examples will have been reported subsequently.)

Case 240/83 *Procureur de la République v ADBHU* [1985] ECR 531

Joined Cases C–430 and 431/93 *Jereon van Schijndel v Stichting Pensioenfonds voor Fysiotherapeuten* [1995] ECR I–4705

Case T–344/99 *Arne Mathisen AS v Council* [2002] ECR II–2905

Case C–556/07 *Commission v France* [2009] OJ C102/8

Case T–277/08 *Bayer Healthcare v OHMI—Uriach Aquilea* OTC (CFI, 11 November 2009)

When pinpointing, use 'para' or 'paras' after a comma.

Case C–176/03 *Commission v Council* [2005] ECR I–7879, paras 47–48

Opinions of Advocates General

When citing an opinion of an Advocate General, add the words 'Opinion of AG [name]' after the case citation and a comma, and before any pinpoint.

Case C–411/05 *Palacios de la Villa v Cortefiel Servicios SA* [2007] ECR I–8531, Opinion of AG Mazák, paras 79–100

2.5.3 Decisions of the European Commission

Decisions of the European Commission in relation to competition law and mergers are to be treated as cases. Give the names of the parties (or the commonly used short name) in italics, the case number in brackets, the Commission Decision number (where available), and the OJ report.

case name | (case number) | Commission Decision number | [year] | OJ L issue/first page

Alcatel/Telettra (Case IV/M.042) Commission Decision 91/251/EEC [1991] OJ L122/48

Georg Verkehrsorgani v Ferrovie dello Stato (Case COMP/37.685) Commission Decision 2004/33/EC [2004] OJ L11/17

2.6 The European Court of Human Rights

2.6.1 Judgments of the European Court of Human Rights

For judgments of the European Court of Human Rights (ECtHR), cite either the official reports, the *Reports of Judgments and Decisions* (cited as ECHR) or the *European Human Rights Reports* (EHRR), but be consistent in your practice. Before 1996, the official reports were known as Series A and numbered consecutively. The EHRR series is also numbered consecutively, but from 2001 case numbers have been used instead of page numbers.

References to unreported judgments should give the application number, and then the court and the date of the judgment in brackets. When pinpointing, use 'para' or 'paras' after a comma. Further information can be obtained from the ECtHR website and the HUDOC database at <www.echr.coe.int>.

Johnston v Ireland (1986) Series A no 122

Osman v UK ECHR 1998–VIII 3124

Balogh v Hungary App no 47940/99 (ECtHR, 20 July 2004)

Omojudi v UK (2010) 51 EHRR 10

2.6.2 Decisions and reports of the European Commission on Human Rights

Citations of decisions and reports of the European Commission on Human Rights, which ceased to function in 1998, should give the year of the decision in brackets, and then refer to the *Decisions and Reports* of the Commission (DR), or, for decisions prior to 1974, to the *Collection of Decisions* of the Commission (CD). If available, a reference to a report of the decision in the EHRR is also acceptable, but if citing the EHRR for a decision of the Commission, insert '(Commission Decision)' after the rest of the citation. If the decision is unreported, give the application number, and then in brackets 'Commission Decision' and the date of the decision.

X v Netherlands (1971) 38 CD 9

Council of Civil Service Unions v UK (1987) 10 EHRR 269 (Commission Decision)

Simpson v UK (1989) 64 DR 188

P v UK App no 13473/87 (Commission Decision, 11 July 1988)

2.7 CASES AND LEGISLATION FROM OTHER JURISDICTIONS

2.7.1 Cases

Cite cases from other jurisdictions as they are cited in their own jurisdiction, but with minimal punctuation. If the name of the law report series cited does not itself indicate the court, and the identity of the court is not obvious from the context, you should also give this in either full or short form in brackets at the end of the citation. When citing a decision of the highest court of a US state, the abbreviation of the name of the state suffices.

Austin v Commissioner of Police for the Metropolis [2009] UKHL 5, [2009] AC 564

Henningsen v Bloomfield Motors Inc 161 A 2d 69 (NJ 1960)

Roe v Wade 410 US 113 (1973)

Waltons Stores (Interstate) Ltd v Maher (1988) 164 CLR 387

BGH NJW 1992, 1659

Cass civ (1) 21 January 2003, D 2003, 693

CA Colmar 25 January 1963, Gaz Pal 1963.I.277

2.7.2 Legislation

Cite legislation from other jurisdictions as it is cited in its own jurisdiction, but without any full stops in abbreviations. Give the jurisdiction if necessary.

> Human Rights Act 1998 (UK)
>
> Accident Compensation Act 1972 (NZ)
>
> 1976 Standard Terms Act (*Gesetz über Allgemeine Geschäftsbedingungen*) (FRG)
>
> *loi* n° 75-1349 du 31 décembre 1975 relative à l'emploi de la langue française

Guides for citations from other jurisdictions can be found in section 4.3 of the appendix of OSCOLA.

3 SECONDARY SOURCES

3.1 GENERAL PRINCIPLES

3.1.1 Authors' names

Give the author's name exactly as it appears in the publication, but omit post-nominals such as SC. When judges write extra-curially, they should be named as in the publication in question. If there are more than three authors, give the name of the first author followed by 'and others'. If no individual author is identified, but an organisation or institution claims editorial responsibility for the work, then cite it as the author. If no person, organisation or institution claims responsibility for the work, begin the citation with the title. Treat editors' names in the same way as authors' names.

In footnotes, the author's first name or initial(s) precede his surname. In bibliographies, the surname comes first, then the initial(s), followed by a comma (see section 1.7).

3.1.2 Titles

Italicise titles of books and similar publications, including all publications with ISBNs. All other titles should be within single quotation marks and in roman. Capitalise the first letter in all major words in a title. Minor words, such as 'for', 'and', 'or' and 'the', do not take a capital unless they begin the title or subtitle.

3.1.3 Parts, chapters, pages and paragraphs

Pinpoints to parts, chapters, pages and paragraphs come at the end of the citation. Use 'pt' for part, 'ch' for chapter, and 'para' for paragraph. Page numbers stand alone, without 'p' or 'pp'. If citing a chapter or part and page number, insert a comma before the page number. Where possible, give a specific range of pages but if you must refer to an initial page and several unspecified following pages, give the initial page number followed immediately by 'ff' (eg '167ff').

3.1.4 Electronic sources

If you source a publication online which is also available in hard copy, cite the hard copy version. There is no need to cite an electronic source for such a publication.

Citations of publications that are available only electronically should end with the web address (Uniform Resource Locator or 'url') in angled brackets (< >), followed by the date of most recent access, expressed in the form 'accessed 1 January 2011'. Include 'http://'

only if the web address does not begin with 'www'. More detailed guidelines for the citation of electronic sources can be found in sections 3.3.4, 3.3.5 and 3.4.8.

3.1.5 Subsequent citations and short forms

In subsequent citations of books and articles, cite only the author's surname and provide a cross-citation (in the form (n *n*)) to the footnote with the full citation. The pinpoint follows the cross-citation. If you cite more than one work by the same author, it may be useful to provide the title as well, or a short form thereof, and the title alone should be used in subsequent citations of unattributed works and some other secondary sources, such as reports and policy documents. Further advice on subsequent citations and short forms is given in section 1.2.

3.2 Books

Cite all publications with an ISBN as if they were books, whether read online or in hard copy. Older books do not have ISBNs, but should be cited as books even if read online.

3.2.1 Authored books

Cite the author's name first, followed by a comma, and then the title of the book in italics (see section 3.1). Where a book has a title and subtitle not separated with punctuation, insert a colon. Publication information follows the title within brackets. Publication elements should always include the publisher and the year of publication, with a space but no punctuation between them. The place of publication need not be given. If you are citing an edition other than the first edition, indicate that using the form '2nd edn' (or 'rev edn' for a revised edition). Additional information should be of a clarifying nature: it may include the editor, the translator or other descriptive information about the work.

> author, | *title* | (additional information, | edition, | publisher | year)

> Kerry O'Halloran, *Adoption Law and Practice* (Round Hall 2010)
>
> Gerard Hogan and Gerry Whyte, *Kelly: The Irish Constitution* (4th edn, Butterworths 2003)

If a book consists of more than one volume, the volume number follows the publication details, unless the publication details of the volumes vary, in which case it precedes them, and is separated from the title by a comma. Pinpoint to paragraphs rather than pages if the paragraphs are numbered.

> Christian von Bar, *The Common European Law of Torts*, vol 2 (CH Beck 2000) para 76
>
> Eoin Quill, *Torts in Ireland* (3rd edn, Gill and MacMillan 2009) 125
>
> Julian V Roberts and Mike Hough, *Public Opinion and the Jury: An International Literature Review* (Ministry of Justice Research Series 1/09, 2009) 42

3.2.2 Edited and translated books

If there is no author, cite the editor or translator as you would an author, adding in brackets after their name '(ed)' or '(tr)', or '(eds)' or '(trs)' if there is more than one.

> Ursula Kilkelly (ed), *The ECHR and Irish Law* (2nd edn, Jordans 2009)
>
> Peter Birks and Grant McLeod (trs), *The Institutes of Justinian* (Duckworth 1987)

If the work has an author, but an editor or translator is also acknowledged on the front cover, cite the author in the usual way and attribute the editor or translator at the beginning of the publication information, within the brackets.

> HLA Hart, *Punishment and Responsibility: Essays in the Philosophy of Law* (John Gardner ed, 2nd edn, OUP 2008)
>
> K Zweigert and H Kötz, *An Introduction to Comparative Law* (Tony Weir tr, 3rd edn, OUP 1998)

3.2.3 Contributions to edited books

When citing a chapter or essay in an edited book, cite the author and the title of the contribution, in a similar format to that used when citing an article, and then give the editor's name, the title of the book in italics, and the publication information. It is not necessary to give the pages of the contribution.

> author, | 'title' | in editor (ed), | *book title* | (additional information, | publisher | year)

> Justine Pila, 'The Value of Authorship in the Digital Environment' in William H Dutton and Paul W Jeffreys (eds), *World Wide Research: Reshaping the Sciences and Humanities in the Century of Information* (MIT Press 2010)
>
> John Cartwright, 'The Fiction of the "Reasonable Man"' in AG Castermans and others (eds), *Ex Libris Hans Nieuwenhuis* (Kluwer 2009)

3.2.4 Older works

Books published before 1800 commonly have as 'publisher' a long list of booksellers; in such cases it is appropriate to cite merely the date and place of publication. When citing a recent publication of an older work, it may be appropriate to indicate the original publication date within the brackets and before the publication details of the recent publication.

> Thomas Hobbes, *Leviathan* (first published 1651, Penguin 1985) 268

3.2.5 Books of authority and institutional works

A small number of older works, such as Blackstone's Commentaries, are regarded as books of authority, and are therefore generally accepted as reliable statements of the law of their time. These works have evolved commonly known abbreviations and citation forms, which should be used in all footnote references to them. A list of some of these works and their abbreviations can be found in section 4.2.3 of the appendix of OSCOLA.

> 3 Bl Comm 264
>
> Co Litt 135a

3.2.6 Encyclopaedias

Cite an encyclopedia much as you would a book, but excluding the author or editor and publisher and including the edition and year of issue or reissue. Pinpoints to volumes and paragraphs come after the publication information. When an encyclopaedia credits an author for a segment, give both the author and the segment title at the beginning of the citation. If citing an online encyclopedia, give the web address and date of access.

Halsbury's Laws (5th edn, 2010) vol 57, para 53

CJ Friedrich, 'Constitutions and Constitutionalism', *International Encyclopedia of the Social Sciences III* (1968) 319

Leslie Green, 'Legal Positivism', *The Stanford Encyclopedia of Philosophy* (Fall edn, 2009) <http://plato.stanford.edu/archives/fall2009/entries/legal-positivism> accessed 20 November 2009

3.2.7 Looseleaf services

For looseleaf services, cite the title of the work in italics, excluding the name of the current author or editor, but including names which have become part of the title. Do not give publication details. Try to avoid pinpointing when referring to looseleafs, but if you must do so, give the volume (if appropriate), and pinpoint to paragraphs rather than pages. If pinpointing, you should also give the release number and/or date of issue at the foot of the relevant page in brackets after the paragraph number, in the form used by the publisher, but without any full stops.

Irish Current Law Statutes Annotated 1997–1998, para 15–15 (R 62 August 1998)

Irish Copyright and Design Law, paras 25–30 (Issue 6)

Consolidated Company Legislation, para A–354 (R 5 April 2008)

3.3 ARTICLES

3.3.1 Hard copy journals

When citing articles, give the author's name as given first, followed by a comma. Then give the title of the article, in roman within single quotation marks. After the title, give the publication information in the following order:

- year of publication, in square brackets if it identifies the volume, in round brackets if there is a separate volume number;
- the volume number if there is one (include an issue number if the page numbers begin again for each issue within a volume, in which case put the issue number in brackets immediately after the volume number);
- the name of the journal in roman, in full or abbreviated form, with no full stops; and
- the first page of the article.

> author, | 'title' | [year] | journal name or abbreviation | first page of article
>
> [OR]
>
> author, | 'title' | (year) | volume | journal name or abbreviation | first page of article

For guidance on journal abbreviations, see section 4.2.1 of the appendix of OSCOLA.
   Abbreviations do vary, so choose an abbreviation and stick with it throughout your work. Some publishers prefer all journal names to be given in full.

Some Irish publications, notably the 'Irish Jurist', the 'Dublin University Law Journal' and the 'Irish Law Times' (formerly the 'Irish Law Times and Reports') have been re-launched in recent decades. These so-called 'new series' re-started their volume numbering when they began publishing afresh in 1966, 1978 and 1981 respectively, and citations to issues of these journals since these dates should contain the abbreviation '(ns)' (short for new series) in order to avoid confusion with the previous publication run. Citations to the older series should omit this abbreviation.

Siobhán Mullally, 'Searching for Foundations for Irish Constitutional Law' (1998) 33 IJ (ns) 333

G F Whyte, 'Natural Law and the Constitution' (1996) 14 ILT (ns) 8

VTH Delany, 'Injuries to Schoolchildren: The Principles of Liability' (1962-63) IJ 15

For journals other than those with a new series, you should use the following to cite articles. Put a comma after the first page of the article if there is a pinpoint.

Terence Coghlan, 'The Copyright and Related Rights Act 2000' (2001) 6 Bar Review 294

Sally Wheeler and Gary Wilson, 'Corporate Law Firms and the Spirit of Community' (1998) 49 NILQ 239, 239

3.3.2 Case notes

Treat case notes with titles as if they were journal articles. Where there is no title, use the name of the case in italics instead, and add (note) at the end of the citation.

Andrew Ashworth, '*R (Singh) v Chief Constable of the West Midlands Police*' [2006] Crim LR 441 (note)

If the case discussed in the note is identified in the text, it is not necessary to put the name of the case in the case-note citation as well. In such a case, the example above would become:

Andrew Ashworth [2006] Crim LR 441 (note)

Even if not separately cited, the case should be included in the table of cases, citing its best report.

3.3.3 Forthcoming articles

Cite forthcoming articles in the same way as published articles, following the citation with '(forthcoming)'. If volume and/or page numbers are not yet known, simply omit that information.

3.3.4 Online journals

When citing journal articles which have been published only electronically, give publication details as for articles in hard copy journals, but note that online journals may lack some of the publication elements (for example, many do not include page numbers). If citation advice is provided by the online journal, follow it, removing full stops as necessary to comply with OSCOLA Ireland. Follow the citation with the web address (in angled brackets) and the date on which you most recently accessed the article. Pinpoints follow the citation and come before the web address.

> author, | 'title' | [year] OR (year) | volume/issue | journal name or abbreviation | <web address> | date accessed

> Graham Greenleaf, 'The Global Development of Free Access to Legal Information' (2010) 1(1) EJLT <http://ejlt.org/article/view/17> accessed 27 July 2010

> James Boyle, 'A Manifesto on WIPO and the Future of Intellectual Property' 2004 Duke L & Tech Rev 0009 <www.law.duke.edu/journals/dltr/articles/2004dltr0009.html> accessed 18 November 2009

Citation guidelines for other electronic works are provided in section 3.4.8.

3.3.5 Working papers

Working papers may be available online on institution websites and on sites such as the Social Science Research Network (<www.ssrn.com>). They should be cited in a similar fashion to electronic journal articles. Because the content of working papers is subject to change, the date of access is particularly important. If a working paper is subsequently published in a journal, cite that in preference to the working paper.

> John M Finnis, 'On Public Reason' (2006) Oxford Legal Studies Research Paper 1/2007, 8 <http://ssrn.com/abstract=955815> accessed 18 November 2009

3.4 OTHER SECONDARY SOURCES

3.4.1 General principles

Follow the general principles for citing secondary sources (section 3.1). If a source has an ISBN, cite it like a book. Generally, cite sources that do not have ISBNs in a similar way, but with the title in roman and within single quotation marks, as for journal articles.

> author, | 'title' | (additional information, | publisher | year)

Additional information may include a document number, a document description, a date of adoption and any other information that may help a reader to locate the source. The publisher may be a government body or an organisation, and it is also possible that no publisher will be identifiable. Depending on the source, it may be more appropriate to provide the publication date, rather than the year. If a source is available only online, then give the web address and the date of access as described in section 3.1.4.

If you wish to use an abbreviated name for the source in subsequent citations, give the short form in brackets at the end of the first citation.

> University of Oxford, *Report of Commission of Inquiry* (OUP 1966) vol 1, ch 3 (Franks Report)

> Simon Whittaker, 'La Protection du Consommateur Contre les Clauses Abusives en Grande Bretagne' (Commission des Clauses Abusives 2009) <www.clauses-abusives.fr/colloque/swhittaker.htm> accessed 19 November 2009

> Lord Bingham, 'Keynote Address' (Liberty conference, London, 6 June 2009) <www.liberty-human-rights.org.uk/publications/3-articles-and-speeches/index.shtml> accessed 19 November 2009

3.4.2 Parliamentary reports

The Official Reports of the Oireachtas are in three series, one reporting debates on the floor of the Dáil, one reporting debates on the floor of the Seanad and one reporting debates in Oireachtas committees.

When referring to the first two series, cite the house followed by 'Deb', then the full date, the volume and the column. Use 'col' or 'cols' for column(s).

Dáil Deb OR Seanad Deb	date,	volume,	column

Dáil Deb 5 October 2005, vol 606, col 1690

Cite debates in Oireachtas committees with the name of the committee, followed by 'Deb', followed by the date and page number.

Select Committee on Enterprise and Small Business Deb 30 June 1998, 3

Special Committee Wildlife Bill, 1975 Deb 1 July 1976, 4

When citing reports of select committees of either house, or joint committees of both houses, give the name of the committee, the title of the report in italics, and then in brackets the document number, which should begin with P, followed by the year of publication, if available and clear. (Not all committee reports carry a publication date. This can sometimes be determined from other sources but it is best not to guess.)

Joint Committee on Climate Change and Energy Security, *Second Report on Climate Change Law* (Prn A10/1448, 2010)

Committee of Public Accounts, *Third Interim Report on the Procurement of Legal Services by Public Bodies* (Prn A11/0171, 2011)

Select Committee on Crime, Lawlessness and Vandalism, *Fifteenth Report: The Prosecution of Offences* (PL 4703, 1987) 11

Sub-Committee of the Committee on Procedure and Privileges, *First Report on Reform of Dáil Procedure* (Pn 2814, 1996) 29

3.4.3 Official publications

Official publications include White and Green Papers, relevant treaties, government responses to joint committee reports, and reports of committees of inquiry. When citing an official publication, begin the citation with the name of the department or other body that produced the document, and then give the title of the paper in italics, followed by the document number (if available) and the year in brackets. If additional information is required, insert it within the brackets before the document number.

The abbreviation preceding a document number should begin with P, is usually Prn, Pn or Prl and indicates that the document was laid before the Houses of the Oireachtas.

All-Party Oireachtas Committee on the Constitution, *Bunreacht na hÉireann: A Study of the Irish Text* (Pn 7899, 1999) 286

Tribunal of Inquiry into Certain Planning Matters and Payments, *Second Interim Report* (2002) 66

Working Group on the Jurisdiction of the Courts, *The Criminal Jurisdiction of the Courts* (Pn 237, 2003) ch 4

3.4.4 Law Reform Commission Reports and Consultation Papers

Cite Law Reform Commission reports by title in italics, Commission number and year, separated by a comma. For Law Reform Commission consultation papers, give the LRC CP number.

Law Reform Commission, *Report on Privity of Contract and Third Party Rights* (LRC 88, 2008)

Law Reform Commission, *Consultation Paper on Legal Aspects of Family Relationships* (LRC CP 55, 2009)

3.4.5 European Commission documents

When citing European Commission documents (such as proposals and action plans), give the body that produced the document, followed by the title in quotation marks, and the COM number. Describe the document type in brackets after the title if appropriate. In subsequent citations give only the COM number.

Commission, 'Proposal for a Council Decision on the conclusion, on behalf of the European Community, of the Protocol on the Implementation of the Alpine Convention in the Field of Transport (Transport Protocol)' COM (2008) 895 final, ch I, art 3

Commission, 'Action Plan on consumer access to justice and the settlement of disputes in the internal market' (Communication) COM (96) 13 final

Commission, 'Proposal for a Council Regulation on jurisdiction and the recognition and enforcement of judgments in civil and commercial matters' COM (99) 348 final

3.4.6 Conference papers

When citing conference papers that were only available at a conference or directly from the author, give the author, the title in quotation marks and then in brackets the title, location and date of the conference. If a conference paper has been published, cite the published version instead; papers that are available online should include a web address and date of access. Cite conference papers that are not publicly available only if you have the author's permission.

Ben McFarlane and Donal Nolan, 'Remedying Reliance: The Future Development of Promissory and Proprietary Estoppel in English Law' (Obligations III conference, Brisbane, July 2006)

3.4.7 Theses

When citing an unpublished thesis, give the author, the title and then in brackets the type of thesis, university and year of completion.

Javan Herberg, 'Injunctive Relief for Wrongful Termination of Employment' (DPhil thesis, University of Oxford 1989)

3.4.8 Websites and blogs

Where there is no relevant advice elsewhere in OSCOLA, follow the general principles for secondary sources (section 3.1) when citing websites and blogs. If there is no author identified, and it is appropriate to cite an anonymous source, begin the citation with the title in the usual way. If there is no date of publication on the website, give only the date of access.

Fiona de Londras, 'Adjudication, Constitutionalism and Trying to "Save" the ECHR' (*Human Rights in Ireland*, 26 January 2011) <www.humanrights.ie/index.php/2011/01/26/ adjudication-constitutionalism-and-trying-to-save-the-ecthr> accessed 30 January 2011

3.4.9 Newspaper articles

When citing newspaper articles, give the author, the title, the name of the newspaper in italics and then in brackets the city of publication and the date. Some newspapers have 'The' in the title and some do not. If known, give the number of the page on which the article was published, after the brackets. If the newspaper is divided into sections, and the page numbering begins afresh in each section, put the section name in roman before the page number, with a space but no comma between the two. If the reference is to an editorial, cite the author as 'Editorial'. If the article is sourced from the web and there is no page number available, provide the web address and date of access.

Carl O'Brien, 'Woman with Cancer Tells of her Abortion Ordeal' *The Irish Times* (Dublin, 21 December 2010)

Shane Phelan and Tim Healy, 'Top Anglo Chiefs are Blocking Garda Probe' *Irish Independent* (Dublin, 5 May 2011)

Paul O'Brien, 'Harney Settles Newstalk Libel Case for €450k' *Irish Examiner* (Cork, 5 May 2011)

3.4.10 Interviews

When citing an interview you conducted yourself, give the name, position and institution (as relevant) of the interviewee, and the location and full date of the interview. If the interview was conducted by someone else, the interviewer's name should appear at the beginning of the citation.

Interview with Irene Kull, Assistant Dean, Faculty of Law, Tartu University (Tartu, Estonia, 4 August 2003)

Timothy Endicott and John Gardner, Interview with Tony Honoré, Emeritus Regius Professor of Civil Law, University of Oxford (Oxford, 17 July 2007)

3.4.11 Personal communications

When citing personal communications, such as emails and letters, give the author and recipient of the communication, and the date. If you are yourself the author or recipient of the communication, say 'from author' or 'to author' as appropriate.

Letter from Gordon Brown to Lady Ashton (20 November 2009)

Email from Amazon.co.uk to author (16 December 2008)

Appendix

2

OSCOLA Ireland Quick Reference Guide

PRIMARY SOURCES

Do not use full stops in abbreviations. Separate citations with a semi-colon. Close footnotes with a full stop.

CONSTITUTION

Article 40.3.3°.

CASES

Give the party names, followed by the neutral citation, followed by the *Irish Reports* citation. If there is no neutral citation, give the *Irish Reports* citation followed by the court in brackets. If the case is not reported in the *Irish Reports*, cite the *Irish Law Reports Monthly* if possible, or other reports otherwise:

> *Riordan v Ireland* [2009] IESC 44, [2009] 3 IR 745.
> *Doran v Delaney* [1998] 2 IR 61 (SC).
> *Friends of the Curragh Environment Ltd v An Bord Pleanála (No 2)* [2006] IEHC 390, [2007] 1 ILRM 386.

When pinpointing, give paragraph numbers in square brackets with the name of the judge at the end of the citation. If the judgment has no paragraph numbers, but does have page numbers, give the page number after the court. If there are no paragraph numbers or page numbers, do not include a pinpoint reference.

> *TD v Minister for Education* [2001] 4 IR 259 (SC) 270.
> *AP v DPP* [2011] IESC 2 [27] (Fennelly J).

Where the case is unreported and has no neutral citation, it should be cited:

> *First Plaintiff v First Defendant* (HC, 22 February 1999).

STATUTES AND STATUTORY INSTRUMENTS

Interpretation Act 2005.
European Convention on Human Rights Act 2003, s 3(5)(a).

European Communities (Electronic Communications Networks and Services) (Data Protection and Privacy) Regulations 2003, SI 2003/535.
Electricity Regulation Act 1999 (Electricity) Levy Order 2005, SI 2005/819.

EU LEGISLATION AND CASES

Consolidated Version of the Treaty on European Union [2008] OJ C115/13.
Council Regulation (EC) 139/2004 on the control of concentrations between undertakings (EC Merger Regulation) [2004] OJ L24/1, art 5.

Pre-1989 cases

Case 272/86 *Commission v Greece* [1988] ECR 4875.

Post-1989 cases

Case C-156/87 *Gestetner v Council* [1990] ECR I-781.

EUROPEAN COURT OF HUMAN RIGHTS

Simpson v UK (1989) 53 DR 188.
Tyrer v UK (1978) 2 EHRR 1.
A, B and C v Ireland App No 25579/05 (ECHR, 16 December 2010).

UK CASE LAW

Corr v IBC Vehicles Ltd [2008] UKHL 13, [2008] 1 AC 884.
Bunt v Tilley [2006] EWHC 407 (QB), [2006] 3 All ER 336 [35].

US CASE LAW

Roe v Wade 410 US 113 (1973) 127.
Arcoren v Peters 811 F 2d 392 (8th Cir 1987).

SECONDARY SOURCES

Do not use superscript for dates and editions (2nd, not 2nd).

BOOKS

Give the author's name in the same form as in the publication, except in bibliographies, where you should give only the surname followed by the initial(s).
Give relevant information about editions, translators and such before the publisher.
Put a comma after this information, but not between publisher and year. When pinpointing, give page numbers at the end of the citation, after the brackets.

Bryan McMahon and William Binchy, *The Law of Torts* (3rd edn, Butterworths 2000).
James Casey, *Constitutional Law in Ireland* (3rd edn, Round Hall Sweet & Maxwell 2000) 126.

Contributions to edited books

Liz Heffernan, 'Evidentiary Rights under Article 38.1: The Right to Fair Trial and Informer Privilege' in Oran Doyle and Eoin Carolan (eds), *The Irish Constitution: Governance and Values* (Thomson Round Hall 2008).

Journal articles

For continuously paginated volumes:
Terence Coghlan, 'The Copyright and Related Rights Act 2000' (2001) 6 Bar Review 294.
Siobhán Mullally, 'Searching for Foundations for Irish Constitutional Law' (1998) 33 IJ (ns) 333.
VTH Delany, 'Injuries to Schoolchildren: The Principles of Liability' (1962-63) IJ 15.

If page numbering re-starts with each issue:
Albert Keating, 'Conditional Wills and Gifts' (2014) 2(3) Irish Probate Law Journal 6.

Pinpoint cites:
Emma Storan, 'Section 117 of the Succession Act 1965: Another Means for the Courts to Rewrite a Will?' (2006) 11(4) Conveyancing and Property Law Journal 82, 85.

Online journals

Graham Greenleaf, 'The Global Development of Free Access to Legal Information' (2010) 1(1) EJLT <http://ejlt.org//article/view/17> accessed 1 February 2011.

Encyclopedias

Halsbury's Laws (5th edn, 2010) vol 57, para 53.

Official publications

Constitution Review Group, *Report of the Constitution Review Group* (Pn 2632, Stationery Office 1996) 45.

Law Reform Commission Reports

Reports

Law Reform Commission, *Legal Aspects of Family Relationships* (LRC 101, 2010).

Consultation Papers and pinpointing

Law Reform Commission, *Consultation Paper on Legal Aspects of Family Relationships* (LRC CP 55, 2009) 67.

WEBSITES AND BLOGS

Fiona de Londras, 'Adjudication, Constitutionalism and Trying to "Save" the ECHR' (*Human Rights in Ireland*, 26 January 2011) <www.humanrights.ie/index.php/2011/01/26/adjudication-constitutionalism-and-trying-to-save-the-ecthr> accessed 30 January 2011.

NEWSPAPER ARTICLES

Carl O'Brien, 'Woman with Cancer Tells of her Abortion Ordeal' *The Irish Times* (Dublin, 21 December 2010).

Index

Abortion, 45
Active listening, 6
Active voice, 65
Amendment of legislation, 53–55
American Constitution, 4
Analogising, 28–29
Annotated Acts, 54
Article citation, 104–105
Attribution, 101–103
Authority, 100–101
Automated referencing, 107–108

Back references, 106–107
Bibliography, 106
Book citation, 105

Canons of interpretation, 59
Capitalisation, 73
Case law
    analogising and distinguishing,
        28–29
    book reading distinguished, 20–21
    case name, 23
    case notes, 31–43
    citation of cases, 21–22, 104
    court, 24
    databases see Databases
    decision, 26
    dissenting judgments, 31
    facts of case, 24–25, 28
    headnote, 23
    importance of reading skill, 19–21
    judge(s), 24
    keywords, 23
    law reports, 21–22, 104
    legal issue, 25
    majority opinion, 31
    more complex issues, 27–29

obiter dicta, 27, 30
overseas cases, 30–31
parties, 23
precedent, 27, 29–31
questions to ask, 27–28
ratio decidendi, 27, 29–30
reasons for decision, 26
same case read in different ways,
    26–27
sources, 21
structure of reported cases, 22–23
unreported cases, 21–22
where did case arise?, 24
written judgments, 22–23
Case names, 23
Case notes
    child custody case, 39–40
    contraception case, 38–39
    format, 31–32
    Norris case, 34–36
    PKU case, 36–37, 40–43
    pollution case, 32–34
Citations
    accuracy, 103
    articles, 104–105
    attribution, 101–103
    authority, 100–101
    automated referencing, 107–108
    back references to previously cited
        material, 106–107
    bibliography, 106
    books, 105
    cases, 21–22, 104
    footnotes, 100, 102
    format, 103
    journals, 103–104
    OSCOLA, 103, 107–108
    plagiarism, 108–109

Citations *(continued)*
    purpose, 100
    quotations, 106
    scholarly works, 101–103
    source not locatable, 102–103
Clinical legal education, 7–8
Colons, 70–71
Commas, 70
Commencement of legislation, 50, 55
Common knowledge, 100–101
Common law, 2
Comparative approach to legal
    research, 82–83
Consolidation of legislation, 54
Constitutional law, 3–4
Constitutionality of legislation
    presumption, 59–60
    referral to Supreme Court, 49
Continuous assessment, 85–86
Court of Justice of the EU, 3
Courts Service website, 153–154
Criminal legislation, 58–59

Dashes, 71–72
Databases
    Courts Service, 153–154
    Europa, 154
    Findlaw, 154
    freely available, 152–156
    Google Scholar, 155–156
    HeinOnline, 151–152
    Houses of the Oireachtas, 154
    HUDOC, 154–155
    Irish Law, 153
    Irish Legal Information Initiative,
        152–153
    Irish Statute Book, 153
    JSTOR, 152
    Justis, 151
    Law Reform Commission, 155
    LexisLibrary, 150
    search tools, 156–159
    Social Science Research Network,
        155
    subscriber-based, 149–152

    Westlaw IE, 150
    Westlaw UK, 150–151
Date of promulgation, 51
Decision of court, 26
Dewey Decimal system, 148
Direct quotations, 66
Dissenting judgment, 31
Distinguishing, 28–29
Doctrinal legal research, 81–82
Drafting of legislation, 46–50

Ejusdem generis, 59
Ellipsis, 70
Em dash, 72
Emotive language, 66–67
Empirical legal research, 84–85
En dash, 72
EndNote, 108
Essay questions, 134
Europa, 154
European Convention on Human
    Rights, 3, 60
European Court of Human Rights, 3
European Union law
    influence of, 3
    presumption of compatibility, 60
    statutory interpretation, 59
Exclamation marks, 71
Expressio unius exclusio alterius,
    59

Facts of case, 24–25, 28
Federal system, 4
Findlaw, 154
Fines for criminal offences, 53
Footnotes, 100, 102
Free Legal Advice Centres (FLAC), 7
Full stops, 69–70

Gender neutral writing, 75–77
Google Scholar, 155–156
Grammar, 67

Headnote, 23
HeinOnline, 151–152

Historical approach to legal research, 83
HUDOC, 154–155
Hyphens, 71–72

ILAC, 135–136
Indirect quotations, 66
Internet research, 147
Interpretation of statutes
 canons of interpretation, 59
 EU law, 59
 literal approach, 57
 parliamentary debates, 60–61
 penal or revenue legislation, 58–59
 presumptions, 59–60
 purposive approach, 58
Interpretation section, 51, 56–57
Irish Clinical Legal Education
  Association (ICLEA), 8
Irish Constitution, 3–4
Irish language, 74–75
Irish law
 common law, 2
 constitutional law, 3–4
 influence of EU law, 3
 influence of UK law, 2
 influence of US law, 4
 legal materials, 5
Irish Law, 153
Irish Legal Information Initiative,
  152–153
Irish Statute Book, 53, 54–55, 153
Its and it's, 73

Jargon, 68
Journals
 citation, 103–104
 databases see Databases
 Irish journals, 5
JSTOR, 152
Judgments see Case law
Juris-M, 108
Justis, 151

Keywords, 23

LaTeX, 108
Latin terms, 68, 107
Law essays
 asking questions, 86
 backing up files, 97
 bibliography, 106
 building argument, 95
 citations see Citations
 conclusion, 95
 cover page, 98
 covering legal issues, 94
 finding relevant material, 88
 following directions, 87
 font size, 99
 general advice, 85–87
 headings and sub-headings, 92
 independent research, 86–87
 introducing concepts, 93–94
 legal research methods and
   methodologies, 81–85, 94
 line spacing, 99
 linking sentences, 92–93
 managing research process, 87
 outline, 89
 overview, 80
 plagiarism, 108–109
 proofreading, 87, 96
 revising and abandoning, 96
 roadmap, 92
 sample essays, 109, 110–129
 serif and sans serif fonts, 98–99
 starting early, 86
 structure, 90–91
 taking notes, 88–89
 topic sentences, 93
 typeface, 98–99
 typography, 97–99
 underlining, 99
 using technology, 96–97
 white space, 99
Law exams
 avoiding 'shotgun' approach, 131
 essay questions, 134
 planning answers, 132
 presenting script well, 133

Law exams *(continued)*
    problem questions, 135–145
    sample answers, 138–145
    time allocation, 131–132
    types of exam questions, 130–131
Law Reform Commission, 155
Law reports *see* **Case law**
Law students
    civic and political engagement, 6–7
    clinical legal education, 7–8
    Irish context, 5
    note-taking from spoken word, 5
    public interest, 7
Legal issue, 25
Legal research
    meaning, 146
    comparative approach, 82–83
    databases *see* Databases
    doctrinal legal research, 81–82
    empirical legal research, 84–85
    historical approach, 83
    internet versus library research,
        146–147
    library-based research, 147–149
    socio-legal studies, 84
    writing law essay, 94
Legal thinking
    arguing for both sides, 16
    authorities and proofs, 17
    avoiding assumptions, 15
    binary answers and fuzzy logic,
        15–16
    clear thinking, 12–13
    identifying ancillary questions, 14–15
    identifying core question, 13–14
    importance of skill, 11–12
    'thinking like a lawyer', 12
Legal writing
    active voice, 65
    capitalisation, 73
    clarity, 62–63
    developing own voice, 77
    direct and indirect quotations, 66
    discussing and disagreeing with
        academic material, 65–66

    gender neutral writing, 75–77
    grammar, 67
    importance of skill, 62
    Irish language, 74–75
    jargon, 68
    knowing your audience, 77
    misspelt words, 68–69
    plain English, 63–64, 68
    possessive case, 72–73
    punctuation, 69–74
    simple sentence structure, 64
    structure: from start to finish, 64
    tone and emotion, 66–67
    word count, 77
legalwriting.ie, 9–10
Legislation
    amendment, 53–55
    annotation, 54
    commencement, 50, 55
    compatibility with EU law, 60
    compatibility with European
        Convention on Human Rights,
        60
    consolidation, 54
    constitutional provisions, 44
    constitutionality, 49, 59–60
    databases *see* Databases
    date of promulgation, 51
    definitions, 56–57
    drafting process, 46–50
    interpretation section, 51, 56–57
    list of Acts referred to, 51
    long title, 51
    marginal notes, 151
    official citation, 51
    parts of Act, 50–52
    primary legislation, 45–46
    reading legislation, 55–57
    referral to Supreme Court, 49
    Regulatory Impact Assessment,
        47–48
    repeals and Schedules, 52
    restatement, 53–54
    rules of interpretation *see*
        Interpretation of statutes

Legislation *(continued)*
    secondary legislation, 46
    short title, 51
    signature by President, 49
    sources, 52–53
    unique form and purpose, 44–45
    websites, 52–53, 54–55
LexisLibrary, 150
Library-based research, 147–149
Lindley Principles, 23
Line spacing, 99
Lists, 70
Literal interpretation, 57
Long title of Act, 51

Marginal notes, 51
Misspelt words, 68–69

Names of cases, 23
Noscitur a sociis, 59
Note-taking from spoken word, 5

Obiter dicta, 27, 30
Official citation of Act, 51
Oireachtas website, 52, 154
OSCOLA citations, 103, 107–108
Overseas cases, 30–31

Parliamentary debates, 60–61
Parties to case, 23
Passive voice, 65
Plagiarism, 108–109
Plain English, 19, 63–64, 68
Political engagement, 6–7
Possessive case, 72–73
Precedent
    overseas cases, 30–31
    ratio decidendi and, 27, 29–30
Presumption of compatibility with EU law, 60
Presumption of constitutionality, 59–60
Previously cited material, 106–107
Primary legislation, 45–46
Problem questions

    analysis/application to facts, 137
    case names, 136
    conclusion, 137
    examples, 138–145
    ILAC approach, 135–136
    issue, 136
    law, 136
Public Interest Law Alliance (PILA), 7
Punctuation, 69–74
Purposive interpretation, 58

Question marks, 71
Quotations, 66, 106

Ratio decidendi, 27, 29–30
ReadCube, 108
Reading judgments *see* **Case law**
Reading legislation *see* **Legislation**
Reasons for decision, 26
References *see* **Citations**
Regulatory Impact Assessment, 47–48
Repeals, 52
Research *see* **Legal research**
Restatement of legislation, 53–54
Rules of statutory interpretation

Scholarly works, 101–103
Search tools
    'and' connector, 157
    date restrictions, 159
    inverted commas, 156–157
    nearby words, 158
    'not' connector, 157–158
    'or' connector, 157
    wild cards, 158–159
Secondary legislation, 46
Semi-colons, 71
Sentence structure, 64
Serial comma, 70
Serif and sans serif fonts, 98–99
Short title, 51
Signature of legislation, 49

Social Science Research Network, 155
Socio-legal studies, 84
Structure of book, 1–2
Subscriber-based databases, 149–152

Tax legislation, 58–59
Textbooks, 5
Thinking skills *see* Legal thinking
Typefaces, 98–99
Typography, 97–99

Underlining, 99
United Kingdom law, 3

United States law, 4
Unreported cases, 21–22

Westlaw IE, 150
Westlaw UK, 150–151
Wikipedia, 101, 147
Wild cards, 158–159
Writing case notes *see* Case notes
Writing law essays *see* Law essays
Writing law exams *see* Law exams
Written judgments, 22–23

Zotero, 108